# Start With Yourself

# Start With Yourself

A New Vision for Work & Life

## EMMA GREDE

**GALLERY BOOKS UK**

London · New York · Amsterdam/Antwerp · Sydney/Melbourne · Toronto · New Delhi

First published in Great Britain by Gallery Books, an imprint of Simon & Schuster UK Ltd, 2026

Copyright © Emma Louise Grede, 2026

The right of Emma Louise Grede to be identified as the author of this work has been asserted in accordance with the Copyright, Designs and Patents Act, 1988.

1 3 5 7 9 10 8 6 4 2

Simon & Schuster UK Ltd
1st Floor
222 Gray's Inn Road
London WC1X 8HB

For more than 100 years, Simon & Schuster has championed authors and the stories they create. By respecting the copyright of an author's intellectual property, you enable Simon & Schuster and the author to continue publishing exceptional books for years to come. We thank you for supporting the author's copyright by purchasing an authorised edition of this book.

No amount of this book may be reproduced or stored in any format, nor may it be uploaded to any website, database, language-learning model, or other repository, retrieval, or artificial intelligence system without express permission. All rights reserved. Enquiries may be directed to Simon & Schuster, 222 Gray's Inn Road, London WC1X 8HB or RightsMailbox@simonandschuster.co.uk

www.simonandschuster.co.uk
www.simonandschuster.com.au
www.simonandschuster.co.in

Simon & Schuster Australia, Sydney
Simon & Schuster India, New Delhi

The authorised representative in the EEA is Simon & Schuster Netherlands BV, Herculesplein 96, 3584 AA Utrecht, Netherlands. info@simonandschuster.nl

The author and publishers have made all reasonable efforts to contact copyright-holders for permission, and apologise for any omissions or errors in the form of credits given. Corrections may be made to future printings.

Simon & Schuster strongly believes in freedom of expression and stands against censorship in all its forms. For more information, visit BooksBelong.com.

A CIP catalogue record for this book is available from the British Library

Some names have been changed.

Hardback ISBN: 978-1-3985-5094-0
Trade Paperback 978-1-3985-5095-7
eBook ISBN: 978-1-3985-5096-4

Interior design by Silverglass

Cover design by Erik Torstensson

Printed and Bound in Italy

*To my darling Jens,
for your belief in me and holding
me accountable to my highest ideals*

# Contents

Introduction ix

PART ONE: **VISION** 1

Yearly Process 12

PART TWO: **MANAGING EMOTIONS** 15

1. Anger 19

2. Fear 25

3. Guilt 31

4. Sadness 35

5. Joy 41

PART THREE: **OLD THOUGHTS** 45

1. Trade-Offs 53

2. Money 75

3. Career 101

4. Family 133

5. Building a Brand & Business 155

6. Leadership 221

PART FOUR: **ACTION!** 269

My Basic Rules for Success 275

Acknowledgements 277

Notes 281

My Favourite Books About Business & Life 285

Thoughts 287

Index 291

# Introduction

Where was Marcus?

I was on the tenth floor of a very grey, very shitty twenty-one-floor apartment complex in Stratford, which for the uninitiated is in East London. It was a concrete dump, but for me it was free. As I walked to the station every day to take a train into town, you would have never thought I was living in a flat with no stove or fridge. Marcus and I would joke that in England, a balcony is sufficient to keep milk cold. It's possible that on this day there was a Gucci diamante thong peeking out from the top of my jeans, as was the (questionable) style of the day, but what's for sure is that I looked fantastic. I've always known how to put myself together, even when everything else in my life is a mess.

And on this particular day, everything was a disaster.

The apartment was small – I slept on the couch in the living room, Marcus in the single bedroom – and so it didn't take me long to deduce that he wasn't there. And then the phone screamed through the silence. It was Marcus.

'Emma,' he said. 'I've been arrested. You need to go on a walk. My mate is coming over to get some of my things. Until he does, Emma, don't go home.'

'Alright, alright,' I replied, scared and thoroughly confused.

So I went for a walk. I stayed away until well after dark, and with each step I turned Marcus's words over and over in my mind. Why was his mate going to our apartment? Why couldn't I be there at the same time? What was his mate going to do? The more I thought, the more scared and confused I felt.

All I knew for sure was that I needed to follow Marcus's instructions precisely. I had known him my whole life, and I trusted him like family.

Marcus ended up spending twenty-two years in jail. Only much, much later did I sort of surmise that his mate must have come by to collect some essential contraband. I didn't want to know back then. And I still don't. For me the main point then, and now, is simply that Marcus, on the edge of the abyss, was thinking of me, trying to keep me safe. That felt meaningful and symbolic. My future deserved his protection – and I carried from that moment onward the knowledge of his faith in me, the belief that I was destined for more and also the realisation that I would need to cross a bridge from the world he and I came from to the world where I wanted to live.

Marcus could have easily told me on the phone that day that I needed to find a place of my own, but he made sure that the rent on the council flat was paid for years, as I had no money and nowhere else to go. I paid his mum twenty quid a week to stay. I was seventeen years old and working my way through fashion school – and that's all I had to spare.

Marcus is not the only family member or family friend who went to jail when I was a kid. This was part of my reality. My extended family and family-friend circle looks like a casting call for a Guy Ritchie movie: they're good-looking, they're fast-talking and they have nicknames like Bonsey and Mads. My mum, Jenny-Lee, is white and British and raised me on her own. My dad, Steve, who is Trinidadian, though born in England, is a good person and really fun, but he was completely absent during my childhood. He's been a British Telecom engineer for his entire adult life, earning a modest income. We're great friends now, but I could no doubt have used his steady presence in my young life.

If a fortune-teller had taken a look at my destiny when I was growing up, she would have predicted I'd become a DJ's girlfriend or a footballer's sidepiece, or marry a gangster. That seemed to be the predetermined path for all the women in my life, women who put everyone ahead of their own dreams and fell into rutted expectations that yielded mostly heartbreak and financial dead ends. My mum was a little different – she'd finagled a job on a trading desk, and while she encountered some hurdles in her life, she had a legitimate job at a bank for most of my childhood. My mum is very smart, though she was a tough role model at times, too.

I didn't officially graduate from secondary school (I was asked to leave for being disruptive, only to learn as an adult that I'm dyslexic and struggled to keep up because they didn't know how to teach me), and I dropped out of the London College of Fashion after my first term because I couldn't afford to stay. I grew up in chaos, with occasional violence, and very few means.

And yet, here I am.

Nobody would have predicted that I'd launch many, many successful businesses and earn a spot on *Forbes*'s 'America's Richest Self-Made Women' list by the age of forty. Nobody would have predicted that I'd be in a loving and warm marriage of sixteen years with a brilliant and supportive Swede from an artsy family. Nobody would have predicted, after a childhood where I was overly involved in raising my three younger sisters, that I'd go on to become the mother of four incredible kids who I am rightly obsessed with. Nobody would have predicted that I'd be able to therapise so much of my anger and have access to so much happiness.

I always knew though. One of the things my mother used to say to me is *You're not more special than anyone else, but nobody is more special than you.* My mum had an inconsistent relationship with reality, but this felt like one of the truest things she ever said, and I integrated it deeply into my thinking. Why me? And also: Why *not* me? While I was a responsible and very overly parentified ten-year-old – somebody had to get my sisters to school, feed them and show up for parents' evenings because my mum couldn't get the time off work – I recognised at an early age that it would be best for me to assume complete responsibility for myself, too. Rather than looking for people and factors to blame for why everything in my life was shaky and unstable, I decided to get on with it – and do *everything* differently from the people around me to create safety and security for myself.

I didn't have any mentors until I'd already become successful, but that didn't prevent me from paying attention: I looked for teachers everywhere, I followed my curiosity into as many books as I could get my hands on, I questioned everything and I learned from every encounter. Nobody was going to give me any breaks, so I asked for them instead. I wedged my foot into any door that was even remotely cracked open. I pushed, I hustled and I showed up, again and again, keeping my word and doing what I said I would do along the way.

I get a lot of questions about how I've done what I've done. People find me on shows like *Shark Tank* in the US and *Dragons' Den* in the UK. They slide into my DMs and pull me aside at conferences or on the street. They want guidance on when, if or how to start a family or a business – and ultimately, how to balance the two and scale. Explaining how I've done what I've done so other women can do it too was the core impetus for writing this book, along with my frustration that there's a lot of marketing for women in business that feels frankly wrong, or like it plays into the insidious programming that keeps us all small.

People often talk about playbooks for success, and I'm here to tell you that there is no playbook, particularly for women. While it's true that the rules of the old boys' club still sometimes work out for men, that's not always true either. What I've learned from operating, scaling and monetising many businesses for more than twenty years is that it's not really about prescribed actions – do this, and do that, and get this result – it's about the thinking that determines those actions.

# INTRODUCTION

This is a book about mindset – about managing your emotions, clarifying your thoughts, and taking the right next step, all while holding a positive vision for your future. It's about collecting yourself after failure, expecting no shortcuts (but taking any you can find) and pushing hard for the wins. It's about thinking for yourself and finding your own path while learning from everyone else's mistakes (along with your own). While a lot of people look to me for guidance on scaling billion-dollar businesses, this book isn't just for entrepreneurs who hope to IPO someday – this book is for *anyone* who is tired of feeling like a passenger in their own life and wants something different for their future. That could be more ease and abundance with money, a balanced home life or a blueprint for building a profitable side hustle that requires no financial investment.

In the following pages, I'm going to tell you about the foundational operating system that guides my life, which I learned in the streets of a very specific place: East London. I'm going to explain how I came to manage and moderate my emotions so that I didn't use any perceived affront from the exterior world as a justification to unload my anger, sadness, fear or guilt on other people, only setting myself back in the process. And then, one by one, I'm going to take down a series of what I call 'Old Thoughts'. Women will recognise these Old Thoughts as core to the way we tend to think about the rules of life *and* business. These thoughts include needing to know the right people or be invited to the right events; that money is inelegant, unspiritual, scarce and dirty; that 'doing it all' is an achievable goal so long as you unlock the code to balancing your work and family life perfectly; and so many more. There are good reasons why we buy into these Old Thoughts: our culture provides manifold evidence that they're true and that we need to abide by them to be socially acceptable – but I haven't. And because of this, I have a lot to show for it on the other side. My life isn't perfect, and I still work on myself every single day, but I live the life I always dreamed of, with a family I'm so in love with, a beautiful house with *two* working fridges, and every day I get to do work that I enjoy.

I can hear a lot of 'buts' rising in peoples' throats: *But what will people think of me? But what will I need to sacrifice to pursue my dreams? But nothing about this world is equitable or fair!* I hear you. I'm not going to gaslight you. I'm not going to bathe you in toxic positivity or rain platitudes down on your head. Yes, the world is typically more difficult for women, people of colour and poor people – and yes, I am and have been all three. There are very few factors that feel ideal for mothers to succeed. I understand that men have much less pressure to be all things to all people and that nobody asked Steve Jobs or Elon Musk how they balanced their parenting while they built Apple or Tesla. Instead, we've largely celebrated their single-minded focus on their goals, even when they've come to the detriment of society. We see the quirks and faults of powerful men through our fingers. I cannot name a single woman who has been afforded the same luxury.

This is all true. And *yet*, we cannot wait for the world to meet our preferences in order to take action. Besides, women are exceptional. In the following pages, I'm going to remind you that your exceptionality is true *and* more accessible when you learn to turn down all the voices in your head suggesting you're not doing it right and turn up your own voice instead. We are full of potential – when that potential meets grit and determination, everything is up for grabs.

And now, we need to grab it. We can't wait for the world to decide that it's our turn to lead and succeed. That ain't going to happen. But we need something different. After all, when I look around at the state of women, I'm both impressed and also very disappointed. The halls of power and cap tables don't reflect our exceptionality, nor do I meet a lot of women who feel fantastic about the balance of their lives. Far too many women feel like they are failing, or creatively stifled or functionally blocked. All women are exhausted. While it's very easy – and we see this all over our culture – to blame men and inequitable systems, that's not how I roll. Not because it's not sometimes valid, but because it's not how change happens. Nothing is fair, it's true. But I don't have time to wait for equity; I'd rather make it. I take full responsibility for my life, and I create my own future, regardless of what comes back at me. If we're going to change the world, we have to start with ourselves. We have to get on our own teams and choose ourselves first. We have everything we need. Let my life be proof that our lives are unpredictable *and* that you can push against expectations and come out (way) on top. I do not follow scripts. I do not abide by prevailing – and often toxic – thoughts. While there's ample cultural proof that these thoughts are 'right' or 'common' or 'foregone conclusions'. I see things differently and live my life accordingly. This has worked out for me quite well.

While nothing happens overnight or without a lot of hard work, you can engineer your life to match your wildest dreams. This process starts by identifying what those dreams even are, doing the work to manage your emotions, and then changing the way you think about what's possible. While my achievements seem singular – especially in the context of where I came from – I'm pretty convinced that I've done what I've done precisely so I can teach you how to do it, too.

Let's begin.

PART ONE

# VISION

*You can't be what you can't see.*

– Marian Wright Edelman

It's a simple image, one that I drew compulsively as a child: a Christmas tree decorated so beautifully and meticulously it could have been in the entryway to Selfridges, piled with presents underneath. This tree stood in front of a gigantic window next to a handsome console table, though I didn't know the word 'console' back then. Twenty years later, I realised these drawings had been a premonition: they matched, detail-to-detail, the first house I bought with my now-husband, Jens. It was December, and I had just brought our first child home from the hospital. I sat there, holding little Grey, feeling tired and blissful, and then I looked up and was startled. As the scene came together, I burst into tears.

Jens looked at me tenderly and said, 'Isn't it amazing we have a baby?'

'No,' I said. 'What's amazing is that I drew this scene five hundred times when I was a kid.' Jens had bought this fancy 1970s Danish console table, and we had a massive tree. I hadn't really looked closely before, but in that moment I realised it perfectly matched my sketches from when I was nine years old. While only about ten miles from Plaistow, that house with Jens was a world away – it represented the future I had been dreaming about, a future that called me forward. This future seemed to have little to do with my childhood, although I've come to understand the way I've stitched them together throughout my life, building a bridge to where I am now.

When I walk into rooms in the US, people think I speak the Queen's English and immediately code me as fancy – but I speak like an East Londoner, which is anything but posh. I've never identified as just English. I will always and forever be from this distinct area, which encompasses one of the most impoverished inner-city areas in the UK. It's a vibrant and incredibly diverse community – large populations of Sikh and Hindu Indians, Somalians, people from the Caribbean, English and Irish – forged together through its own culture, down to the way we dressed. In East London, you wear every good thing that you own at the same time – all your jewellery, and your best clothing is visible. And the trainers? The trainers are always fresh and never dirty.

While in many ways I'd have loved to have been born in the suburbs, into a stable upper-middle-class family with two parents and the promise of a pedigreed education, I'm so grateful that I grew up in those streets, as it was there that I learned my basic operating manual. In East London, you learn manners: you respect your elders, and you don't talk shit about parents or kids. Your mum's your mum. In East London, people say what they mean – your word is king – and people do what they say. There's no real room for meaningless pleasantries or loose talk when you're trying to survive. And, if you lie, flake – or cheat, you're going nowhere – or worse.* I've learned over the years – especially working and living in Los Angeles – that this is not standard for most. So many people make promises they have no intention of keeping, shy away from unpleasant truths because honesty makes them uncomfortable, and operate under the delusion that things should just happen for them because everything has always worked

---

* There's lots to recommend about East London, including the fact that if you were hungry as a kid, you could go into anyone's house and they'd make you a sandwich. We'd stay out in the streets playing until late because, even though it was dangerous, if you lived there, you felt protected and safe. I knew every single adult in my neighbourhood, and every kid. It was a proper community.

out before. This has not been my reality. I have never been a bullshitter, and I've never felt entitled to success – even now. I credit my East London upbringing for this: when I say I'm going to do something, I do it. I never spare people from the truth. And I am always in motion, working to make my next dream materalise.

My dreams are big – bigger than my fears and bigger than the console table and the Christmas tree that I drew as a little kid. Throughout my childhood, I knew I didn't belong in Plaistow – not in a bad way, just that it wasn't my destiny. Plaistow is etched in my heart and a huge part of why I'm successful and who I have become, but it didn't feel like home. I remember watching as the neighbour kids played with the gravel in the driveway and thinking, *I'm not supposed to be here. This is not me.* They were my best friends, and I loved them, but I always felt different, certain I'd been dropped into the wrong place as a baby. I definitely couldn't imagine signing up for the same fate I saw around me. I shared a room with two of my younger sisters, and at bedtime I liked to read to them and make up stories from our grand future. I would cut up pages of old *Vogue* magazines and fill scrapbook after scrapbook, dreaming about a different life for us. I knew it was out there. I could see it in the magazines – and more importantly, in my mind's eye. Intuitively, I understood I could trust the visions in my head and use them as signposts for what might be ahead.* As with all the visions I've received, I never assumed they were foregone conclusions or eventualities. I knew I simply didn't quite know yet how to achieve them but would figure it out. From a young age, I understood that my dreams would require work.

---

* These visions were different from my desires, too. For example, I've had a recurring dream throughout my life that I collect an award at some point – I see an orchestra and a stage, and a setup that is similar to the Academy Awards. I have no idea what this is – and no, it's not the CFDA Award that I won in 2022 – and I feel zero attachment or even excitement. I just know that someday this will happen.

I got my first job delivering newspapers when I was twelve, which taught me two things: first, it exposed me to the early-morning workers, a whole host of people who got up at the crack of dawn to get ready for real jobs (the grafters) – as opposed to the nightlife crowd that I was more familiar with who didn't get out of bed until noon and then hustled to get by.* As I did my round, I could see these early risers through their windows as they sipped their tea and read the news. I wouldn't have had this language then, but it was a meditation – and made me maniacal about creating my own morning routine. To this day, I set myself up in a very specific way. Because I'm up early, I don't overdo it with alcohol, and I don't stay out late on weekdays. The second thing my paper round brought me was a fascination with the news and information gathering. I would always buy a paper for myself so I could read about the world. I couldn't get over the idea that you could buy that much info for fifty pence! While I wasn't yet fully living in the world I dreamed of, that didn't stop me from wanting to understand it. I credit this 'always in learning mode' mentality for being a huge part of my ongoing success. I operate from a place of feeling like I don't know what I don't know, but I can learn anything.

From twelve until fifteen, I continued to get up at five o'clock every morning for my paper round, even though I found additional – and somewhat easier – ways to make money. I worked at a shop, I sold fireworks seasonally (even though I was too young to buy them) and I made sandwiches at a deli. With each one of these gigs, I did an impeccable job: I made a beautiful toastie (and still do). I also managed to strike up a big business making hundreds of pounds selling Ralph

---

* Most of my family members are workers, but even so, I watched many of the women in my life, including my mum, hook themselves up to husbands, boyfriends and partners who blew it. I knew that would never be me. My mum, however, never relied on a man financially, and I give her a lot of credit for this given our circumstances.

Lauren and YSL shirts that 'fell off lorries' to teachers during breaktime, and real Fendi Baguette bags to old ladies who won big at the bingo hall. (I still have a beaded Baguette that I knew was too beautiful to sell.) As a tween, I often had a wad of cash in my backpack, but because my fashion supply chain was uncertain, I kept my gig selling papers for thirty pounds a week. Plus, that morning ritual anchored my entire day. I learned from my family that you could never rely on a consistent flow of cash, so you should always hedge your bets.

I don't know if it was this early experience as a hustler in the playground or the fact that my mum focused *all* her maternal energy on making sure we looked put together despite whatever shit was happening at home, but I've always been obsessed with fashion – and finding a job working with clothing felt like a foregone conclusion. I also didn't have a lot of other models for what was possible, especially for women. There seemed to be more options for the boys – they were going off to football academies, they were becoming mildly famous rappers, MCs, and DJs – and because of this, they were making a lot of money. There just didn't seem to be as many roads out of Plaistow for the girls. I still remember the pamphlet I picked up at a school fair for the London College of Fashion: it was thin, matte, long and so chic. I chose the business course, mostly because it was the cheapest programme, but also because I didn't think I could sketch like a real designer, though I was certain that I could run Topshop someday. I scraped and saved half of the £6,500 tuition and borrowed the rest from my uncle Joe, my mother's brother, who was very good to me throughout my childhood.

When the course started, I was sixteen and I knew I was in trouble – I was sleeping on Marcus's couch and essentially living on my own, as my mother had moved to Spain. I didn't really even have a place to unpack my bag or the wherewithal to organise my life, much less the functional support I needed to help me be successful at college. At the time, I didn't realise I had dyslexia either – while I felt motivated, I literally could not get through the work.

There was that, as well as the reality that the London College of Fashion was then in London's West End, five minutes from Selfridges and Browns. I told myself I was doing 'market research' by stopping in to see the new Alaïa or Dolce & Gabbana instead of going to class, but I found myself constantly distracted from college by my growing interest in flipping through racks of high-end fashion. And then I became sidetracked even more when I took a part-time job at a shop across the street and performed so well I started taking on additional days. The upside of my time in retail is that I came to understand one of my genius spots: I can sell anything to anyone – even account cards, which are like a store credit card. I used to sell more account cards in the two days I worked a week than the rest of the team who worked in the shop full-time. I loved being the number one salesperson – plus, for each account card I opened, I'd earn fifty quid. *Nobody* wanted to open an account card – at the time, it was even more time-intensive and manual, as you'd have to fill out a lot of physical forms – but I could convince *everyone*. Even when someone would be declined, I'd get them to come back with proof of income so we could finish the process. I was relentless. The money was tantalising, and by the end of the first term, I'd effectively worked my way out of college. I didn't finish the year; I dropped out.

While I found studying difficult, I had an endless appetite for work – via my time in college, I understood that you could get apprentice-like work placements. I wrote about a hundred letters. Every single designer in London received a letter from me, along with every showroom and every PR agency. When I didn't get a response, I showed up in person and rang the bell, hoping I could engage someone, anyone, in a conversation to really underline my interest. Ultimately, I landed gigs at Aurelia PR, which at the time was the shit; I worked for an amazing label named Gharani Strok, which was the hottest thing at London Fashion Week; and I did some time at a concierge company called Quintessentially.*

These work-study jobs were unpaid, and you would spend sixteen hours a day toiling away – nobody was worried about your welfare or worker rights – but these apprenticeships were invaluable.† Beyond beginning to build a network, I went around London figuring out everything I didn't want to do, which is probably the most important thing you can do early on in your career. I worked and I also watched. The fact that I was a few steps removed and not an employee gave me an interesting vantage point to study the fashion world as an outsider, an industry I was intent on joining.

When I was eighteen, I landed a real job at a fashion show production company, where I stayed for six years. We produced a lot of London Fashion Week and worked on sponsorships for the best designers in London, so I got exposure to Alexander McQueen, Matthew Williamson and Vivienne Westwood as they realised their visions every year. It was so exciting to work in any proximity to those creative geniuses. But for most of the less-famous fashion talent, I couldn't understand why there seemed to be no money in any of it. The economics made no sense as I watched young, talented designers go upside down producing their shows, completely disconnected from their own businesses.

---

\* I bartered for this internship after one of the founders came into the shop and needed to exchange a Juicy Couture tracksuit that he'd bought at Bloomingdale's. He was with a girl, and it was clearly not her size. He offered to take me to a P Diddy White Party that weekend if I'd swap it out for him. I asked him who he was and why he was going to a P Diddy White Party, and he told me that at Quintessentially, they could get anything from anywhere for anyone: 'If Gwyneth Paltrow needs an organic turkey, we're the guy.' He was flamboyant and fun, and I felt like he was doing things and going places. I told him I had no interest in the party but that if I did him a favour and swapped his tracksuit, I'd like work experience instead.

† We need to bring unpaid internships back. Sure, it would have been nice to have been paid, and I desperately needed the money, but that's not why I pursued the placements. The experience and connections were far more valuable.

Ultimately, I found this production company incredibly toxic. At times it almost felt like a parody of stereotypically bitchy bosses who pitted us all against each other and made us feel terrible – *but* I learned an awful lot. And for that I'll always be grateful. I didn't think they were great businesswomen, but I was so close to what I wanted to do and what I loved. I was close to the creativity, I made a lot of contacts, and I got to know the industry from the ground up. Much of it was deeply unglamourous, but such is the reality of most careers, even the most glittery ones. While I was there, I learned how to budget, I learned how to be organised, and I learned how a designer moves from concept to collection – and the hard reality that these shows were a terrible waste of money for most, and they had no clue how to transition their artistic vision into the retailer orders that would ensure their labels would thrive. It was only ever about creating a show and the corresponding pressbook. There was so much ego attached to the artistry that nobody was talking about a merchandising plan, or the ROI you'd need to see to justify spending £150,000 on a runway show.

Ultimately, this chasm between vision and reality became my bridge to build – and this turned into the beginning of my career. From what I recall, it began with the need for TVs. A designer wanted a wall of TVs for their show backdrop, similar to one Donatella Versace had done – and naturally these aspirations did not line up with their budget. So I called Toshiba and somehow convinced them that it would absolutely be in the best interest of their brand to align with this young designer. They shipped me a load of TVs in exchange for their logo on the credit sheet, and I was off to the races. I worked in the sponsorship division for the next few years, where I would call and call for money. I had a friend of the family who was a football agent, and he told me to commission brands 10 per cent, but that felt like too little – so I asked for 20 per cent and got it. The problem is, though, that none of this revenue was going to me. Six years in, I was bringing in millions of pounds but only netting a £26,000 salary. We were the only division of the company generating any profit. I went to my bosses to renegotiate my compensation, and after arguing for a while, they told me they'd give me a £4,000 pay rise. And so I quit, as I realised that what I was doing for them I could create on my own. Rather than waiting for these women to take care of me, I needed to take care of myself. Nobody else could do that for me.

For the first time, I got really clear about my vision for my future, and I started a process that has done well for me over the years: I made a plan for turning thirty and forty, and I'm currently working on my plan for fifty. I write these plans down. I write them as a vision statement about how I want to spend my time and what I want to be doing. I assess where I am and where I want to be, and often connect this to concrete financial goals: when I was in my twenties and building my plan for my thirties, I decided I didn't want to be a salary girl forever, and that someday I wanted to fly in the front of the plane – and that I wanted a housekeeper to come once every two weeks. My current list – Emma @ 40 – lives in a sticky note on my phone so I can look at it every Sunday and ask myself whether I'm moving closer to where I want to be or shifting offtrack. Once I write it down, I work backward and then break it into yearly/monthly/weekly chunks. I know that changing habits and engineering results requires consistency, routine and focus – and continuous improvement, as nothing happens overnight. Every year on my birthday in September – my "new year" – I assess the year that's passed and plan for the year to come, a plan that needs to be realised by the actual new year. I think of this as grounding my vision, or the beginning of the process of materialising my future. I highly recommend you do this with me so you can establish the map for where you'd like to go and use it as a touchstone for the weeks and years ahead. Plus, I can tell you from experience that it's fun to understand how much you actually control in your life.

## YEARLY PROCESS[1]

**1. Looking back at the goals you didn't achieve this year, what were the main reasons you couldn't get there?**
This question requires brute honesty. You must examine the answers that come up first, and continue to ask yourself *why?* It's critical that you look to yourself and don't blame external factors.
    Write it down.

_____

_____

_____

_____

**2. What are three things you wish you did more of last year?**
Don't overthink this. It should be easy to come up with a list of three things that give you joy, feel aligned with your purpose, make you feel accomplished, have a positive impact on you, etc.
    Write it down.

_____

_____

_____

_____

**3. What are you avoiding? And what are you scared of doing?**
This could be something small like learning a new skill, or something life-altering. You choose your 'hard'. I always try to think about this one for a long time. What would you do if you didn't give a shit about what anyone would say?
    Write it down.

_____

_____

**4. How do you plan to learn and grow in the year to come?**
For me, this past year was about going to the Hoffman Process, taking a course in Transcendental Meditation and learning to swim – yes, at forty-two I was learning to swim. I try to find progress each year.
   Write it down.


**5. Habits and boundaries: what habits do you want to create, and what boundaries should you establish?**
I put these two together because to me they are both about defining limits and nonnegotiables. I never write more than three for each, and I rarely achieve all six, but that's a good start. The mere act of writing them down moves me forward.
   Write it down.


Once you've committed to a vision for yourself, it's time to move on to managing your emotions, because an inability to regulate your reaction to the world can undo any plan.

PART TWO

# MANAGING EMOTIONS

*The greatest discovery of my generation is that a human being can alter his\* life by altering his attitudes.*

– William James

---

\* (Or her . . . !)

If you were to poll a group of people, they'd probably tell you that women are more emotional than men. That's certainly the stereotype, even though there's little scientific evidence to suggest that this is a biological fact.[1] It's definitely possible that this is a cultural reality, though, and that women are more in tune with their emotions, simply because we're allowed to be. In fact, the stereotype that women are more emotional than men grants us licence to be that way. While there's a certain amount of stoicism expected from men, women are allowed to feel their feelings. This is a clear advantage. Emotional literacy and emotional intelligence (EQ) are critical skills for reading a room, tapping into cultural trends, understanding the motivations of other people, and even understanding what you want. Our emotions are often our best connection to the intelligence of the body as well – if you know how to listen.

To reap the benefits of your gut-based intuitions, and to use your emotions in a healthy way, you need to learn how to modulate and manage them. While your feelings are an essential source of information, you cannot live a healthy or functional life if you're running a decision-making process based on your anger or fear – and many of us, dare I say most of us, are. This very much used to be me. It's very human. Almost every woman I meet is terrified of messing things up and frequently so paralysed by fear that there's a refusal to start working on a dream outside of fantasising in her head. Meanwhile, some of us can't get beyond guilt, whether it's guilt about the ones we feel like we're leaving behind or neglecting in the process (children), or guilt about doing too well.

It's important to rightsize all your feelings – even your enthusiastic ones – as you consider how to best move forward. This does not mean that you run your feelings over or suppress them. In fact, because emotions are body-based, your body will have its vengeance on you in time if you leave it out of decisions completely – a lot of us ignore our own body-based 'no', for example, and agree to do things all the time that we absolutely don't want to do. This is a type of betrayal; we need to stop doing it.

I've worked hard throughout my life to get a clear read on my emotions, in part because my childhood ensured that, like many of us, I'd occasionally be flooded and overwhelmed. Since I was largely left to figure out life on my own, I didn't learn proper emotional coaching or regulation from the adults in my life – in fact, it was a boyfriend in my teens who suggested I needed help learning how to manage my feelings. I'll always be grateful for this intervention and the community-based programme I found (I could not afford therapy, nor would I have known where to look), as I learned – in time, with patience – how to listen to my emotions without letting them colour my thoughts or destroy my relationships. This takes practice, but it's one of the most productive things you can do.

These coming pages are about precisely this: before we get deeper into mindset and assessing the Old Thoughts that shape the way so many of us show up in the world, we need to clear the emotional decks first.

# 1. Anger

*One of the hardest things in life to learn is which bridges to build and which bridges to burn.*
– Bertrand Russell

'Excuse me! . . . Excuse me! Excuse me!' I was yelling. I was definitely shouting. We were underground in a tube station in London, and the woman in front of me was fumbling with her card, which was stopping her – and me – from moving through the turnstile and getting on the incoming train.

'Excuse me!' I screamed, the politesse of 'beg your pardon' completely obscured by my very explicit anger, which was about to become physical. I wanted to shove her out of my way.

She turned and gestured to me, her mouth making sounds. 'I'm deaf.'

'Well, are you blind, too??????? MOVE!' She stepped aside and I pushed past her.

Even as I type this, I feel horror, and my throat burns with deep shame. Can I even include this in my book? It was so embarrassing. And as I sat on the train, my frantic pulse finally slowing, I put my head in my hands. *What the fuck is wrong with you?* And then: *You have totally fucking lost your mind. You just blew up on a deaf woman.* I knew in that moment that if I didn't deal with my anger, it would deal with me. I could not and would not vacate the driver's seat and let my full, unthrottled rage take the wheel again. More than that, I couldn't even let my anger ride unchecked, whispering in my ear that I had every right to unleash my fury on the world. I must have been about nineteen, but that night, I enrolled myself in a free anger management course with meetings that I went to for three years. I still practise what I learned there today. In the years that followed, I also quit smoking weed, which I hadn't realised was a contributing factor for me.

Until I took this course, nobody had ever taught me the power of simply closing my eyes and taking a few deep breaths until I felt myself come back into my body. In those sessions, I plumbed my anger deeply, until I really understood the roots of my despair. For the first time, I realised I had a choice to not ever let anger get the better of me again. I walked away recognising that the goal was not to avoid feeling my anger, but to become much more skilled in expressing it. I knew it would ruin my life if it stayed unmanaged and uncontained. I had ample evidence for that all around me. I understand that anger made it difficult to stay in relationships with people and that I would need to forge stable relationships as a bridge out of my old life and into the new. Burning relationships down was not an option; I was working too hard to set myself free.

I've done a lot of work on myself to access and process all my childhood anger. I spent all my teens, and most of my twenties and thirties, feeling mad at my mum until I realised that not only did she do her best with what she had, but that she couldn't give me what she didn't have – she wasn't withholding from me; she just didn't have it to give. My mum got up and put on a suit and went to work, and she gave us what she had left over after a long day in the office. Staying angry didn't magically give me a different childhood; it only hurt me.

This type of self-work isn't fun, or pleasant, but it is essential – particularly as I've needed to prove to myself that an adult *is* in the driver's seat, an adult who is equipped to look after that younger, indignant version of me that is still inside. I do a lot of work to keep that inner child settled and calm. I also came to understand that I had learned anger as my default emotion, and I needed to learn how to choose something else instead.

This does not mean that I'm now 'soft' or that I don't get angry. I have fierce boundaries about what is okay and what is not, boundaries I don't feel badly about patrolling and enforcing. Too many of us are afraid of our anger, and we leave it bottled to fester inside – or it leaks out of us in unproductive and passive-aggressive ways. I am not that. I am direct. If I'm unhappy about something, I say it. There have been a few people in a business context in my life who have pushed me too far, and in turn, they have seen my harder side. I am not someone who feels compelled to operate according to Hollywood standards, or who abides by the insidious idea that a good woman should swallow her discomfort, allow injustice or not have her own back. I am not a pushover; in fact, I will push back. All that said, moments of intense anger are quite rare for me, in part because I try to practise impeccable emotional hygiene, dealing with things as they come up.

Most of the time – and *always* when the power dynamics lean in my favour (I *never* punch down) – when I find myself overcome with anger, I take the time to calm myself until I'm ready to express myself without destroying the people around me.

My team at work would say that I have incredibly high standards, but that I have a very fair way of ensuring those standards are met. I'm kind in how I ask for stuff to be done, though I have a low tolerance for what I perceive to be a lack of care. You can make a million mistakes, and you can ask a million questions, but if I think you don't care about the quality of your work or how you show up with your colleagues, then we're probably not meant to work together for long.

We're living in a culture where everyone feels aggrieved and takes the world personally. I don't think this is a productive way to live. This isn't to say that I don't understand why people feel resentful. I understand. I, too, was full of blame – and I grew up in a blame-drenched culture, too. Nothing was ever anyone's fault. It was always the neighbour's fault or the government's fault. Nobody was talking about personal responsibility. A culture of blame is infectious, and it was in me, too. When I got to the London College of Fashion and found myself in a sea of girls who had been privately educated, I felt furious with blame and feelings of injustice that I hadn't had the same privileges. I told myself that I'd never get through these classes, it would be impossible to succeed, and because everyone had a better start than me, they'd have a better ending, too. I'm not the sort of person who can suffer getting second place, much less last, so I dropped out.

But soon after, I snapped out of this headspace. Of course, I was watching Oprah, and she was talking about taking responsibility for yourself – that you couldn't change the world, but you could change your relationship to the world – and it clicked. My attitude shifted, and the way people responded to me shifted, too. I dropped the blame. I picked up a sense of steering my own ship.

These days I see myself as the creator of my own experience; I do not see myself as its victim. To that end, I'm generally not looking to 'get even' or settle scores publicly, or to prove myself right. I do not live my life as a giant 'fuck you'. Honestly, that's a terrible waste of energy. When one of my first bosses threatened to take legal action against me after I left her company to start my own agency, I was angry – but it never occurred to me to try to get back at her.* I simply cut her out of my life. Psychiatrist Phil Stutz calls our need for payback, or an apology, or to be vindicated, 'the Maze', and I believe that's an apt description. As he writes in *True and False Magic*, 'The only way to get out of the Maze is not to win. The only way you can get out of it is to say, *I don't have enough time to waste on this shit, so I have to let the other guy win*. The moment you do this in your mind, you can move forward.' He continues, 'The Maze represents your posture, or your interpretation of life, when you say, *I've been wronged; it's not*

---

* I'm not perfect, and I *might* laugh to myself a little when this woman's partner rings me up for new business quarterly. I will never give it to them.

*fair. The person who wronged me – robbed me, punched me in the face, disparaged me – has to make up for that in some way. I refuse to take even one more step in the direction of my goals and my needs until I get paid.* It is predicated on the idea that the universe is fair and is supposed to be fair. But if you're waiting for someone who has harmed you or hurt you to apologise, you're an idiot.' Well said, Phil. After all, what do you get if you win? This is actually a very deep question. The next time you feel like you need to 'get even' or be proved right, sit with it.

While I've made a lot of progress in managing my anger, there's an essential part of its cycle that I have yet to master: I am not good at forgiveness. As mentioned above, my instinct is to cut people out of the fabric of my life and move on because I don't want to spend any energy maintaining a relationship that doesn't feel positive or productive. In some cases, it's probably easy to argue that I should do the work to reintegrate this person on new terms. But at this point, I'm not there, and so there are plenty of people who are no longer in my inner orbit. I've either removed them from my galaxy altogether, or I keep them at a distance where I can function around them, because I do not yet have the time, energy or skill to forgive and reach for renewed closeness. I give myself grace here. To quote trauma therapist Prentis Hemphill, 'Boundaries are the distance at which I can love you and me simultaneously.'[1] I choose this type of peace instead. It's important to remember that forgiveness and repair are a process, and some people can't give you what you want because they simply don't have it to give. This is okay. Continue to move forward anyway.

---

*Anger is an essential emotion – it can show us what's important to us – but you need to become skilful in dealing with it. Do this work for yourself as early in your life as you can (though it's never too late to begin).*

## 2. Fear

*If you can't beat fear, just do it scared.*
– Glennon Doyle

'Hey, are you good?'

I leaned into the partition that separated me from the driver.

'Yeah, I'm good,' he replied. 'Are you good?'

'Well,' I offered, 'we're being followed.'

I was in South Africa as part of a delegation for the Obama Foundation, in a car with a husband and wife I'd never met. I looked in the rearview mirror, pulse racing, and clocked the cars on our tail, convinced we were about to be kidnapped – or worse. I continued to confer with the driver.

The wife tapped me on the shoulder. 'It's our security, we have a car behind us.'

'But do you have two cars?' I asked. 'There are two cars tailing us.'

She looked at me, pausing. 'How did you know that? We have one car tailing us and a second you're not supposed to know about.'

'Well, I see them. A heads-up next time would be appreciated. I thought we were about to die.'

---

I learned my hypervigilance in East London, which is, to this day, a very tough place. Twenty years ago, my husband, Jens, thought it would be a good idea to get down on one knee and propose there. As he held out a large diamond, I pulled him to his feet.

'Are you mad?!?!?! We are going to get robbed.' We were on a little cul-de-sac where I had lived for the first twelve years of my life. The primary landmark in this tiny stretch of Plaistow during my childhood was not my school; it was a pub that featured the sign *No blacks. No dogs. No Irish.* When I grew up, this neighbourhood establishment was frequented by skinheads – and naturally, one of the regulars was obsessed with me. He'd ask me out repeatedly with his braces and Doc Martens and army trousers, and I'd have to say, 'I'm sorry, but from what I understand, that would not be cool – I'm not your demographic.' I can laugh now, but danger was palpable, and dark stuff went down all around me, though I had a veil of protection from my family. Nobody messed with my uncles, and by extension, nobody messed with me. Or that's what I told myself. In reality, I didn't operate with the belief that I should be protected from fear – it didn't even occur to me that that was an option. Nobody cushioned me from reality. I was scared as shit, but I didn't have the privilege to use that as a reason not to go about my life. My family's DNA revolved around toughness. *You are strong. You don't get to be scared. Other people are scared.* I needed to push past fear and survive, which meant learning to function in a world that was a little terrifying. Today, aside from rare moments – like when I found myself hurtling through traffic in South Africa with two cars on my tail – I can easily recognise that most of the time, I'm not in 'real' danger at all, even though, yes, I am frequently scared. I think we all are.

I credit my ability to navigate fear in business to my upbringing: what I encounter now in business is not going to kill me, even if it might feel that way. I'm usually unfazed at the prospect of gambling on a product or investing in a first-time founder or starting a new business venture. This doesn't mean I'm not scared – I'm scared all the time. But I've developed the ability to use my fear as a signal that there's something important on the other side – that I'm being faced with something big, whether it's an opportunity to grow and learn, or a space to win. If fear isn't present, I know I'm not pushing my edge. I know it's so difficult, but I do believe that if you want to achieve in business and more generally get what you want from life, you will need to learn how to push through this discomfort; too many of us let it stop us in our tracks. The number one statement I hear from women I meet is *I just don't know where to start.* But they do, they're just scared. Scared they'll lose money, scared they'll fail, scared they'll embarrass themselves. I totally get it. Here's the thing, though: you're going to have to shit your pants a little bit to get to anything good on the other side. Unsavoury but true.

Now, I get it. We are taught that fear signals something life-threatening: Don't walk in a dark alley, don't wear a skirt that's too short, don't put yourself out there. Because of this, fear holds many women by the throat: fear of not being enough, fear of not doing enough, fear of messing up, fear of failure, fear of screwing up our kids, fear of losing our partners to younger and hotter people, and so on. It's an exhausting list, and I'm not even rating the existential and cultural fear that many of us mainline daily as we scroll the news over coffee. I understand that people feel the world is scary as shit. What I want you to grapple with though is that you can't let this stop you.

German psychiatrist Fritz Perls said that 'fear is excitement without the breath'.[1] I love this frame, as the two are partnered in my mind. When I feel low-grade scared about pushing into a new opportunity, or a new venture, or a new space, it's a signal for me that there's something there that I need to move toward. A little twinge of fear is the starting point for most of the big moves I make in my life. I find it extremely motivating to pick up the phone, start asking questions, and begin to sort out whatever new problem is in front of me to solve. Another word for this is 'eustress', or challenge stress. Challenge stress is when we feel called to rise to the occasion – it could be interviewing for a new job, it could be presenting at an important meeting, it could be getting married. It's those moments when you feel your pulse start to race in anticipation of doing something new or difficult. While we're understandably all convinced that stress is going to kill us, this is *good stress*. Learn to not only welcome it but embrace it.[2] While it can feel scary, it's typically misunderstood excitement.

I love the idea of challenge stress because it underlines the role we can play in being actively engaged with the world. When this is your mindset, you are rising to meet whatever is in front of you and choosing to make an impact on your life directly, rather than feeling like the world is happening *to you*, where there's little you can do to protect yourself in response. I'm convinced that if you're going to do anything interesting, if you're going to take any action in your life that's outside the lines that have been prescribed by our culture, you will have to learn how to contend with fear – and if that feels overwhelming, reframe it as challenge stress instead.

Before we move on, I want to underline this idea that when it comes to employment and our financial future, many of us do not feel in control of our destinies – we feel we operate at the mercy of our bosses. And that is, in fact, very scary – especially when we feel like we are in trouble, or that we've done something wrong. I'm going to talk about 'employee mentality' later in the book, but I'm going to argue that I used to have a propensity for looking for a 'boss' everywhere until my husband brought it to my attention that this was a debilitating way to see the world. I'm not arguing with the reality that most of us have bosses – even many CEOs report to their boards – but I do want to point out that when you see yourself as doing the bidding of someone else, stress will not feel positive; it will feel terrifying. Women in particular are exceptionally good at finding someone in the world to be in charge of them – we will outsource our decision-making to Fred, our bank manager; or Joe, our lawyer; or a critical Instagram follower any day. If we don't have a boss, we will frequently invent one to subordinate ourselves to someone who must know better.

The other day, I was in my office with several members of the executive team – my CFO, my head of HR and a handful of others. Besides me, there were two women and two men. We called in several members of the senior leadership team for some guidance on a project one by one. As we called them in, the other women and I locked eyes: 'The women are going to think they're about to get fired,' one said. The men looked at us like we were nuts. Sure enough, both of the women we called in to the meeting asked, as soon as they had stepped into the room, if they were being canned, while the men sauntered in with an inquisitive, 'What's up?'

I don't run ruthless organisations where people get fired willy-nilly – these women had no reason, at all, to think their jobs were on the line. (They run essential functions of the business – and admirably!) But their predictable reactions are a testament to a wider culture, one where women operate as though they are always under threat. I get it. I don't want to discount the way so many of us feel. And yet I want to acknowledge that this is not a good way to live, nor is it an efficient use of energy. We must stop giving other people permission over our lives. We need to shift our mindsets. We cannot let strangers dictate how we feel. Instead, we must learn how to manage our emotions so we can stay calm, centred, and in control over the right next step.

---

*If I'm not a little scared, then I know I'm not pushing enough. I use fear as a signal that something important, something that demands my attention, is in front of me. And then I move forward through the discomfort quickly and without delay in order to embrace what's on the other side. Speed is very important, because stalling and overthinking comes at a very high price.*

*Perfection is not the goal, forward motion is. If helpful, use a visual like a doorway to represent fear. You need to walk through it to get to growth and expansion. This is a muscle that you can build. In time, you will come to trust your instincts even more – that you will be okay regardless of what happens, which will help you override your fear even more.*[3]

# 3. Guilt

*Don't let yesterday take up too much of today.*
– Will Rogers

I am the oldest of four, with three younger sisters: Charlotte (one and a half years younger), Rachelle (five and a half years younger) and Katie-Beth (ten years younger). Growing up, the joke was that my mum was our dad – she worked long days making money at a bank and came home late, all out of energy. This left me to be my sisters' mother: I packed lunches for them every morning, I ironed their uniforms and I took them to and from school. Sometimes I went to school, too, and sometimes I went back home and watched Oprah on TV. As a result, my sisters still treat me like I'm their mum to a large degree. When they need something like a deposit for a flat or a bit of advice, when it's time to celebrate a happy occasion, everyone calls me or shows up at my house. My mum is a passive observer, a bit like a divorced dad who gets invited to drop by on major holidays – she's a fantastic grandmother though. My kids adore her.

It's obviously not natural or normal to be a parentified child – and there was a big sacrifice in this, as I skipped my own childhood – but I would argue that I was pretty good at it. It certainly gave me a time advantage on wrestling with mum guilt, as I learned early on that I could never do enough for my sisters to reassure myself that I had done a good job. At a certain point, I felt like I had to abandon them – they moved to Spain with my mum on a seriously misguided romantic adventure – while I moved in with Marcus and put myself through London College of Fashion.

Anyone reading this might think, *Well, Emma, don't beat yourself up. You were just a kid – of course you needed to look out for yourself,* and yet I don't think the guilt I felt then is all that different from the guilt some mums feel today. We live in a culture that subtly insists mothering should be our primary remit and ambition, that anything beyond those bounds that you might do in the 'outside world' comes at a cost to a child's health and happiness. Having experienced money scarcity in my childhood, and not having anyone who was focused on my education or future prospects, I realise I can provide both to my own children now – and that gives me some relief, as well as some authority to tell you that being the *only* safe and reliable adult your kids have access to is not emotionally realistic. For anyone.

We don't have time for a romp through our prehistory, but we evolved with affiliative care – alloparenting – which is a concept mainstreamed by anthropologist Sarah Blaffer Hrdy. We raised our children collectively and communally, with help from multiple generations. While that feels incredibly far away from our modern reality that insists on nuclear and patriarchal families, we're going to have to figure out how to approximate it through chosen family, teaming up with resources, and if one is lucky enough to afford it, hired help – there's simply no other way. Even if a mum or dad doesn't want to work, the reality of a single-income family maintaining a middle-income reality disappeared in the seventies – it's very rare to find a family that can pull that off. In almost all scenarios outside of the 1 per cent, both parents need to work outside of the home.[1] We need to accept this as a cultural norm and get over it, i.e., stop making women feel like they are being derelict in their duty by having – and maybe really wanting – a career.

We're going to talk more about this in the section on family and trade-offs, but I believe that in order to be an effective leader in business, you must contend with your ambivalence and cut yourself some slack. And as a culture, we need to make this the norm and not the rule. I have four kids at three different schools, and it's a great week when I manage a couple of school drop-offs. I have been known to snap back at security guards and teachers who comment – with surprise – that it's good to see me. Just the other week, I was ready to pick a fight at the school gate, as I said to one, 'It's not good for working mums for you to be exclaiming that they showed up.' She responded that she 'could receive that'. Good: receive it! For what it's worth, I cannot imagine a teacher saying anything like that to my husband, who is about as present as I am – and for what it's worth, I also can't imagine him noticing if they did, as men do not feel constantly on their back foot about their competency and visibility as fathers. We don't think of them as bad fathers when they're not present all the time.

Clearly, this is touchy for me as it is for so many other mothers. I'm in a constant conversation with myself about what I'm prioritising and why, and whether I'm making the right decisions. What I've learned over time is not to leave *myself* out of that calculus. I don't just think about my family's well-being; I also think about myself and what I both want and need. I make choices from that perspective, as honestly as possible – *and then I own them* and I don't equivocate. This is critical, because too often I hear my friends blame their children and their families for keeping them from a job because they refuse to own their ambition – or they shift their own guilt about working outside the home back on their kids by explaining that they *have* to be employed even though it's not what they want. We don't think about it this way, but that's what we're doing: we're making our children responsible for our choices, and that is a heavy burden. As Carl Jung wrote, 'Nothing exerts a stronger psychic effect upon the human environment, and especially upon children, than the life which the parents have not lived.'[2]

I had Michelle Obama and her brother Craig Robinson on my podcast, *Aspire with Emma Grede,* and naturally, I hit Michelle up for parenting advice. 'If you are choosing to drive in your career, don't parent from guilt,' she offered. 'I always say that kids have nothing to do but watch us. They don't have jobs. They don't have responsibility. They're figuring it out based on us.'[3] Whenever it's appropriate, I make my decision-making apparent to my kids – especially to my oldest daughter, Lola. She knows I love my work. She understands I find a lot of identity and fulfilment at the office. I do hope by modelling this for her, she'll carry less anxiety about the choices she'll have to make someday, too. We're going to talk a lot about trade-offs in the coming pages, because I want to leave you with a concrete plan for tending to them when they invariably come up.

---

*Expect guilt – it can be a helpful and healthy check when you're out of balance in your life, have fallen out of integrity or need to put something wrong right – but it's not helpful at all in excess. And before you give guilt any attention in your life, make sure that it's coming from inside of you as a signal about your values, and not from failing to meet the expectations of others.*

# 4. Sadness

*If you want the rainbow, you gotta put up with the rain.*
– Dolly Parton

The other week, my oldest son, Grey, said, 'No one sits with me at lunch.' This broke my heart until his friend came over for a playdate and confided in us that, every day, she picks Grey's lunch up and brings it to her table because everyone wants to sit with him – and then he moves away to sit by himself. When he heard this, Jens howled with laughter.

'Ohmigod, Emma, Grey is exactly like you. You always say, "I have no friends in Los Angeles," yet people are hunting you down for dinner and drinks – you always say no.' Jens isn't wrong. I don't suffer from a lack of invitations; I just rarely want to go. I have a lot of casual friends, but my closest confidantes live in London and knew me long before other people knew my name.

In some ways, I've always been a loner – and I've always felt lonely. I spend a lot of time by myself, and often by choice. Spending time by myself is critical to my mental health, and I've found that I can increase my feelings of loneliness when I spend too much time with people I don't really like or know that well. Small talk is not my friend. I find it disorienting and sad, as we all really want to be known on the deepest levels. And I don't trust anyone who doesn't know me really well. I'm also conscious of the fact that if everyone sitting at your table is on your payroll, you have a problem. The people I spend the most time with, the people I feel the closest to, the people I love, respect and have chosen to be with every day are people who work with me. Quite simply, they are the people I like the most. It's a conundrum: I know I can't just hang out with my staff, even though that's often my preference.

There is a fair amount of mental illness in my family, including a tendency for prolonged and debilitating depression. This has always served as a warning sign for me. I knew I would need to tend to my emotional health so that I never found myself taken out at the knees. And instead of denying my sadness and pain, I would pay attention to it. When I was in London and first working in fashion production, I would try to power through hard days – without fail, I'd get a migraine and need to get in bed. Later, when I started my company, every six weeks – like clockwork – I'd be overwhelmed, and I'd have to allow myself to take a pause and process my feelings. I promise: if you don't deal with life, life will deal with you. But it's also very normal to expect some sadness.

I always talk and think about my life as a 'Rule of Thirds' because I believe that if you're doing something difficult, or you're chasing your dreams with the rigour that you should, or you're going outside the norm to push yourself into a new space, you can expect to be happy about a third of the time. The other third of the time, you're going to be all right, and the last third of the time, you're going to feel a little shitty. *And that's okay.* This is part of the human condition, and we all need the resilience to deal with it.

The expectation that you should wake up every day and feel that everything is fantastic and you're killing it – that you're the best wife, the best mother and the best at work – is not realistic, and you're setting yourself up to fail. This is why I feel it's so important, as a highly visible mother and woman in business, to be honest that I have difficult days and not everything is easy. I always use the Rule of Thirds as a barometer for how I'm doing. If things are too good, then I'm probably not pushing forward enough, or I'm not seeing clearly or missing something. And if things are too difficult, then the balance is out of whack, and I need to dial it back a bit. Throughout it all, I use my emotions as a way to tune in to where I am in space and time. I let myself experience them so I don't project them onto other people. And I allow myself to take the room I need and have my process.

One of the things I grieve continually is all the people I've left behind. Some of this is geography: Bel Air is far from East London. But some of this is a function of living a very different life than I did when I was thirteen. Every time I've made a seismic move – whether it was moving to Essex to live in my uncle's house while he was in jail so I could go to a better secondary school, giving up weed and all its corresponding compatriots, leaving my first job in fashion production to start my own agency, or leaving London to launch Good American in LA – I've lost people. I've managed to pull some relationships forward, but many are lost to time, or exigency. Certain habits and ways of being, certain social groups, and sometimes my comfort zones needed to be firmly left behind.

There's a great quote attributed to Tupac: 'Just because you lost me as a friend doesn't mean you gained me as an enemy. I'm bigger than that. I still want to see you eat, just not at my table.' This is exactly how I feel about my childhood and my upbringing: to move forward, I had to prune a lot of relationships and then cauterise those wounds so I wouldn't feel too much pain about moving on. But those wounds still needed to heal. There's a lot of sadness that comes with slowly tending to that pain of loss. When I was young, the only way I knew how to cope was by quickly moving on and away from situations. Now, I can sit with discomfort and know that I can handle it. Or at least I'm better at it.

I have always kept a journal – not so much so that I have a record of my days but so that I have a container for my feelings. Honestly, it's one of the best ways to get a handle on what I'm really thinking, as it pushes my thoughts past my judgmental mind. When I feel my emotional well getting full, I know I need to rest for a bit and write things down. I don't reread it much; I just write. This always levels me out.

I've noticed that motherhood has also evened me out a bit. This is partly because my kids create a natural break in my day – when I get home, my phone goes away for a few hours, and only those with access to my bat phone landline can reach me, which gives me a mental reprieve from work and other people. It's also calibrated my concerns. The minute I had a baby I had a revelation that I had been completely worried about the wrong things. Before I had Grey, I would wake up in the middle of the night to do amendments to contracts I'd be negotiating; I haven't done that since. And, on the flip side, as soon as I had Grey I also felt a surge in ambition. I wanted to be back in the world and at work almost immediately. As much as I loved also being with him, having him made me realise how much I am capable of, and the bigness of my life. But I will say that having kids put a boundary on my energy in a way that's been very helpful. I don't kill myself during the week thinking that I'll recalibrate at the weekends. A weekend with four kids isn't restful, so I need to find a way every day to break the chaos and focus on myself, even if it's just for ten minutes. I suggest you do the same.

Another way I apply the brakes is meditation. I started doing Transcendental Meditation this year and have miraculously managed to find twenty minutes almost every morning to practise. I've trained myself to think of it as a different kind of work so I don't feel so selfish when I slip away to do it. When I find myself overwhelmed by politics, existential dread and concern for my kids, it's become an essential way to return to myself and fill my tank. I feel far more grounded and resourced when I'm done. I need space and time like this because I get hundreds and hundreds of emails and texts a day, and I'm pulled from pillar to post – it's become increasingly important to find ways to slow myself down before feelings of overwhelm force me to. A lot of people think of meditation as a way to calm down the mind before bed, but it actually plays the opposite role in my life: I sit for twenty minutes, about three or four times a week, and clearing my mind fills me with energy and the space for creativity and problem-solving. Finding out what gives you energy is really worth spending time on.

I also drop everything anytime for the people I love. I will walk out of a meeting to take a call from one of my sisters. I will fly to London for twenty-four hours so I don't miss a close friend's birthday. When I love, I love deeply. We all need people in our lives whom we don't need to explain ourselves to, who are massively supportive of us outside of our primary romantic relationships. For me, Chenelle, Melissa, Holly, Etty and Poppy are these women. They are friends I found in my late teens and early twenties when I was working my first real job. I was broke, and because I never went to university, I was the youngest alongside Chenelle. Without fail, when I headed off to the night train, Melissa would insist on giving me twenty quid for a cab to get home. They paid for all my weed and every single cocktail for years. I'm forever indebted to them for showing me a different side of life, helping me have fun, never judging my choices, and loving me so hard.

As I think about it, it's not that surprising that I feel lonely, particularly because as much as there is to love about Los Angeles, its relationships are largely transactional, and that can be a tough pill to swallow. It's rare to find an opportunity where you really get into someone's life story and come to know them deeply, without any expectation that there's something to *get* from the encounter. This is why I love meeting cab drivers when I travel. I love hearing what people are about when there's absolutely no agenda outside of getting from here to there. People are so interesting, and warm, and good, especially when you can both settle into the present moment without any expectation of a return on that time except for a great conversation.

Ultimately, as a culture, I wish we were all more comfortable discussing our loneliness and sadness, particularly when we're people whom others perceive to be at the pinnacle of success, who surely must have it all figured out. I've figured a lot of things out, it's true, but you can't 'solve' sadness. And sometimes I'm very sad. I believe it's important to speak about this: it's easy to use social media as a glossy highlight reel of permanently good times and 'winning' moments. Not only do I experience a lot of sadness, but I experience deep disappointment, discomfort and hard-to-hear feedback a fair amount, too. This is okay. Being sad won't prevent you from achieving greatness; it's an essential part of the human experience. I've come to not only expect it but to embrace it as well.

---

*Social media will try to convince you that you should always feel great, but the reality is that life is sometimes hard, and in its own way, that's great, too. When we start with ourselves, sadness is a signal to listen to. It invites us inward, asking us to take responsibility for ourselves. Sadness, when you welcome it rather than resist it, becomes a mirror – showing us not what is wrong, but what is unfinished. To expect sadness isn't about being pessimistic, but about being prepared. Sadness is a natural response to living. In this way, it is not weakness but a useful tool for self-ownership.*

# 5. Joy

*If you're not positive energy, you're negative energy.*
– Mark Cuban

Several years ago, I went to the Hoffman Institute in Northern California to do their 'process'. You can't really go out in Los Angeles without hearing about the 'Hoffman Process', which is a week of group therapy where you 'bury your childhood' and better understand your patterns. People are really fanatical about it. Ultimately, I had high hopes for finding forgiveness, but that's not the moment that stands out for me.

I can naturally be quite lighthearted – I love to laugh, and I love to dance. I'll dance until 6:00 a.m. if I'm left to my own devices. But on this particular day, a group of us were in a circle, and we were supposed to be doing a series of silly things. I was sober, it was the middle of the afternoon, and I just couldn't bring myself to dance around with a bunch of people I'd only known for two days. I told the leader I was tapping out. 'Nope, sorry, this is not for me.'

He approached me on the sidelines and said, 'You know, Emma, you have four kids – you might need to learn how to play.' Now that was a gut punch.

I thought about that a lot in the weeks and months after. I don't know if it's because I felt saddled with responsibility so young, but I don't remember ever playing. Kids would come around to our cul-de-sac and ask me to come out and hang out, and I remember feeling offended: *As if. Please tell them to go away.* I refused to even go to the door. My mum would urge me to go and hang out with kids my own age, but I was definitely that child who only wanted to sit with the adults. I don't know if I'm serious by nature or I just skipped that part of childhood where you learn how to be carefree, but I couldn't relate to the other kids. I've never been carefree; I don't know what that would even feel like. But I have found ways to feel a lot of joy.

While you need to manage your anger and fear, you really can't 'manage' joy. And you can't manufacture it either. In my experience, it comes unbidden and leaves just as fast. But joy is a better goal than 'happiness', which as a steady state seems unreachable. This insistent cultural idea that we're supposed to be consistently content and happy, or put that idea of ourselves forward on social media, really holds us back, because it feels like we're failing when it doesn't feel as perfect as it looks.

What I've come to understand, though, is that while joy doesn't come on demand, you must take responsibility for clearing the barriers that make joy hard to find. There are a lot of things in my life that threaten to take my joy away: I get calls all the time from people who want money from me (and nobody ever wants a hundred dollars from me; they want $10,000 or more); there are endless hurdles at work; I need to navigate a lot of business complexity both in and outside of the office. It's in my hands to create my joy despite the basic reality that life sometimes makes it hard. For me, this comes down to habits, routines and rituals that I know I can rely on for an infusion of joy: girl trips with my friends, family time with my husband and kids, getting good sleep, and taking care of my mind and body. No one has made me happier than I make myself. I take this responsibility very seriously.

I talk about the Rule of Thirds a lot because we live with a false belief that you can *buy* happiness – that money will solve your emotional problems and deliver you to a place where you wake up smiling and content. Money can solve a lot of problems, it's true;

specifically, money can solve all your money problems. And I'm a fierce advocate for women making more of it – but money doesn't make everything easy or okay. You can believe me on this point: I've experienced all sides of the wealth spectrum. At many points in my early life, we were scraping pennies, while some members of my extended family were frequently quite flush (not always from the nicest or most savoury sources). Those family members were typically the most miserable. Meanwhile, my father, who as a British Telecom engineer made about £35,000 a year for the majority of his life, is *joyful*. He's a happy, mellow soul – everyone in his house is mostly content and chill, most of the time. Now, to be fair, he wasn't present in my early life. My mum was twenty-eight and single, with three kids under five, so I don't know that joy was as easy to come by for her. But joy is not contingent on having everything dialled in. I was chatting with Mark Cuban recently on my podcast, and he told me the story of his first entrepreneurial venture, born out of a desire to get a reasonable place to live (he was sleeping on the floor in an apartment he shared with five other guys). 'My attitude is if you're happy when you're broke, you'll be happy when you're rich. If you were miserable when you were broke, there's no amount of money that's going to change you from being miserable. When I was sleeping on the floor, I was still having fun.'[1]

I have a pretty low bar for feeling like things are pretty good. I'm optimistic and inclined to see the upside. I wake up every day feeling thrilled to be alive and so happy to be in my bed in Bel Air. As it were, I could still be in Plaistow, or worse. I held a meeting with my business managers a few months ago – my holding company is called E13, which is the postcode for the area where I grew up. So we all looked on Google Earth to see from whence I came. As they peered around, I watched their faces in amusement. It's one thing to say a neighbourhood is rough, but it's another thing to watch people experience it from afar.

'I thought I grew up in a terrible place, but most of these cars don't have wheels? I don't understand.' The woman who made the comment grew up in Long Beach.

'Yeah,' I responded, 'that's how it was when I was younger, too. People would just steal the wheels off cars, and these vans would stay abandoned on the street. It's nice to know some things never change!' There's a marked difference between my bedroom view as a child and my bedroom view now.

While I left Plaistow behind, it's a huge part of who I am. I've made a new life and created an entire world for myself across the globe, in part because I've always understood that I'm responsible for my inner state. My happiness is on me. I've never looked for anyone else to make me happy. I don't expect my husband to make me happy. I don't expect my children to make me happy. And I don't expect the outside world to make me happy. I'm the only person who can do this for myself. I control my thoughts, which we'll turn to now.

---

*Treat your emotions – including the hard ones – as important information. Your emotions are not your enemies. You get to choose how you respond to life; it's a choice you get to make every single day, maybe the most important choice of them all. While it's easier to be joyful when life is being kind to you, it's up to you to decide how you're going to show up in the world. It's a skill to choose how you respond to whatever you're feeling, but it's one I practise every day.*

## PART THREE
# OLD THOUGHTS

*Maybe the journey isn't so much about becoming anything. Maybe it's about un-becoming everything that isn't really you, so you can be who you were meant to be in the first place.*

– Paulo Coelho

'Emma, aren't you so grateful for all that you've done in your life?' It was early morning, and I was in a TV studio, somewhere, bathed in stage lighting.

Wait, *what?* I felt a flash of anger as I processed the question, confused for a second by my own irritation.

'I don't feel grateful,' I responded. In my mind's eye, I could see my publicist shift uncomfortably just out of frame behind me. 'I don't feel fortunate. I earned my right to be here.'

The anchor smiled uneasily and we moved on, though I didn't want to. I wanted to ask her if she'd ask a man the same question, but I played nice on TV at the risk of coming across as an ungrateful bitch.

Now, first, I have a gratitude practice like so many of us. I know the science behind gratitude and that it can lower stress and promote feelings of well-being. I practise this, too. I'm grateful for my beautiful and peaceful home. I'm grateful that I have a wonderful husband who keeps me happy and entertained all the time. I'm grateful that my kids aren't spoiled brats. I'm grateful for many, many things. I make a list and run through it as I brush my teeth in the morning, and I know the list is long because I brush my teeth for the full two minutes that my dentist prescribes.

But I also know how psychologists Robert Emmons and Michael McCullough define it, explaining that gratitude requires two steps:

the first, 'recognising that one has obtained a positive outcome' and the second, emphasis mine: 'recognising that *there is an external source for this positive outcome*'.[1] There you go.

So, no, I'm not grateful for my success. I'm *proud*. I did that. I didn't do it alone, certainly – I chafe when businesspeople are described as 'self-made', as I recognise I've been supported by an incredible team and great business partners, including people who have believed in me before I believed in myself – but that doesn't diminish the reality that I am responsible for the trajectory of my life. I've made something beautiful and significant. *I am so proud of myself.*

There is a tendency among women to ascribe our success, our achievements, our accomplishments to external factors. We speak in the passive voice: *This job was given to me because this person made a call on my behalf. This business became successful because this person posted it on TikTok.* There might be some truth to those statements – we encounter and impact each other's lives all the time – but you are not a bystander in your own life. Your success and ability to move forward is not merely a function of lucky happenstance or a grateful mindset or being in the right place at the right time. To be in the right place at the right time, *you* must put yourself in motion. *You* must take action. And you must take responsibility for that action.

When we assume the state of *hoping* for something to happen to us or *credit* some external party for determining our future, we do a deep disservice to ourselves and other women. When we attribute our success (or lack thereof) to other people or systems or unseen forces, we are disowning our own power, suggesting that we don't have much agency in creating our own lives or charting our own destinies. In this view, we're simply the recipient of a good, or bad, hand of cards. When we're in this mindset, we see ourselves as victims of circumstances. Of course, there are real victims in our world, but that's not what I'm talking about. I'm talking about our tendency to blame or credit other people for what happens with our lives. Stop that. Stop playing down your gifts and your efforts. Instead of: *My kids really need me, so I shouldn't take a bigger job, even though it would be a major next step*, how about: *Yes, my kids need me, but they also need a parent who is fully expressed. Instead of blaming them for holding me back, I'm going to take responsibility for managing my guilt and ambivalence.* Or: *I got passed over for that promotion because Andy is a show-off and is always in everyone's face.* Instead: *I don't care if people think I'm full of myself. I'm going to do great work, draw attention to it, and ask for a promotion. If they say no, I will figure out my next steps.* If you need some inspiration, I love the Snoop Dogg video when he received his Hollywood star. First he thanks the academy and his fans and family. And then he says: 'I wanna thank me. I wanna thank me for believing in me. I wanna thank me for doing all this hard work. I wanna thank me for having no days off. I wanna thank me for never quitting. I wanna thank me for always being a giver and trying to give more than I receive. I wanna thank me for trying to do more right than wrong. I wanna thank me for just being me at all times. Snoop Dogg, you're a bad motherfucker.'[2] Try this little speech for yourself as you brush your teeth!

You can certainly live your life like you're a passive actor in a larger play, hoping a director offstage gives you a good part with good lines and tells you where to stand so the spotlight is directed on your best side. But I don't recommend this, and it's certainly not how I live my life – nor is it how I assess founders and potential hires. I see myself as the creator of my own life, someone who acts directly on the world and both suffers and celebrates the results. While it's so much easier to blame others when things don't go our way, I resist this impulse with all my might. I create my own reality – and then I own it.

This is one of the reasons why I chafe at the way that we talk about 'empowering women'. This is part of our collective script,

I get it, I'm sure I've said these words, too. They're one of those throwaway phrases that sound good on Instagram or a business panel. But as I think about the idea more deeply, it bothers me. It suggests that whomever we are 'empowering' – typically women, people of colour or others whom we perceive to be disadvantaged in the cultural hierarchy – don't have power already, so we need to give them some. We are all very powerful. It may not always feel like it – often, it can feel like you're swimming upstream – but I would argue that this type of resistance builds strength and flexibility and endurance. It might feel painful at times, but it is definitely a less acknowledged type of power. I am here for that. So, instead of talking about empowering each other, I'd like us to use more specific language: we can stand behind each other in a show of protection, strength and support; we can put our resources and energy into each other's work to expand its reach and add fuel to its growth; we can help create a strong foundation – through sharing advice, expanding networks, making recommendations, investing capital – on which people can both stand and build. We can do this not from a place of scarcity but only from one of abundance.

I'm being a stickler about words because our thoughts dictate our actions, and our actions (or lack thereof) create our reality. Going back to the difference between feeling proud of what you've achieved versus feeling grateful for what's 'happened to you', I want to acknowledge that I know saying 'I'm proud' is difficult for us. We immediately try to diminish our own light before others do it for us. We do this out of fear of being destroyed by those who might think we're arrogant braggarts, women who need to be put back in our place. But I also think we do it because it's the script handed down by other women. It's modelled for us everywhere, so we run these same words and thoughts as though they are our own. We are moving through our lives on autopilot, mimicking the thoughts and actions of those who have come before us.

There's some wisdom in doing this, as there's much to bring forward. I love a shortcut. But when I look at what women have achieved, I'm not convinced that we've charted a path to the top of the mountain, or one worth printing on maps and passing to our daughters and friends. This is one of the reasons I wanted to write this book – to add my route to our collective wisdom about women and success. And it's one of the reasons I push back so hard on abiding by the prevailing thoughts of the culture; doing this isn't working out so well for us. As Albert Einstein may have (apocryphally*) pointed out, 'Insanity is doing the same thing over and over again and expecting different results.'

Before we dig in, I want to be clear that I'm not suggesting you have control – or that I have control – over the world. I'm not suggesting that I know with any specific certainty what will happen because of my direct actions. Life is wholly unpredictable, which is also what gives it its meaning. (Think about how freaky a cause-and-effect world would be: if you knew what would happen, without fail, there would be no point to life.) While you can't control the outcome, you can control the way you relate to and respond to the world. That's what I'm interested in cultivating, both in myself and in all of you. The following pages are about the role we all have in choosing our thoughts carefully – and what's possible when you take full responsibility for yourself in your life.

None of us have time to wait for equity; we have to make it.

---

* The internet seems to be divided over whether Einstein or a mystery writer named Rita Mae Brown said this. I think we should give it to Rita – regardless, it's sound wisdom.

# 1. Trade-Offs

*There are no solutions. There are only trade-offs.*
– Thomas Sowell

I'm convinced that a key part of my success is my ability to both anticipate and accept trade-offs. I call these the 'unavoidable choices' we all make. I'm a gifted operator, but I can't be in two places at once. I recognise there are limits to my time, energy and power, *and* more importantly, I allow this to be the reality without constantly beating myself up about it. It's one thing to not make it to your kid's basketball game because you have a big meeting; it's another to miss the game and then spend hours feeling guilty and looking to your child to reassure you that they won't be seeking therapy for your absence when they're an adult. You must make the choice, accept the trade-off and move forward – or better yet, the other way around: predetermine what the trade-off will be. You can do all the things – you just can't do them all at the same time. As Michelle Obama said to me, 'It's impossible to have it all, so stop with that. You can have it all over a period of time, but the impatience of like, "I've got to have the exact job at the top of the game, and I want to be the best mum. I want to be there, be at all the stuff, and I want to look my best and be in my best shape and be emotionally in tune, la, la, la, la, la. And my marriage has got to be on point." You can't do all of that. There are trade-offs and it's okay. If we're blessed, we can take care of ourselves emotionally and physically. Life is long and you can have chapters, and you don't lose out because you didn't read the whole book in one sitting.'[1] As someone who also thinks about her life in chapters, this really resonates.

It's a type of insanity that women are convinced they'll pull this having-it-all ruse off. Practically, what does 'having it all' even mean? Life is not a to-do list; you're not going to tick all the boxes every day. You must find a way to give yourself grace and accept that perfection here is not only impossible, its pursuit will limit the joy you find in your life. It's time to cut yourself some slack and prepare to pace yourself through life.

### 1. Old Thought: It's either/or . . .

> *We don't have to be smarter than the rest. We have to be more disciplined than the rest.*
> – Warren Buffett

A few weeks ago, I took my twins to school – every Friday there's an all-school gathering in the chapel, and I try to make it occasionally. I felt like I was winning that morning until a fellow mum asked me if I had made my twins, Lake and Raffi, birthday crowns. I immediately panicked. First, what the fuck is a birthday crown? And second, was I supposed to make one?

She asked me if I had seen the school email, and my panic subsided. Easy answer: I hadn't. 'I don't read any school emails.'

'What?' She looked at me like I was nuts.

'They go into the same pile as the Aritzia or Gap emails. I don't really read any of them.'

She looked at me again quizzically and then turned her attention to her son and *his* birthday crown, and I realised the source of her question: apparently, when it's the twins' birthday, I'm supposed to jazz up some paper crowns so they can be celebrated. And if I miss the email alert? Should I feel terrible and beat myself up, or can they use their imaginations to summon a crown for their heads? I'm thinking the latter. They certainly won't die of disappointment. One of my least favourite things about the culture is this expectation that mums are supposed to be some sort of superhero for everyone except themselves. Jens definitely isn't losing sleep over school emails and birthday crowns.

Women ask me all the time whether they can have kids, or whether it will derail their careers. *Can you have kids and be successful?* My answer is always the same: yes, so long as you refuse to let the culture get to you. You need to resist a culture that insists you perform perfectly in both spheres simultaneously.

A lot of life comes down to timing and questioning the presumption that there's a right way to do things, and the only 'right way' is to throw yourself full throttle at everything that presents in your life – *especially* when it comes to your kids. There's an idea that, yes, you can have a job, but only so much as this career requires no pull on the attention that should otherwise go to your children. For this reason, there are a lot of women who are overextended and exhausted – *and* loaded with guilt because they're not living up to some sort of cultural ideal – and a lot of women who don't think it's worth the fight to even consider doing both. There aren't many of us who are easily wearing a successful and vibrant career while feeling like we are also a good mother – and there also aren't many of us who don't have to work, whether we have a partner or not. I'm the product of a single mum – we were already poor, and we would have been homeless if she hadn't worked. A 'good mother' is one of those really tough concepts: who exactly counts? When have you done enough for your children to make it into these hallowed mother-of-the-year halls? When have you done too much and limited your child's ability to figure out life for themselves? Who gets to decide if your child is a success story, and along which factors? The whole concept is flimsy. If someone offered me a catalogue of mother archetypes as a kid, I probably would have picked Clair Huxtable over mine, and yet I look at where I am in my life and I have to tip my hat to my mum. Either I forged myself out of my environment *or* perfect parenting might not be as essential as we've been led to believe. I watched my mum leave the house every day and not return until after dinner. This was tough but perhaps not damaging – it was certainly an inspiration of sorts.

I believe that our kids don't need us as much as we've either been conditioned, or sometimes *wanted,* to believe. I really think that mothering need not be so intense. I have four kids – that's a lot of drop-offs, playdates and needs to meet – and I am wise to pick my battles. I also married a Swedish man and fully drank the Kool-Aid of being with someone who comes from a country with far better standards of gender equity. I never once assumed that I would be a better parent than Jens – and as a result, neither does he. This balances our parenting and marriage in a way that has given me a lot more space than many of my other married friends enjoy – this is space I then don't beat myself up for taking. I do myself the service of not feeling bad about seemingly having more freedom than other mums, who let the lead parent role default to them.

The maintenance of this balance – particularly in an American culture that bends so insistently toward the idea that a woman's primary job needs to be in the home (#tradwife) – requires me to check my own masculine energy at the door when I come home at night. And I have a lot of masculine energy. I give direction and tell people what to do for most of the day. By the time I get home, not only do I want a break, but I need a reprieve. I do not parent my husband. I once watched my dearest friend explain how to make a sandwich, step-by-step, to her husband. I have never done that shit and I never will.

The other day, I was scrolling through Instagram and I encountered a post from a mum influencer explaining her child's perfectly bento-boxed school lunch. Veggies were cut into elaborate shapes, the macros were balanced and there was nothing 'fun' in sight. Everything was gluten-free, sugar-free and so on. (I'm guessing that this perfectly architected lunch was not consumed by her kid.) There was so much anxiety in her voice. The whole thing is bananas when you think about it, except that this guilt-based, fear-fomenting content is like catnip for mums. When I was living in London, a friend's four-year-old daughter went into anaphylactic shock the first time she went to a birthday party because she had a piece of cake – a regular old cake from Marks & Spencer – but she had never had sugar like that before. Her system freaked out. Is this the best use of this family's energy? If I take my kids trick-or-treating or get them to a birthday party, I feel like I've won the day – and making them fork over the sweets they've dressed up in costume for is not a good use of my time. This level of over-parenting is not good for kids either. Who is it good for? It's killing women, who already feel so overburdened by all the things they're supposed to think about: the ingredients in their kids' snacks, the way they speak to their children, how they put them to bed, the lotion they put on their skin . . . we are now being sold scripts on Instagram for engaging with our own offspring. It's a type of madness. Honestly, parenting is not that deep. It's just not that deep. What your kids need: a lot of love, someone who sees them, someone they can depend on no matter what, moments of repair after big upsets, and guardrails. I don't think my kids need me to hover over them in anxiety, worrying about every meal and every after-school enrichment opportunity. That's not what my kids need from me, and I'm not a bad mum because I feel that way. I've come to believe that my kids have fewer 'real' needs than other mums feel their kids do. I'm comfortable with this.

It can feel very countercultural to not participate in mum guilt. Many of my friends make a sport of this, lamenting everything they miss while simultaneously resenting how much of their own lives they've thrown on the sacrificial pyre for their kids. This is a cop-out – it's fun to be friends with me, I promise! – and too many of us use the cultural pressure of being an ever-present mother as a reason not to pursue our own dreams. Don't misunderstand me though. I'm deeply indebted to all the people whose mission in life is working with kids. This is a calling for many, whether it's as a parent, a teacher, a childminder or a coach. This is simply not where I feel called to serve. And because of this, I'm very clear about controlling expectations and communicating clearly so that I don't embark on an impossible balancing act where I'm under-delivering all over the place – and making others help me carry the guilt that results.

I do this by being incredibly clear about the trajectory of my life and my own nonnegotiables. I think clearly about my goals – including my goals around the time I spend with my kids, and the other things that give my life deep meaning – and say no to everything that doesn't get me closer to them. Sometimes this also means saying no to things that I really want to do. And it makes it easier to say no to things I don't want to do, too. For example, I don't do anything at my kids' schools that doesn't involve them. It isn't meaningful to them that I volunteer for the mums' coffee or go to the school gala; it is meaningful to them that I'm at their school play if they are taking part. As I mentioned, every September around my birthday, I spend a few weeks working on my annual plan, my own New Year's resolutions, which involves carefully planning out my year. I do this so that when trade-offs inevitably present themselves, I'm prepared to meet them and better able to manage the pressure. These resolutions become my blueprint for the year ahead. As part of the visioning process for my career, I also ask myself the following questions as it relates to my family – and I reassess every few months.

- What would a great year look like?
- What am I willing to sacrifice?
- What progress do I want to make and where?
- What gives?
- What am I not willing to sacrifice?

- How do I want to look back at this year in twelve months' time?
- What is important to my kids?

Once I've committed this to paper, I start the time-consuming task of working my way backward, step-by-step, in chronological order, until I arrive at today. I use this master blueprint to make to-do lists, and I keep the bullet points on my home screen to hold myself accountable throughout the year. Not only does this blueprint help me architect business success, it helps me to ensure that my kids take priority in the year, too, and that I'm buttressing intense work periods with opportunities to spend deep time with them as well. This allows me to be fully present wherever I happen to be, rather than feeling like I'm being pulled in multiple directions.

This clarity of intent is important because we can often feel that we are never enough, and that whatever we do, we should really be doing something else. Planning allows me to create a shield against these pressures, and it gives me the time in advance to get comfortable with the inevitable trade-offs that are coming my way. And there are many: you cannot be a mum with perfect attendance and have a demanding career. You cannot be a leader and a people pleaser. You can't please your children all the time. You will miss out on things. Feelings of guilt are to be expected, but these feelings are not a good reason to put off going after what you want.

While balancing between career and family certainly puts pressure on trade-offs, I've been noticing a cultural trend among younger women I encounter who don't yet have families, a trend that worries me as well. It's the insistence on prioritising self-care and a soft life over career. Listen, I do a lot of self-care – it counters the amount of energy I expend in my career. But I see it as part of a balance: energy in, energy out. It can't just be energy in. While I understand all the impulses that make this generation want to push back against hustle culture, I don't think this is the right trade-off. I worked my arse off in my twenties – yes, I got an early start because I didn't go to university, and I still made time for fun, especially in my teens,* but I was mostly pedal to the metal. By the time I hit thirty I had built and scaled my own agency. I didn't yet have kids. I didn't have a mortgage or other looming responsibilities or concerns, so I applied all my energy to my career.

This story might make you groan, but when I had my agency ITB, I used to wake myself up in the middle of the night to see if I needed to respond to any lawyers' questions or comments on a celebrity's contract. I couldn't bear a long turnaround time when I was trying to close a deal and keep a client happy, so given the time difference between London and LA, I'd wake myself up to make sure it all got done. While I'm not advocating unhealthy work habits, I'd be lying if I didn't say that there will be moments in your career where it will make sense to push it beyond typical expectations.

Looking back, it's easy to put my friends in two buckets: those who worked hard in their twenties and those who were unfocused. When I look at how successful they are now, the difference in the two buckets is very, very clear. When I was in my twenties, I very much recognised that this was my time to make considerable headway in setting myself up for a career that would give me a shot at financial freedom. I intuitively understood that I had outsize ambition, and I was never going to make it with a low work ethic. As I tell members of my team, you're never going to be able to do what you say you want to do working three days a week. You can't do Pilates, walk your dog, go surfing, work three days a week and then come to me for a pay rise.

For anyone saying, *I don't want to give my life to work,* I'd say don't. But if you're an ambitious little monster like me, then I'd tell you that

---

* I once found hourly ironing work so that I could support myself while couch surfing through Ibiza when I was seventeen. Those were some of the best months of my life – ten out of ten, would recommend. But I knew it was a temporary reprieve from my life back home and not my fate to date club DJs and dance until 6:00 a.m.

you're thinking about it completely wrong if you're not planning on applying yourself fully for a decent period of time – like ten years minimum. I would think of devotion in the earliest years of your career as being an investment in yourself. When you're evaluating any opportunity, you need to assess compensation (salary, bonus, potential equity), the value of the brand on your résumé and, most importantly, *what you can learn and gain for yourself.* When you're young, this last part should be of primary importance – go where you can learn and grow. You probably won't make much cash, but take that as an acceptable, often necessary, trade-off. Money will come. Go where you can get the most leverage to use your experience as a stepping-stone to your future. Recognise that throwing yourself into your career in your twenties when you're relatively unbound by responsibility will be good for you later. I can't compare because I didn't graduate from university, but it feels like a master's degree. My twenties were a grind and I didn't make much money, but I set myself up for my thirties and forties. While there are certain moves that led to failures, fundamentally I would have done it the same way again with no regrets.

The other thing I've observed on my teams is that many women are overly concerned with other people. They're worried that this person isn't getting paid enough. They're worried that that person isn't getting enough rest. They're worried that this person isn't fulfilled. It strikes me as a uniquely female trait. I recognise that nurturing might be conditioned into us, or perhaps it comes more naturally to women, but I also believe the tendency can be attributed to the fact that putting yourself first – and surging forward in your career regardless of everything else – is simply *hard.* And we don't have enough models in the culture of women doing it without misgivings. Instead of focusing on what you want, and how you want to distinguish yourself, it becomes easier to look around and find other places to spend your energy. Ultimately, rather than focusing on meeting our own needs, we feel pressured to look around and try to meet the needs of other people instead. I so understand this urge – and it's a beautiful thing – but I'm not sure we can afford it. I want us to stop doing that. *I want women to stop caring for other people in a way that they aren't caring for themselves.* Start with yourself. Putting yourself first is self-care, self-care that is not about a spa day. It's nailing down your career, your financial future and the freedom to find your own way, whatever your choices. This pays off considerably down the line and creates all sorts of options and possibilities that then let you take care of people in an even more powerful way.

It sounds like a stereotype, but in my experience, men have a much easier time sticking to the mission and keeping their eyes on the prize. I wonder sometimes if it goes back to vision and whether we are willing to dream big dreams and commit them to paper. It sometimes feels like we don't have a plan for ourselves. Yes, we want a promotion. Yes, we want to make more money. But we don't necessarily have a bigger vision for our lives. When I push women to tell me what they ultimately want, I tend to point out that if that's what they really want, they don't seem to be trying to achieve it. 'Have you thought about the necessary steps it's going to take to get there?' Often, the answer is no. It's not that they're without ambition, but they are often operating without a clear strategy.

We partly get tripped up in our visioning for the future because we aren't prepared for trade-offs. Culture conditions us to believe that you shouldn't have to sacrifice anything to achieve your dreams, that you shouldn't be forced to compromise at all. This is one of the most unpopular things I say, and I get a lot of grief for it – in fact, get ready to throw this book across the room – but things in your life will have to give, and you're not going to get what you want quickly. Nobody wants to hear this part, but it's the truth: they're called trade-offs for a reason. To win, you will often feel like you're losing – and sometimes losing a lot. And it's not easy. If it were easy, everyone would be doing it. Really throwing yourself into your career and life doesn't always taste nice – and it's definitely not always fun. But if this is what you want, it is worth it. What are you willing to give to get what you want? You need to get very clear about that answer. Many women look to me thinking I've found a magical way to make packed lunches for my kids really quickly, or that I must have found a secret portal to get home for bedtime every night, regardless of where I am in the world. I haven't found any shortcuts that you can't figure out for yourself. I don't make packed lunches. I'm often not there for a goodnight kiss. It looks like I 'have it all', but I've traded off a lot – and I continue to do so every single day.

I get that there's a tremendous amount of disillusionment in the culture. We're at a moment where it's hard to imagine an end goal. We can't buy a house. We can't find a good guy. And we feel really far away from having a kid. I hate that this is stopping so many of us; we can't let it. Find your nonnegotiables, write them down and prepare yourself to trade off the rest. This will give you peace. I hope my legacy helps change the thinking about this and encourages more women to focus on themselves in the context of business to make the rest of the vision more accessible. If you circumscribe your ambition at the beginning of your career, you will leave your life partially unfulfilled, thinking about what could have been. This is one thing I cannot accept for my own life – or for yours.

New Thought: **It's both/and, which requires anticipating trade-offs and planning for them.**

---

2. Old Thought: **Not only is there a right decision, but the 'rightness' of your decisions should be apparent right away.**

*Things turn out best for the people who make the best of the way things turn out.*
– John Wooden

A few weeks ago, a fellow school mum called me to rage about an issue at our kids' school – I let her go on for a bit and then told her I had no idea what she was talking about.

'Ah, it must be so nice to never really be tapped into what's happening.'

It was passive-aggressive, yes, but it's also her loss. I'm very comfortable paying for a service and then letting the people I've hired get on with it. I don't need to be in my kids' school curriculum. I've trusted them to do their job, and I don't need to check their work.

Early on in my career, I learned the power of delegation; I hire people I trust to make decisions on behalf of the business – or in the example above, in my kids' education. One of my mantras is *no small details*. Don't ask me what time my flight is or what day we're meeting. I don't know, and this is a superpower. I trust other people to manage the small details, and I see no upside in trying to micromanage or control people or spaces where I have little expertise. Granted, I have a lot of support and people I can delegate small details to, but I learned this mindset from my mum, who had no support and no people. She accepted help wherever she could find it: my aunt would babysit; the local grocer would sub my mum milk and eggs until she got paid. Find a way to make your life easier. There are so many tech-enabled tools to outsource to now: auto-pay settings, shared calendars, food and grocery delivery services, WhatsApp parent chats if you need someone to pick up your kid from school because you're running late – and there's a lot of energy to be regained by not obsessing over the minutiae of daily decision-making. Where can you find help or outsource part of your to-do list? What are you willing to give up to make your day less frantic?

We need to shed the idea that we're the only ones who can and should do it all. To that end, I'm realistic about outcomes. I know how to form the right questions, when to get more information and when to seek help. I might have a lot of ease with this because of my early anxiety about my credentials or the fact that I lack a formal education, but whatever its cause, it has served me well. I'm confident about my ability to find excellent people to whom I can outsource what I don't know. My role is to hold the bigger vision for companies – and mostly, this doesn't even require me to be the CEO. I'm an excellent people picker. For the big decisions I do take on myself, I make my choice and then I move on.

Ellen Langer, a famous Harvard professor and psychologist, has done most of the mindfulness research that's made it into the mainstream. When she says 'mindfulness', she's not talking about meditation; she's describing the power of attention and the impact of the mind on the body. In many ways, she is describing mindset. Langer asserts that there is no such thing as the 'right decision'. In fact, people who are effective in their lives are so simply because they make decisions – and then they make those decisions right.[2] There are very few circumstances in our everyday lives when we get to run an A/B test, i.e., try two paths (or two headlines, or two web designs, or two variations of a product) simultaneously and see which option rates best. Instead, we're stuck with our choice, which involves cutting off the other option. You can't live in two places, or take two jobs, or maintain two fully committed relationships simultaneously. You must make a decision and move on. Langer's advice is to act without ruminating about what might have been. There's even a term for the goal here, which is to make a choice that's good enough: it's called 'satisfice'.[3] Ruminating is a waste of time because *we'll never know what might have been* – there's no rewind button on real life. Langer also points to evidence from other researchers that thinking too deeply about what to do is bad for mental health. As she writes in *The Mindful Body*, 'Barry Schwartz and his colleagues found that considering more options and taking in a good deal of information results in a decrease in happiness, self-esteem, satisfaction with one's life, and optimism. It was also correlated with an increase in depression, perfectionism, and regret.'[4] No thanks to that.

Psychiatrist Phil Stutz works with a lot of industry titans, and he explains that the most exceptional leaders in his practice are not those who make the 'best' decisions, but those who make the *most* decisions. By taking action repeatedly and quickly, these leaders develop confidence. They come to trust their guts. This absolutely checks out with my own lived experience. As Stutz explains, you never have enough information to be certain about the right action to take, and to *wait* until you have enough confirming information means you'd be dead – or at least highly ineffective – as a leader. As Stutz writes, 'An ability to tolerate consequences and recover is the only certainty you can have.' In *True and False Magic*, he writes about a tool he calls the Instinct Cycle, which develops your intuition and trains your unconscious to work with reality: 'It is an exercise that requires a committed and proactive willingness to be wrong. It's not the person who is right the most times who is the most confident, or who trusts the universe more completely – it's the person who works the cycle the most times.'[5] While Stutz is not the sort of person who looks for proof (and neither am I), for the scientists among us, Professor Sunita Sah offers some: while she resists the idea of 'trusting your gut', there is a concept called 'expert intuition'. In *Defy*, she explains that this is 'an accelerated cognitive process, borne of a high level of experience and knowledge, many thousands of repetitions, and a stable environment that provides immediate feedback.'[6]

There's another word for feeling the right thing to do, which is *super scientific* – it's 'vibe'. It may sound like a light word, but I drive many of my decisions – specifically ones that involve people – off vibe. It's very important for me to get into a room with someone to determine whether we'll be a good fit, whether I'm considering an investment or looking to add someone to my team. I wouldn't be able to tell you all the bits of information that I'm picking up subconsciously, but I can tell immediately and intuitively whether it will work with someone – and while I sometimes mess up, I'm rarely wrong. It's an energy, a sense of someone's perspective and point of view on life, that feels like magic.

When it comes to object-based decision-making, it's not all vibe – I refer back to my list of goals to see whether the opportunity in front of me ladders up to what I'm hoping to achieve. It can be hard to let go of opportunities that seem fun or exciting, but when it's not clearly aligned, I say no. I've watched many other founders and business leaders get distracted and pulled into side alleys and cul-de-sacs that seem far from their stated values or concern – I know I don't have the time or energy to pursue everything that comes across my transom. I continually work through my fear of missing out – which has largely come through experience – because I trust that great opportunities and business ideas will continue to arrive at my door.

This isn't to say that I've managed to avoid regret, or there aren't do-overs that I wish for, though in some ways, I believe the universe always gives you another chance. In my experience, if you mess something up, or more specifically, fail to learn the lesson, you'll get another crack at doing it differently down the line. I think this is why so many of us have repeating patterns: sometimes this is from trauma and re-creating situations that feel familiar until you heal the core wound, but it's worth holding it as a prompt to do something differently this time and get on the right path. One example of regret is when I quit the fashion production company early in my career after they refused to give me a decent pay rise. Not only was I furious, but I couldn't afford to stay. It had been six years, I'd paid my dues and learned a lot, and needed to make a livable wage. When I left, I went to Saturday Group, which my now-husband, Jens, ran with his business partner Erik Torstensson, to start my own business. In response, the fashion production company threatened to take legal action if I continued to do my job offering any services that they deemed competitive. It scared the shit out of me, as I didn't know the law and didn't have any resources to fight back. Jens was unfazed though, and I got behind him as his legal team took my old company on and told them where to go. I regret this though, as I had never *not* stood up for myself. Because I didn't face them head-on and skirted the confrontation, I found myself dodging these women at parties for a long time. This was a huge waste of energy, and it was a pattern I found myself repeating in the years to come until I learned the lesson of direct and immediate confrontation. That's always the decision I make now: I go straight into it and never around it.

**New Thought: You make decisions, and then you make those decisions 'right'. Life requires constant iteration – you see everything as a learning opportunity to inform what you choose to do next.**

---

### 3. Old Thought: Perfection is the right goal.

*Experience is simply the name we give our mistakes.*
– Oscar Wilde

During my childhood, on any given Saturday, you'd find me or my sisters with a giant wrapping-paper roll covered in adhesive tape – my mum had fashioned this strange contraption so we could lint roll the navy blue carpet. My family called my mum 'Bleach' – and not because of her bleach-blonde hair. She earned the nickname because she's obsessive about cleanliness and compulsively fastidious. Vacuuming the floors wasn't enough for her – she wanted the whole operation to be finished off by hand. If you wore white socks on that carpet that left any lint behind, she would murder you.

At the time, I knew this wasn't totally normal, but I went along with it because where I come from you don't argue with your mum, and it was a relatively easy give. She was a perfectionist in this way. But it wasn't lost on me that she focused an awful lot of her attention and energy on the appearance of being tidy and put together, while as a family unit we didn't quite match up. I don't ever remember her asking me about my homework, but she did insist on dressing me, Charlotte and Rachelle in coordinating outfits – with perfect, tight French plaits that matched. (Luckily, my sister Katie, who is ten years my junior, never experienced the coordinated outfitting.) We didn't leave the house unless we looked perfect – while we were not well-off kids, you could have taken us to Buckingham Palace any day of the week. She felt we had to 'present' well. This was about living in East London, and also perhaps about race. 'Emma, you are a little Black girl, and people are going to judge you – you're going to have to stand up for yourself and have thick skin.' I think she felt that looking perfect would help. That, and she loved the affirmation she'd receive about our appearance. 'Your girls are so beautiful, Jenny. Your girls are so polite.' This was the stamp of approval and only validation she needed when it came to her parenting. To be fair, my mum also loved clothing and had an unexpressed creative part to her – she even worked as a shop window dresser for a bit, and I sometimes wonder if my interest in fashion came from her.

This is pretty typical – and it's definitely similar to the social media manoeuvres that we all pull off to some degree. We are all engaged in showing our best angles, and sometimes to an extreme, whether it's stories of abuse like with the Franke family in Utah or that friend of yours down the street who puts out a perfectly manicured feed while crying into her hands after school drop-off. So many of us are hard at work cultivating an image of perfection to project to the world – images that are often quite far from reality. Or even if they're true, they are momentary snapshots of a much more complex life, a life that has many more moments that aren't exciting or glamourous. The end effect though is that we're stuck in a cycle of comparison, where we're convinced perfection is both achievable and an admirable goal, that our image is what makes us interesting.

I'm not immune from this. I put out my share of aspirational content and want to share tidbits from my life, especially as attention on my life has grown. It's a natural inclination when you have a face full of glam for an event, or you're loving your outfit, or you're doing something interesting in the world. I see it as part of my job, too. Personal brand, unfortunately or not, is inextricably linked right now with professional success – *particularly* for women. This is even truer when you're in the business of image, which anything in fashion and beauty and lifestyle invariably is. I want to see this change, and yet I also understand that there's a fair amount of fascination with women who seem to have a fair amount figured out. With this comes scrutiny and pressure to make it all look good, to glamourise the pursuit to tempt other women to follow you down the path. I don't think this is an entirely bad thing, so long as it feels joyful and connected to the truth.

What's deeply unhelpful though is putting out an idea that perfection is possible – or the ultimate goal. In this relentless pursuit of perfection, we often lose what it means to live our own success story, primarily because we're so busy trying to please everyone else and keep up with an impossible ideal. The bigger headache is when we sell women the idea of *effortless* perfection. This is the reason I post so much behind-the-scenes work and glam rather than pretending like I roll out of bed with my face fully done – or pretending like I don't wear makeup at all. (It takes a team.)

The pursuit of perfection really doesn't work in business because you must take risks, stumble and fall on your face. The ascent to greatness is rarely pretty, and you will learn the most from failure. If you're not failing, you're not learning or getting stronger, and your ambition probably isn't big enough. *What is this here to teach me?* is the most important question I ask myself every day – if you're doing life 'perfectly', there's no opportunity for growth. In fact, to achieve perfection, you would need to circumscribe your life and ambition to ever-smaller goals. You would be self-restricting to a zone of things over which you have direct control. (A small number of things, truly.)

Now, I also understand that we live in an incredibly lookist society.

There's no getting around the fact that women are penalised in both directions in a type of Goldilocks impossibility. We're damned if we're considered attractive and we're damned if we're not, whereas this really doesn't matter for men. For one, there's something called a 'perfection bias', where studies suggest that men are evaluated on one criterion for jobs (competence), while women are rated on the perception of three criteria (competence, morality and sociability). And it actually gets much worse, as research suggests that we're still attached to the idea that external beauty reflects internal goodness. Several studies support the idea that people who are universally rated as attractive are more socially desirable and receive better treatment across the board. People go out of their way to please hot people. That said, this can backfire on women in the workplace, as studies show that the perception of beauty indicates a lack of competence. Yep, it's difficult for people to compute that a woman can be clever *and* hot. It's the age-old beauty versus brain conundrum. Attractive women are desirable for entry-level jobs and then perceived as too pretty to lead in any job considered to be the dominion of men.[7]

I'm generally rated as an attractive woman, and I recognise this is a privilege that benefits me in significant ways – *and*, throughout my life, I've been continually underestimated because of the way I look. This still happens, despite my success. Many men still think I'm just the 'face' of the business, while my husband must be the brains. Recently, I was doing a deal with a man known for being difficult and domineering. At one point in our negotiations, I kept pushing him to accept terms he wanted to reject. He looked at me perplexed and completely confused, unsure of what to do, before he ultimately gave in.

'You're like a beautiful Rottweiler.' I took it as a compliment, though it underlines the idea that somehow toughness and acuity in business and attractiveness are incongruous, at least to men. He didn't seem to know what had hit him in the face. Just last week, a man called me a 'little darling'. If he only knew. For my part, I've tried not to dwell on this while continuing to push forward, but I'm conscious of the fact that it is a thing, and I wish it wasn't, since I'm convinced that the way I look is the least interesting thing about me. I believe this is true of every woman I've ever met.

Every day, I ask myself what it would look like to meaningfully support other women in a way that does not enforce standards for women that are unachievable. One of the ways to resist our dominant culture is to ask yourself – deeply – whether something is important to you or truly aligns with your values. Sometimes you have to stand back and say, 'Does this matter to me based on my principles and what I think is right? Is this the right use of energy?' I often stop myself from simply going with the flow of cultural pressure – especially when it comes to wellness or beauty trends – when I realise that I simply don't care enough to spend any time on it. I'm convinced that a giant slice of why men seem to be more successful in business is that they don't spend an inordinate part of their days on the way they look. This is a huge advantage.

My husband, Jens, never suffers from an outfit crisis. He's never concerned about whether he's having a bad hair day. Meanwhile, I often find myself with girlfriends falling into a pattern where we bitch about ourselves because it's a socially accepted thing to do. (There's research to suggest that if you *don't* bitch about yourself, you'll be perceived poorly by your peers – in fact, there's an entire *Sex and the City* episode where Samantha refuses to speak poorly about herself and chaos ensues.) It's an autopilot form of conversation, and as women, we need to consciously shift it. I'd love to have all that time back. Can you imagine if at the end of your life, you had the opportunity to reclaim the 10 per cent of your life spent on body dysmorphia? I've been thinner in my life, and I certainly wasn't happier. Whenever I find my mind wandering in this direction, I quickly pull it back.

Now, again, *I am not perfect at this*. I have plenty of days where I feel less good about myself. Sometimes I stand in front of the mirror in the morning and bitch about my hair. But I have made a lot of progress with my body. I love clothing and I love getting dressed, so putting together outfits feels like a pleasure – and I truly dress for myself. At times, members of my team will tell me that I'm wearing something that's not flattering, which really drives me nuts. Because guess what? I don't care! Am I supposed to go around showing you how narrow my ankles are? I think not. Clothing brings me joy. If clothing brings you joy, or makeup, or doing your hair, so be it – you don't need to deprive yourself of this time indulgence if it truly feels good and self-expressive. But when you find yourself wasting your time and precious energy on something that is making you miserable to maintain, *pull back*. Not only is this better for you, but it's better for other women as well – the less time we spend enforcing a culture that insists women maintain a certain level of perfection, the less energy we'll all need to spend upholding it.

Research suggests the antidote to body anxiety, eating disorders and all the ways in which women belittle our own appearance is not positive self-talk. Nope, you read that right. In fact, complimenting a woman's body will make her feel worse, as it creates self-consciousness. It sounds crazy, but research underlines that this is true. We need to stop talking about women's bodies and their beauty, even when we think we're being kind. The antidote for us is to *not* talk about the way we look at all, and to instead think about our bodies and brains in the context of all they can *do*.[8] Wouldn't that be hugely liberating? Imagine how the world might change if women everywhere unhooked from self-consciousness and spent their energy flexing their big brains instead. I can't wait for the day when we pay far more attention to what women achieve in the world than how they look doing it.

> **New Thought: Perfection is both futile and boring – the process is much more interesting.**

# 2. Money

*You get in life what you have the courage to ask for.*
– Oprah Winfrey

Besides scaling mentorship, one of the reasons I wanted to launch a podcast is because the business landscape is dominated by men – and I wanted to have public conversations with other women about *money*. But I've had a really hard time getting *any* of my female guests, many of whom are titans in their respective fields, to speak candidly with me about the subject. Whenever I ask about capital raises, compensation and cap tables, they demur and deflect. Meanwhile, when I drilled Michael Rubin, founder of Fanatics (a $30 billion business), with money questions, he answered them all, to a one – with glee. No shame, no anxiety, no fear of judgement. Most women do not want to talk about money. I can't get many women to be straight with me about one of the most important topics of all – even off the mic. I hate making things about gender – *and yet*, the following pages largely are, simply because men don't seem to have the same hang-ups about scarcity and negotiation. I hope you don't feel like I'm screaming at you on these pages, but all I want is for women to have access to more cash and capital – we *need* women to have more access to cash and capital – and I get really fired up about the topic. So bear with me and forgive me if you feel attacked by what's to come. I promise, I just want you to be rich and successful so you can make other people rich and successful as well – or at the very least be properly compensated for what you do. My greatest dream is to ignite one million Emmas who hear my story and realise they can do this, too.

Meanwhile, there's an unspoken rule among women in business, especially women who have some money – whether by dint of their own efforts, or family, or marriage – that they're going to pretend like access to cash isn't foundational to both the function and enjoyment of their lives. They don't want to talk about it. Money is gross, it's unspiritual, it's inelegant. It's beneath them, despite money being at the centre of their lives (none of them are living in an ashram). They argue that money is not the only thing that matters. This is true – I'd argue time and energy have a higher value in many instances – but you will find your time and energy extremely hampered by lack of funds and financial stress, in part because you will spend a lot of both trying to get your basic needs met, which requires . . . money. Money buys space, ease, convenience, support, some types of physical security, access to opportunity and a lot of really fun things – it's not the only thing that opens those doors, but it sure is a shortcut. And yet, I consistently find that most women want to gloss over this. And that's a problem, if not the biggest problem when it comes to women and our capacity to succeed.

I am a woman who has existed in every tax bracket. I've lived without two pennies to rub together, and I've lived as someone who makes the lists of the wealthiest 'self-made' women. I spent years earning less than I should working for other people. What I want to stress is that money is important. While it's true that money can't solve all your problems, money sure will solve all your money problems.

Money is not bad or unspiritual. It is *foundational*. We live in a capitalist society that runs on money – and the power this money buys. You don't need to worship money or pray at its altar, you don't need to sacrifice all meaning in your life just to earn security, but you do need to manage your relationship between the two. Consider the section of the book on trade-offs: this is not an either/or equation . . . it's both/and. You can be a good person and make a really good wage. You can create culturally significant work and be compensated well for it. You can care deeply about money *and* a lot of other things, too. I recognise that our society doesn't always value the right things – our teachers, our essential workers, our nurses, as some examples, should be paid a fortune for the care they deliver, and they are not – but you can't wait for the culture to shift before you work to meet your own needs. And to meet your needs, you're going to need money. Plus, it's a lot easier to shift the culture when you're not worried about feeding yourself or paying your bills. Start with yourself. And if you *really* want to shift the culture, it's good to have some levers to pull. Money talks, often louder than everything else in the room. Women are great at making money, often for other people; we need to be better at taking money for ourselves.

### 1. Old Thought: Nice girls don't speak about money publicly. (Or think about it.)

*Every morning you have two choices: Continue to sleep with your dreams, or wake up and chase them.*
– Carmelo Anthony

Many of us – most of us likely – have a somewhat distorted relationship with money based on our family of origin and lived history. There are very few people who seem to have neutral feelings about cash. Most of us see it as something that's loaded with story. And many of us see it as a 'necessary evil', as something that we want to avoid. In that sense, business for many of us becomes about creating enough wealth so that we can avoid money altogether, which is kind of ironic. My feeling is that we are never going to stop thinking about money. Yes, it's true that if you make enough money, it won't rule your emotional life in the same way and you might not experience as much money-based fear, but money is an ever-present reality. You can't escape it. You can ease your relationship with it though.

This is why it is so important that we heal our relationships with money and begin telling ourselves a different story about what it means. Otherwise, we're going to think the *same thoughts* about money that are based in trauma, scarcity and lack – or just avoidance altogether. And we're going to continue to make that story come true. In my experience, if you don't do the work of looking inward and interrogating the way you're thinking about money, you're not ready to take control of it in your life. Even in the best of times, the economy is uncertain and risky and will tip you into a place you're not ready to take on if you can't stay balanced and grounded in reality. I was watching Pinky Cole, founder of the restaurant chain Slutty Vegan, at Masters of Scale one year, and she said it best: 'Scared of money? You're going to make no money.'

Furthermore, unless you're taking your cash and sequestering yourself on a remote island somewhere, you don't get to escape money once you've made it. For much of my early life, I just wanted to be someone who didn't need to check prices on menus. After I ticked that goal off my list, I wanted to be able to fly in whatever class of travel I chose. What I've imagined for myself financially has expanded over time along with my bank balance – and as businesses have scaled, so have expectations. Once you have a successful and vibrant company, you're employing more people and ensuring those people have good benefits, best-in-class pay packages and viable futures. And once you have multiple successful and vibrant companies, you get to multiply those concerns as well.

You can't run away from money; it's a baseline reality of business. Money continues to matter, in increasingly consequential ways. The people who think, 'I'm rich now, I'm excused from looking at my bank balance' are often the ones who run out of cash – or see their business valuations vanish overnight.

This holds true even if you are not entrepreneurial. You still need to do the work to excavate your stories about money and get more comfortable with it. There was a hilarious TikTok meme recently of a series of women telling their partners that they didn't think they'd be able to pay their rent or mortgage that month – and the joke every time was that their boyfriends and husbands laughed in their faces that they wouldn't even know *whom* to pay, or for *what* amount. About fifteen friends sent this to me with a laughing face emoji because I'm the one who tells them constantly that they need to learn the basics of their finances instead of relying on said boyfriend or husband to make it all invisible. I've seen too many women in my life get fucked over for one, but also: start getting comfortable with money by digging in right there. Despite having people who take care of this for us in my marriage, I am in all the paperwork and in all the details; even though Jens and I are fifty-fifty partners in most things, I still have my own lawyers look at everything. This might sound extreme, but then I know exactly where I'll stand should my circumstances ever change.

I learned about the careful stewardship of money from my mum, who would sit at our kitchen table at night and budget – she was meticulous with money. While we didn't have much to go around, when she was able to work full-time, we never went without because of her vigilance. I've heard stories from other daughters of single mothers that their mums would stuff bills under the sofa cushions or toss them in the bin unopened because they couldn't bring themselves to look at them, but my mum treated them like a basic reality. Every month, she would sit with a stack of bills, writing cheques and balancing her accounts, and teach me about the price of electricity and gas. At eight or nine, I knew exactly how much everything cost, which gave me an understanding of market value in the world.*

---

* I was not perfect, at all, with money when I was young. It took me a long time to learn not to spend it as soon as I made it. A boyfriend used to call me a 'squander bird', which was an appropriate nickname considering I spent all my wages on shoes and drinks at the club.

My mum watched every single pound and knew where every penny went, which is why I'm still known in my house as a careful bitch – and why I insist on giving my kids an allowance in physical cash rather than ephemeral Apple Pay. I will take their money off them when they want to buy an app or spend money on Roblox. I want them to transact in real dollars and understand that money is concrete and not a vague digital concept. They think I'm tight, but I don't care. Jens would tell you that I measure the amount of my moisturiser he uses and get after him if he's being wasteful. I'll cut a bottle of body lotion in half with scissors so I can scrape the last bit out of the bottom. And if he throws out a piece of mouldy cheese, I'm right there to dig it out of the bin, cut away the mould and finish it off. I don't like waste. It offends me. I don't let prices determine what I order on a menu, but I still look, and I respect the underlying value. It means something to me.

This is partly why I'm an excellent merchant: I know what every single component on a pair of jeans costs and how that might negatively affect either the margin or what the customer needs to pay. I am fastidious about pricing because I understand its psychology and people's relationship with money. I know the price of everything. I know how much lettuce costs. I know how much milk costs. I know how much a newspaper costs. It's a grave error in business to lose connection to your customers' value system, even after you get rich and decide *you* don't need to think about money anymore. This is very fallible thinking. While you don't need to *worry* about money in the same way – or let scarcity dictate the choices you make for yourself in a way that it might have early on in your career when you didn't yet have a lot of optionality – if you're going to be successful in business, you can't pretend like money doesn't exist. You can't see money as something that needs to be escaped or ignored – or as something that has little value once you have a lot of it. If you can't tell, I really like to talk about money – and I want everyone to do the same. We must stop pretending that it's off-limits or impolite. 'Emma, you talk about money too much.' I hear this all the time. This is the feedback I get from all my rich female friends. Some of them have made their own cash, and some would have not a sausage if it weren't for their husbands. 'Your obsession with money is really not elegant.' 'When we feel like it's inelegant to talk about money, money has a way of elegantly passing us by,' I like to offer in retort. 'Also, know what *is* elegant? Buying your first house, travelling at your own expense and not having to ask for shit . . . and while *you* might not have had to pay for those things, somebody did.' At this point, they typically shake their heads and chuckle and move on: *What are we going to do with her?* But I know underneath it all, many of them are terrified. Many of these women have educations, intelligence, wit and social power – yet they're entirely unwilling to have a conversation about the one thing they don't have under control: their own cash and the financial security that comes with it. I get invited to a fair number of business conferences, and I'm frequently asked to sit on panels, though my tolerance for this type of conversation is increasingly low – in part because the advice that's dispensed is largely PR-driven platitudes. I'm uninterested in skirting the issue. (If you can't tell, I can't get over this, so I'm going to really hammer it home.) I believe we don't like to discuss it because we think it's inelegant, as my rich friends like to tell me – that money is not for us, that it's impolite, that it's not the prerogative of nice girls and good women to really think about it, much less discuss it at length. Case in point, a friend who is a powerful female venture capitalist told me she was recently at an event where a female investor on a panel said something to the effect of: *I don't invest to make money; I only invest in things that are good for the world and good for women.* My friend pulled her aside afterwards and told her that she can't say that again. Making money is the point of investing. Even though it *sounds* good and more palatable to suggest that you do it out of the goodness of your heart, it's a massive disservice to women to suggest that making money in business is secondary to caring about women and the world. It just confirms the same unhelpful story that so many of us carry around about money being unsavoury and bad. We need to be able to get down

to the crux of it – after all, you're holding a book about business in your hands! What are we doing here? We need to take some responsibility for the fact that we're not in the conversation, and that women are only getting 3 per cent of VC funding. It's not because we're not competent, and hardworking, and brilliant, and full of fantastic ideas. And it's also *not* because the world is misogynistic. There might be some of that, sure, but we need to own that our refusal to speak plainly about the investable opportunity around money – to put profitability and financial achievement at the centre of our plans – does not serve. We often shove the hope to build a big, powerful business under statements about helping the world and helping other women, and this means we are missing out.\*
Start with the money. Start with the business proposition. No investor is going to pat you on the back and write you a cheque for your warm, cuddly idea.

I sat on a panel recently with some very impressive women engaged in different sectors. While the moderator called me out as being invited for the 'cool factor', I realised that I was the only one who had actually made hundreds of millions of dollars myself. (And yes, that is cool.) As we talked, I felt my impatience rising, because we weren't talking about what mattered. We were vaguely discussing inequity at the office, sexual harassment and whether fertility treatments should be a corporate benefit. We weren't giving the women who were listening in the audience or watching the video back after the fact what they actually needed to know about negotiating for their value at work or driving better outcomes for themselves or women in the wider world. That all came out *after* the tapes stopped rolling and the mics weren't hot – and mostly because I'm a pushy bitch and I will ask. I wanted to know how much each woman was being paid. I wanted to understand how one woman's deal structure had shifted

---

\* Obviously, your big, powerful business *can* help the world and help women, but you can't do anything for anyone without profit.

pre- and post-IPO. I wanted to know how, when the VCs rolled in, one woman had changed her deal, and which lawyers she had used to structure her contract – as well as how much she had paid them. Many of them shifted uncomfortably at my questions.

The next day, one of the women reached out to me for coffee and said, 'Never in my life have I disclosed what I am paid on any of my deals. And as a result, I'm pretty sure that I'm the lowest paid CEO of any of the other highly visible companies in my industry.'

I told her that she is living proof of exactly what I'm talking about, and that I would refuse to be the lowest paid if I were her, specifically because she is arguably the most accomplished. For the past few years, this woman had been murdering her competition and driving up considerable and measurable shareholder value – all while likely being undercompensated. As she told me, 'I'd love to have a coffee, because clearly I have a lot to learn.'

I'm not telling you this story as a flex (though if I could teach women one thing, it's this). I'm telling you that even the most admired and successful women in business today stumble when it comes to talking about money. They avoid the conversations and try to navigate around them, even as they themselves are dealing with vast budgets and decisions that affect legions of employees and stakeholders. They cannot extend their competence with money to themselves. Their concern is only for everyone else. They will advocate for everyone else before they advocate for themselves. Mellody Hobson, co-CEO and president of Ariel Investments, has had similar experiences to me, explaining, 'We're loyal, and we're team players, and we expect good things to happen to us. I think I've been naive at times, too, so I'm not saying this in a condescending way, but sometimes it will work out, and at other times, you have to ask and put people on the spot.'[1] Sometimes you have to ask, i.e., you have to talk about money.

Men have no problem talking about money. I overhear these conversations all the time. Just the other day, I was having what was supposed to be a lunch date with Jens when we were interrupted by some big, powerful bankers. One of them carefully outlined how he had just pulled off a major real estate deal. Now, listen, I was annoyed, and my first instinct was to be grossed out that this man interrupted my hot lunch date with my husband to flex about his business acumen. But Jens was listening carefully, and as they walked away, he turned to me and told me that he now knew what to do with a commercial building we had just bought. I was so busy being grossed out, I hadn't followed the breadcrumbs to see what this man was offering that I could apply in my own life. Men don't get grossed out; they pay attention. Men disclose deal structures, pay packages and trade intel about bankers who are jerks and should be avoided, or the lawyers who are creative thinkers and can get any deal over the line. If you ask a bunch of women about their banking relationships, they will demur from disclosing or they will lie. I've thought a lot about what stops us from telling the truth in public, and I don't believe it's because women intend to mislead or want to be dishonest – it's because the truth can sometimes be perceived as 'mean' in a culture where we women are determined to be seen as nice, gracious and good. I was standing backstage with a female business paragon a few months ago who unleashed about a banker who had done her dirty and all that she had learned in its aftermath – but as we stepped onstage her whole demeanour shifted to present as someone who has it all nicely under control. In turn, she had nothing meaningful to share. When this happens, we all end up leading each other down a garden path.

Money is not negative. It's a neutral tool. And it needs to be explored – and explored thoroughly – from that perspective. You need to speak about money with your partner. You need to think about money with your kids. You need to think about it from a professional point of view. How well are you spending your money? And on what? Every angle needs to be explored. Because money is neutral *and* it's important. And what it can buy you – freedom, optionality, space, time, support – can be fucking great. The more comfortable you can get talking about it, asking questions about it, and handling it without projecting a bunch of stories onto it, the more effectively you can make more of it. Here are my requests:

- Speak freely about money in both personal and professional contexts with your friends and colleagues.
- Teach yourself about finances: understand mortgage rates, savings options, retirement accounts and investment vehicles.
- Always look at comps for what you do professionally.
- Offer and share information with all the details intact that you would normally keep to yourself.
- Make introductions to accountants, bankers, lawyers and other dealmakers who have helped you navigate financial situations.
- Never allow anyone to make financial decisions on your behalf without your understanding and consent.
- Never undersell yourself or give your services away for free without making it clear that you are doing so.
- Make financial plans.

New Thought: **Take the fear out of money by facing it and thinking about it constantly – it's a type of exposure therapy that will build comfort over time.**

---

2. Old Thought: **Scarcity is real, and if you ask for more, someone will get less.**

*If you don't sacrifice for what you want, what you want becomes the sacrifice.*
– Anonymous

At the beginning of my work experience in fashion, it was clear that I was different – an interloper in a world that was all about being an insider. For one, I was the only Black girl. But the bigger deal in London, at least, was that I was the only poor girl. I'd sit at my desk with my sad supermarket sandwich while the others would head out for lunches. I had no cash and no connections; it was clear to everyone that I did not know anyone in the office, and I had written a letter to get a job. I was always a little destroyed when I realised whom I was sitting next to – the owner's friend's son, the niece of someone, such and such's daughter with a triple-barrel surname. Once I got over my self-consciousness about how I was not supposed to be there though, I realised that being different gave me an opportunity to see the playing field more clearly, an advantage in perspective-taking that I've maintained for my entire life. I also reframed these differences not to be disadvantages, but to help me stand out. For one, I took nothing for granted and worked hard, maximising every opportunity. And for two, thanks to my East London accent and big, curly hair, nobody ever confused me for anyone else in person or on the phone.

I quickly became comfortable in multiple worlds – an outsider who could behave like an insider or at least understand the operating system enough to navigate it well. I also seemed to be the only one who could clearly see the office politics at the fashion production company, where the owners too often made attention and praise a scarce commodity and pitted us against each other to try to win it. We would regularly compete for both their affection and the plum assignments that would come with being the chosen one for a few weeks or maybe a month. This kept us squabbling like a group of hungry dogs, rushing to get the L'Oréal job or the Zac Posen show. As I saw it, it was incredibly effective at making a hostile work environment, where we would see each other as foes before friends. It was very formative in helping me determine the type of leader I did not ever want to be.

At my level of the business, there were two of us – me and Lauren – who had to continually face off against each other, though this wore on me quickly. Finally, I went to Lauren and said, 'Listen, why don't we not do this? Let's stop fighting it out in this fake competition. You do one job, I'll take the next one, and so on. We don't have to fight for attention like this – we can work this out amongst ourselves.' It took her a minute to concede that I was right, and then we moved peaceably on. It not only gave us emotional energy back but worked out better for us and the business – and gave me early insight into how the perception of scarcity incites so much fear in women. Most importantly, it showed me that all you need to do to make it end is to break the spell: scarcity is a magic trick; it's not real. I think that the owners sometimes kept us running around mainly for their own amusement and sense of importance. Perhaps, they got their power kicks out of making us beg for crumbs. The irony is that it did not serve their business well.

As I've been working on this book, I've been thinking a lot about scarcity around money, and how this is the most insidious story we carry. I'm fortunate that I don't have it, and I believe it's because I saw early on that engineering scarcity is a type of game. Historically, it's been one of the primary marketing levers companies pull – and it works in the limited-edition trainer world, too. Scarcity is mostly created. You might feel like you have less today, but then you suddenly have more tomorrow – time, money, opportunity and energy are all liquid, they shift and move. The story of scarcity that we're led to believe, though, is that there's a finite amount of money, or time, or attention to go around, and because it's limited, if I get more, you get less. Philanthropist Lynne Twist, author of *The Soul of Money*, describes scarcity like this: 'When we believe *there is not enough*, that resources are scarce, then we accept that some will have what they need and some will not. We rationalise that someone is destined to end up with the short end of the stick.'[2] From where I stand, women are the first to raise their hands, not only in support of this story of *not enough*, but to believe that the short end of the stick belongs to them. You hear variations of this all over the place, whether it's Anne Lamott writing about her mum always taking the worst piece of cake or the broken egg, or the female founder who refuses a pay cheque and works for free because it seems to her to be the 'right' thing to do.

I don't know if it's because we are raised to be more relational – and to caretake, nurture and put other people's needs above our own – but this idea of scarcity grounds many of us before we've even begun to take flight. It's hard for us to think about our needs and wants and our value in the marketplace as discrete – our tendency is to contextualise it against the needs, wants and value of other people, or to assume that there must be a relationship to the group. We don't want to be an outlier or to stand apart. In watching many men move through business, men are not concerned by this at all. They have no problem openly competing with each other, for one, in very direct ways, but they also seem to see their value and worth as distinct and related more to objective facts and less to subjective *fairness*. They don't take it personally. As women, we often take it *all* personally. We love to talk about fairness, and in reality, 'fair' does not exist. Fair is always looked at in comparison to other people or situations – it's not a helpful concept in business. In my experience, you do not get what you deserve; you get what you negotiate.

I see this most clearly when we determine pay rises at our companies. Every year, the male leaders take their budget allocations and distribute it to their teams without comment; the female leaders come back to me, before they've allocated any of it, totally bent out of shape on behalf of their teams. It doesn't matter what the facts are, or that we pay team members at the very top of market (often establishing new market values for roles in the process), my female leaders feel a lot of feelings about it – and when I dig into it with them, we often arrive at the same place: they feel badly that as thirty-year veterans, they make a lot more than their most junior hires and worry that it's not *fair*. They feel uncomfortable with their own compensation and want to balance it out. They want to be closer to the group so they don't stand out, even though their experience and wisdom is unparalleled in the organisation and a huge asset to our success.

It's not that wanting parity is *wrong*, but it means that women are in a constant comparison play, wondering how we stack up against everyone else – and we feel terrible about the idea that we might be outpacing the group or distinguishing ourselves in any way. In my experience, this means women invariably earn *less*. (We will talk about negotiating shortly.) Take the story at the beginning of this section: my bosses at the time were pitting us against each other, leveraging scarcity to suggest that any opportunity, affection or money that went to one of us was being taken from someone else. In reality, the performance of my peers had absolutely nothing to do with my ability to drive money to the bottom line – what they were up to was literally none of my business.

It's not lost on me that scarcity is so big for women in business because we also have so few models of success. Men look around and see a world built for them, and men killing it in every industry with plenty to go around. Women are fed a constant diet that when it comes to us, it's winner-take-all: you're either in the seat at the table or you're nowhere to be found. I don't think we should underestimate how deeply this sits in the minds of women – and how we need to get behind each other rather than against each other to create the shift change we want to see in the world. Men do not see their pay, or their bonus, or their opportunity as coming out of some other guy's pocket. They look at each other and say, *If him, why not me as well?* Women on the other hand think quite differently: *If I do that or get that, I'll be taking it from her.* Men see opportunity; women see limitation. If you are carrying this story, you need to make it really visible to yourself. Look outside the company you keep for models – and look to the men as inspiration, too. Because of scarcity for women, men are better exemplars of what's possible. They are our competition, not each other.

While I don't carry the scarcity story about money, I do have a money story that drives my husband nuts. My story is that what goes boom can also go bust. This is a pattern I experienced in childhood, not so much with my mother but with my extended family and the community at large in East London. Someone would hit it big and go big . . . and then have nothing again. When Jens and I started dating, I told him, 'I don't go backward in lifestyle'. And I meant it. He would tell you I am deranged about this, and I concede that I probably take this to an unhealthy level, but I am fastidious about understanding every facet of our financial lives. I do mega long-term and short-term budgeting and planning. I trust my husband implicitly, and yet I can trust him because I know I am taking care of myself rather than blindly relying on him to do it for me. While it's arguably extra work and expense for me, it takes the stress of dependence out of our relationship.

I still laugh at the lines in Chris Rock's 2008 special, *Kill the Messenger*: 'I had to make miracles happen to get that house. I had to host the Oscars to get that house. And to this day, I don't even believe it's my house. That's why I keep a bag packed right by the door. Just in case the white people that really own the place show up one day. Time to go, blackie. Hey, I knew this day would come. Good thing I'm packed.'[3] I feel like this sometimes, like I'm an interloper in my own life, even as I recognise that if I'm going to pack it all up, it'll probably be to move into a nicer house.

I experience a lot of financial freedom right now, but I don't think the reason I've had so much success is so I can be more successful – I've made plenty of money, and it no longer drives my decisions about where to invest my time. Instead, I'm 100 per cent certain that the reason I've become so successful is so that I can share with other women how to be successful, too. I realise that my programming is different from other women and so I can be a model for a different way to behave.

I don't take the financial lightness I now feel for granted. Everything around me in childhood was so heavy. People were depressed; they couldn't make ends meet. It was a scary way to live. Everybody's life was so hard. I realised – and it was incredibly motivating for me early in my career – that if you could take away the grind of not knowing where your next pay cheque would come from and remove the pain of having to do utterly unenjoyable work, life looked really different. It's been an incredible gift to find things I've been good at, and to make money doing those things. I wish this for everyone.

Like me, Michelle Obama grew up in tough financial circumstances, and we chatted about the survivor's guilt you can feel when you make it, when others don't. It can be incredibly tempting to try to rescue friends and family – it can also feel like an expectation or a responsibility – but you can't do this effectively until you yourself are secure. As she explained to me on the podcast, 'I have this conversation a lot with minority kids going to college in particular, because . . . the need to leave behind the people who need to be left behind gets a lot of young people in trouble. . . . We have kids who go to college, and they take their student loan money, and they're trying to pay the light bill at home. They're grappling with survivor's remorse. And the thing that I remind them is that you've got to put your oxygen mask on first. And it's a long climb to get to a place where you can really, really help others. And if you stop too soon and try to help too early, you'll all fall.' She and President Obama's combined student loan debt was larger than their first mortgage – and they didn't get out of it until President Obama wrote *Dreams from My Father* and became a bestselling author while he was a senator. 'It wasn't until *after* we got out of the White House that we were in a position to buy my mom a safe place to live with a doorman, which she didn't understand she needed. "You're the former first grandmother. You can't just live in the hood." But I say that to young people to explain that that's how long it took before we really could afford to bring others along.'[4] This is coming from two of the most powerful people on the globe, people who do as much as they can for others. It's not selfish to make sure you're safe and secure before you extend your generosity to the world. It's essential.

> **New Thought:** Money is not relational – advocate for yourself first, then you can think about other people.

---

> **3. Old Thought:** You should be satisfied with what you have, as there are people out there who have so much less than you. It's greedy to want more.

> *When I get ready to talk to people, I spend two thirds of the time thinking what they want to hear, and one third thinking about what I want to say.*
> – Abraham Lincoln

'Stop having an employee mentality.'

When Jens first said this to me, it stopped me in my tracks. 'Wait, what?'

'Your board follows your direction as the leader of the company – stop pretending like you have six bosses instead.' This idea of an 'employee mentality' was a massive unlock for me, but when Jens first brought this phrase to my attention, it was in the context of negotiating my salary with the board of ITB Worldwide, the agency I had built in London. I had been running through scenarios in my mind, thinking defensively about all the ways they might counter my ask and tell me no, when Jens told me to cut the shit.

'So, what – I just tell them what my compensation package will be?'

'Yep. Go be Emma. Tell them what's what. They are looking to you to lead.'

I walked into the meeting, laid out the plan and told them how I'd be compensating myself and why – I didn't pose this as a question but stated it as a fact. Nobody batted an eye, and we moved on to the next agenda item.

This was a breakthrough for me, if only because I started to do for myself what I had already been doing so effectively for other people. My entire livelihood and business came down to my ability to negotiate on behalf of designers and eventually a wide roster of brands and talent. I simply didn't yet have a ton of skill in doing this on my own behalf, partly because there is no way to triangulate when you're negotiating for yourself. When you're playing the role of the third, or the broker, it's not personal. You can take some distance and understand what both parties want and need to successfully close the deal without getting emotionally invested in an outcome or feeling offended when it falls short. This ability is why women tend to be the best negotiators for other people and businesses: we're excellent at modulating emotional information, reading the room and ensuring that everyone walks away feeling happy.

When I interviewed her for my podcast, Mellody Hobson confirmed that this has been her experience as well. When she negotiates, she tells her opponent across the table that she won't ever ask for something that she doesn't actually need – and she expects the same consideration in response, particularly because the negotiations she undertakes are massive, intense and typically strapped for time. As she explained, 'If you call me and say, "I need it," I believe you. But I need you to believe me, too.'[5] That is a powerful negotiating tactic – and my guess is that women are especially good at it. In my experience, we tend to not domineer or bully or take a win-at-all-costs approach, which generally ensures that everyone is satisfied.

But when you're negotiating on behalf of yourself, you can't get any perspective because it's you versus someone else, and your ability to take emotional distance tends to collapse or at least get very cloudy. It feels personal and scary and, for many of us, like it's more important to please the other party than yourself. Unless you build your negotiation muscle, it's likely you will constrain yourself out of the gate – until your resentment and anger about doing *yourself* dirty forces you to move your arse, either to advocate on your own behalf or take yourself elsewhere.

While negotiating on my own behalf is now a superpower, my inability to do it for myself launched my career. Back at the fashion production company, I asked my two female bosses to double my wages, which seemed like a great deal for them (I made £26,000, or about $35,000), as I created a lot of revenue for that business. They essentially laughed in my face, we argued about my value to the bottom line, and I walked. I didn't have a financial safety net, but my compensation was thankfully *not* golden handcuffing me to my job (a real risk for some people), and I was *pissed*. While it didn't feel like I had any leverage in that moment – no competing job offer, for one – I knew I should bet on myself and my ability to build the same business somewhere else. More importantly, I knew I couldn't afford to stay – not in wages and not in the opportunity cost, i.e., my time and energy were becoming far more valuable than my current compensation. I'd already been there for six years, starting as an unpaid intern, slowly building my network and my reputation. I had paid my dues, and it was time I more directly benefitted from my experience.

My friend Sara, who was the hottest fashion publicist in town, had recently been hired by these two very cool Swedes named Jens Grede and Erik Torstensson, who had a company called the Saturday Group. They were in the process of acquiring all these fashion companies. She put us in touch, and I met Jens at the Shoreditch Soho House, where I told him what I'd been up to – putting designers together with brands to underwrite fashion shows, special projects and collaborations – which was still a novel form of business development at the time. I told him about the money I'd been able to drive and the potential value of the business I could build if I were properly supported, as well as what I could see coming down the pike in terms of influencers (at that point, we still called them bloggers). I didn't reveal my measly salary or ask him for a specific amount. I wanted to understand how he would size the opportunity first. On the spot, he wrote out a deal for me in a little MUJI notebook – a notebook I still have – and I told him I'd have a think about it even though, honestly, I was desperate for a job. The offer was good – commissions and a fifty-fifty stake in the business line I would build, with full back-office infrastructure and support – but I emailed a follow-up and asked for a more significant salary guarantee up front. I knew I needed cash and security (he didn't need to know that, so I didn't tell him), but I also wanted him to understand that I knew how to drive a deal. I got what I asked for, and I started at the Saturday Group shortly after.

For the first six months, I ran my hustle inside a PR agency that the Saturday Group owned. I worked intensively, and soon after, my business unit started to blow up. I was making a ton of commissions. They didn't know me from any of the other girls in the office, but I was killing it, so Jens and Erik asked to meet – they wanted to make my business its own entity, divorced from the P&L of the PR agency, and they believed I could take it far. They had so much faith in me, I could feel myself borrowing their faith in the meeting, convincing myself I could and would go all the way. We aligned on a vision – an agency built around collaborations and brand deals that extended beyond fashion to encompass celebrities, influencers (i.e., bloggers) and cultural figures. Erik and Jens predicted I'd stay with them for three years while I built the business, after which we could sell it or spin it off, and I'd be free to do my next thing. Jens is now my husband, and we've built businesses together, though he believed in me as a businessperson well before there was any inkling of romance, and that meant a lot. One of Jens's genius points in business is that he knows it when he sees it, and in that instance, he saw me.

When women ask me for negotiation advice, I tell them that on the face of it, it's super basic: (1) You are almost certainly being paid less than you are worth, so start from that assumption and ask for more. (2) Do not overexplain, just state your ask or expectations and leave it there – including space for silence – as sometimes shit is really simple. Don't rush in to justify. (3) Never take the first offer, always negotiate. (You also never want the other party to think a fast and easy 'yes' means they've overpaid.)

These sentences may sound simple, but this advice seems incredibly difficult to take.

Every time HR approaches me at one of our companies about approving an offer for a potential hire, it's *always, always* because a man is asking for more and they need sign-off to lift the salary band. He's negotiated his way up to me.

The biggest stumbling blocks women seem to face are low self-worth (*Who am I to think I deserve that?*) and a fear of displeasing other people or making them uncomfortable with an ask (*Am I going to make this other person feel bad? Am I asking for too much? Am I taking this from someone else?*). Mori Taheripour, a professor at Wharton who wrote a great book on negotiation called *Bring Yourself,* tells her students that before they can become effective negotiators, they need to heal their stories about themselves. As she explains, 'You can't be the person who diminishes your value – others will too often do that for you.'[6] This is hard and deep work, and sometimes the best way to understand your value in the context of business is through experience. The more you move around in your career, the more you'll be able to feel into the market and ground your expectations in reality. I know this entire section is about how difficult it is to get other women to talk about money, but do your research. (And ask men! They'll tell you!)

Mellody Hobson has experienced people coming to her in what she calls 'the right way'– and also the wrong way – to advocate for themselves. The wrong way, in her estimation, is when 'you really don't know what you're talking about. You have overstated your significance or your value. That's the biggest thing. It's a killer. If you do that, [your boss] will never look at you the same way. When this happens, I think, "Well, you don't know anything. How valuable can you be?"' This sounds harsh, but Mellody works in finance, and she relies on her team members to understand market value – including their own. 'There's nothing worse than the person who is asking for something that literally doesn't exist. They're like, "I want to be your chief of staff, and I want five hundred thousand dollars." That's not going to happen *anywhere*. If you can get that job, go get it!'[7] Instead, Mellody recommends going to questions rather than statements if you're in a difficult negotiation for yourself. She likes to hear questions like, 'What do you think I could be doing better, or what do you think I could do more of to achieve my long-term goals?' Then you need to take the feedback and not argue. If the feedback doesn't feel valid, if you disagree, it might not be the right place for you. Or you might learn something valuable in the process.

If you're negotiating in a space where there is no reliable information to level-set against, you need to blindly adopt the belief that you are worth more until your belief catches up with this assumption. Remember: by the time you're at the point of negotiation, it's because both people want a deal. You need to ask for more.

This brings us to fear. Worst case, someone tells you no. Or maybe laughs at your entitlement. (See above.) Both might sound like terrifying outcomes, but when you think deeply about this, *Who really cares? Who are you trying to please if not yourself?* For one, even if you have a bumpy or contentious negotiation experience and you end up with the job, everyone moves on. And even if you don't end up getting everything you ask for, you'll still end up with more, including the self-respect to know that you didn't sell yourself out. If you don't get what you want, you have agency: you can accept the offer and look for leverage down the line *or* you can always walk away. But don't let your fear cut off your ask. As Taheripour writes, 'Fear takes up so much room in our psyche that we don't want to put ourselves in the position where we hear it at all. We either don't ask for what we should, or we rush to fill up a silence that we fear will lead to a negative response. Think of how often we end conversations or emails that contain an ask with "If it doesn't work for you, I understand" or "This is of course negotiable." Why? Why do we immediately offer an easy out? Because we've already told ourselves they'll come back and say no, and we're so afraid of that word that cushioning it makes it less scary.'[8] We modify emails all the time with statements like the ones she outlines – and then some. (*No worries if you don't have time . . . You've probably already thought of this . . . I was just wondering . . . Sorry to bother you, but . . .*) Start building your muscle for difficult conversations like negotiations by striking all this language from your everyday email vernacular. Say what you think and make your asks on the daily without offering easy outs. Practise with the discomfort of asserting yourself. It gets easier over time.

I wanted to lay the groundwork on scarcity in the last section because negotiating from a place of scarcity sucks. And it rarely works. To be an effective negotiator, you need to approach conversations from a place of abundance – that everyone can get what they want and get their needs met. A good negotiation is effectively relational, but not in a way where one party subjugates everything they want and need so that the other party wins. I'm good at negotiation because I'm able to see all sides. When I sit down with someone who is making their ask of me, I take their position to understand where they're coming from. *What does this person ultimately want? What are their nonnegotiables versus their nice-to-haves? What does success look like for them when this negotiation is over?* I try to see the entire map from their point of view. My goal is always the same: find something mutually advantageous. Nobody wins and nobody loses. I never want to push someone's back against the wall.

Keep abundance front and centre when you set out to negotiate, think first about yourself, what you want and what you're bringing to the table. Do not prioritise the other party. And do not think too deeply about how you might be received or how they might rebuff your ask. As Taheripour writes, 'Those who have a healthier sense of worth . . . start their preparation by identifying their value and strength of their asset(s), then devising the argument that will persuade their counterpart. They do consider the counterarguments. But they don't consider them first. That order of thought makes a huge difference. They don't start from a point of fear and weakness but rather confidence and leverage.'[9] While you can fake confidence, leverage is real – and ideally, you have some. This might be another job offer, one that confirms a higher market value and is compelling enough to take if your current employer won't match their terms. This might be enough cash in the bank to guarantee some runway for you to find a better fit or deal. This might be the pull of going out on your own as a freelancer, consultant or entrepreneur if you can't find the right FT situation. Your leverage might be a staunch belief in your own value. I always recommend looking for and creating optionality so that you never feel stuck. That way you're not backed into a corner where you must accept an offer. If it's a bad deal, you can walk away. If it's a bad job, you can quit. You don't want to cling to a bad outcome out of fear that nothing better will ever come your way.

> New Thought: **You need to think about yourself first; *nobody else* will do this for you. Everyone else is too busy thinking about themselves.**

# 3. Career

*I never dreamed about success. I worked for it.*
– Estée Lauder

There's an amazing scene in *Sex and the City* where Carrie and Miranda are sitting in a shoe shop. Carrie's trying to figure out how to buy a house after her breakup with Aidan. I'm paraphrasing from memory here, but she turns to Miranda and asks, 'When was everyone buying houses? Nobody told me. I must have earned some money?'

Miranda says, 'Well, of course you earned some money. How many pairs of these shoes do you own? Fifty?'

'Oh, come on, more like one hundred.'

Miranda responds, 'Well, there you go – one hundred times four hundred – that's your down payment.'

'Well, that's only four thousand.'

'No, that's *forty thousand*.'

'I spent *forty thousand dollars* on shoes and I have nowhere to live?'

This is funny because for many women, *it's true*. When we pull a Carrie and refuse to think about money, neglect to plan financially, or assume someone else will sort out a house for us, it stops us from really thinking about money as a tool.

I'm an employer; I rely on excellent employees. My ability to build an incredible team is part of what has enabled me to be successful. And I still don't want anyone to sacrifice the vision for their life to my business plan – good employer–employee relationships work when everyone is being served by the partnership. Any job you have is an excellent training ground for becoming the type of leader or thinker you feel destined to be – and I would recommend approaching your career through that frame. What would you emulate, and what would you leave behind? Which decisions would you have executed differently? Where would you have invested, and where would you have pulled back? Use your current career as both a sandpit and school – a place to learn, to play, to test, to grow. And use it to wrestle some of the stories you might have playing in your mind to the ground. After all, if you don't attend to them now, these stories will grow bigger in your mind when you're on the hook for meeting payroll yourself. So let's start with one of the biggest stories of all: you're an impostor.

### 1. Old Thought: You don't know enough and you're not qualified for the role you want.

*Work ethic eliminates fear.*
– Michael Jordan

At 9:00 a.m., my investors thought I was a genius. At 11:00 a.m., I was a CEO who was not fit for purpose. And to be fair, this was kind of true: I had no idea what I was doing. I had never done it before. But as I've come to understand, while my inexperience might have been really obvious that fateful October morning, nobody really knows what they're doing. And if they're doing something interesting, they've likely never done it before either.

Let me back up. On this particular day in 2016, I was huddled with five other people in a conference room at Frame, a denim brand cofounded by my husband, Jens. Jens and I had moved to LA not long before, and I had just had Lola, my second child. I had recently sold my first company, the agency I built under the Saturday Group umbrella, and I was itching to do something for myself. I had grown tired of seeing my ideas build brands for other people.

Besides the initial booking fee, I would see zero upside for my ideas and my work; it was starting to create resentment and irritate me to the extent that I knew I needed to do something different.

I had also started doing equity deals for clients – I had cut Pharrell Williams and Will.i.am into businesses, for example, and I knew that this would be the future. I had also watched as those businesses ballooned. This happened again and again. But because of the structure of ITB, my agency, potential upside from equity couldn't be our future – we were set up for fees, not equity – and so there was no functional way for me to benefit from this shifting business ecosystem. The world was changing. Nobody wanted to just be a face anymore; they wanted real skin in the game. And I did, too. Because I functioned as an exporter of US talent to the rest of the world, I handled a lot of brand work for celebrities outside America – and I had been doing business with Kris Jenner and her lawyer Todd for many years. Over time and trust, we had become friendly. I wanted to create an inclusive denim brand – in a much wider size range than what was generally available – because almost every woman I knew struggled to find jeans that looked good and didn't make them feel bad. I knew Khloé Kardashian would be the right person to partner with and bring it to the market.

First, I went to Jens and Erik and pitched them to invest in me. I asked for $3 million, and they gave me $1 million. (Jens's response: 'You're an unproven apparel person, so go elsewhere and raise the rest.') I raised the rest in a friends-and-family round mostly composed of clients I'd done great work for over the years. At the beginning, I flew back and forth from London to Los Angeles, eight months pregnant,* spending most of my time in the factories in Vernon, where I learned the process of how to make denim. I watched them wash denim, I watched them distress denim, I watched them

---

* Don't do this, as the customs officials were certain I was trying to have an 'anchor baby' so I could stay in the United States. I told them my husband would kill me if we had to stay in the US, though look at us now!

construct pockets. I realised I had no clue what I was doing. I would stand there and watch how many pocket squares could be sewn in a minute, not knowing how to put the whole process together or how to price it. I had a lot of questions: *What's the cost if you change the way the belt loops are sewn in? What's the cost if you do something special on the hem? What's the cost if you change the construction of the waistband?* The level of my naivete was stunning.

But I also knew Good American could be huge – and different. I wrote a mission statement for the brand, and Khloé went on the radio and read it. It described how ridiculous it is that so many women can't find clothes anywhere that fit well – and there was a massive resonance and response. People rushed to follow the brand on Instagram, and when we held an open casting call at Milk Studios, thousands and thousands of women applied. We wanted to find women to represent a brand made to fit them, and not the other way around. I'd been present at so many marketing campaign shoots over the course of my career that advertised 'inclusivity', knowing that if you turned the few plus-size models on set around to the camera, all the clothing had been cut down the back to make it look like it fit. This was the opposite of that. That day at Milk Studios was one of the most emotional days I've had in my career: *Are you really going to make jeans that will fit me? Is this actually going to happen?* The women were cautiously excited, wondering if we were really going to stay true to our word. We were addressing a profound need. That was also one of the most clarifying days in my career: I knew that Good American was going to work.

Launch day came, and I was very nervous. The team was tiny: just me and a handful of people, along with Jens to offer emotional support. We set up a TV screen for the Shopify dash and started testing the site at 6:00 a.m. to make sure the checkout worked. Even then, we could see the customers sitting on the home page waiting for launch, and I panicked: *We aren't going to have enough stock.* Eventually, there were fifty thousand people on the site waiting for us to release the collection. At 9:00 a.m., when we launched the site, everyone thought I was a genius.

At 10:00 a.m., one of my investors, Andrew Rosen, called: 'Oh, darling, you may have underestimated the opportunity a little bit.'

At 11:00 a.m., another investor called to tell me I was a fucking idiot and that I didn't know what I was doing.

And I really didn't. I had worked with a merchant named Melissa Anderson on the collection, and she had warned me that we were 'off-calendar', which means we didn't have production cycles lined up, but I didn't know enough to take her seriously. I had used all my start-up capital to make this first collection of jeans. Not only did I not have any more collections planned out, I didn't even have any fabric ordered and on hand to meet the demands of the first day. My inexperience could only afford me visibility to the launch.

I did some things right, even though a seasoned denim merchant probably would not have made the same choices. In my naivete, I only made nine SKUs total, three fits, in three washes: Good Legs (skinny fit), Good Cuts (tailored boyfriend) and Good Waist (high-waisted skinny). But I made these three fits in an unprecedented range of sizes, which went from US 00 to a plus-size 24 (UK sizes 4 to 28). I based the launch on the iPhone: we told a story about the unique features of our product – the difference in our denim – and we showed the product from all angles on three different size models, which at the time was totally unprecedented. We explained how it was made and, better still, how it would make you feel. We told our story, how we wanted to make a jean that's a perfect fit for women's bodies, especially women who have curves and encounter a lack of options when they go shopping.

We promised we would never make them feel bad. We named the fits after what we knew customers would want to achieve: a Good Waist, Good Legs, Good Curves. We also stressed the differences in the smallest details we had spent a year perfecting, like our signature recovery fabric, the reinforced belt loops and our four-piece trouser waistband, which ensured you'd never have that gap in the back. Our concepts were so simple, it was memorable for customers: the names of the jeans stuck, and women felt to the core that we had seen them. I learned, then and there, that people don't buy when they understand what you're doing; they buy once *they* feel understood.

We sold $1 million worth of jeans on day one and were out of stock by hour two. I had to frantically figure out how to reorder and make more. Except I didn't have any fabric, and I didn't have any factory space. We wouldn't have any stock for at least twelve weeks. I sat there for three days straight and emailed, texted or phoned every single disappointed customer, telling them that I would get them their jeans . . . eventually. I didn't realise it at the time, but that original group of customers – those who heard from me directly – would become key advocates of the brand as we grew. They never forgot the direct contact.

Understandably, I was in a panic, so I started calling everyone I knew in Los Angeles, asking if I could buy fabric or factory space from them. I had some relationships from Jens and my ITB days, but largely I was a stranger in a strange land. It was a great forcing mechanism to put me more deeply into the denim community, particularly because I had just moved to LA and was running a business I fundamentally did not know how to run or fully understand. Though I was theoretically a competitor, people were really kind. They gave me information, they gave me space in their factories, they gave me advice for getting my costs down with the logistics provider (every time they 'touch' your product, it costs a dollar – so if they're folding your jeans into thirds instead of in half, or adding a paper insert, or including fancy packing materials, you're suddenly blowing your product margins with costs you don't really need).

We got a ton of press about our 'Million-Dollar First Day' – and we experienced some backlash. I knew the Kardashian family did well at an accessible price point, and that's what people expected from them, but we were selling $300 jeans, priced at $179 because they were direct-to-consumer. Even then, I had not properly thought through my margins (unsustainably small!), which took a long time to clean up because these jeans were of a quality that was expensive to make. No one knew what 'four-piece trouser waistband' meant, but everyone knew about a gap in the back, or sitting down and exposing your thong to the world. I remember going to a *Forbes* conference and saying that women didn't need to experience that anymore and hearing a gasp from the audience. They understood what we were doing straightaway. One of my sole focuses was translating all the knowledge about denim and trouser construction I was accruing into problem-solving for women – specifically for women who had never been considered.

It was an interesting moment in my life because I was being praised left, right and centre for making something women loved and wanted, but behind the scenes, my investors thought I was a not-fit-for-purpose CEO and that I was wasting a massive opportunity because of my inexperience. But I knew, despite the company being teeny-tiny, the launch wouldn't be a flash in the pan and that we were holding a really big, if not revolutionary, idea. These days, it's somewhat inconceivable to build a brand without including a much wider array of sizes. But back then, we were the only one taking this on.

The team at Nordstrom believed in it, and before we even launched, they told me they'd put the brand in fifty stores. I negotiated it down knowing that I would need to manage the growth and test and learn in a wholesale environment. I had gone to them with a half-made prototype and convinced them to believe in the vision: an incredible fabric, a size run not seen before, and an incredibly desperate customer who was entirely underserved by the existing market.*

---

* The other reason this was a big deal is that sizes 24, 26 and 28 take up more space in stockrooms, and most businesses have built their fulfilment centres around a more limited offering. For this reason, the CEO of Bloomingdale's at the time told me I was crazy and that they would never take on that type of size assortment. They are one of my best accounts to this day.

Some companies believed in it less. After the launch, Net-a-Porter wanted to put in a sizable order, which would have been validation for Good American from a fashion point of view, but they refused to take all the sizes: they wanted sizes 2–10 (UK sizes 6–14), so I told them no, as that undermined the entire principle of the brand. 'Have you been listening? Have you read any of the press? I've taken a *pledge*, a pledge of fucking allegiance, to do nineteen sizes.'

After the launch, everything got very serious. We launched in October, and if we had managed to maintain inventory, we would be on a $40 million trajectory for the year – if full inventory had been available, I could have done $60 million in the first six months. As one of my investors said, 'Emma, you have a tiger by the tail. Please don't fuck it up again.' As soon as we were able to get Nordstrom their inventory, they blew out of it, too, but they had bought in a much more considered and better way, with a more accurate size curve. They have a powerhouse team of planners and merchants who really understand the American customer, and I credit them with teaching me almost everything I know about the denim business. I was lucky to encounter a team of incredible women at Nordstrom – Trisha, Holly and Shea – who took me under their wings. I ate up everything they were willing to teach me. (Coincidentally, these women now run the biggest retailers in the US.) At the beginning, I didn't know *anything*. They sat me down and really helped me understand what the customer in America goes for from a wash point of view, the fabrics I should be developing and what fits might be next. It was Denim University at Nordstrom, and I was their best student, in part because I knew I didn't know shit, and I was open to learning.

Nordstrom also asked me to go to stores all over the country to meet and talk to customers and train the staff. I jumped at every opportunity to learn about my customer. I gave away as many jeans to the retail team as possible, pinpointing people on the shop floor who

I knew would be good advocates for the brand: 'You – you're a size 16, put these Good American jeans on.' From that one experience with the brand, they'd sell Good American all day. I learned so much about the country, about people's tastes in different markets, and about what people want. In reality, I've come to understand that operating a business requires this type of mindset: if you go into every encounter with a beginner's mind, believing you have so much to learn, you will.

When Michelle Obama talks about her own impostor syndrome, that maybe she doesn't have anything wise or relevant to share, she offers a 'secret' to the rest of us: 'I have been at probably every powerful table that you can think of. I have worked at nonprofits, I have been at foundations, I have worked in corporations, served on corporate boards. I have been at G-Summits, I have sat in at the UN: they are not that smart.'[1] I honestly think that when you think you have it all figured out, when you're certain that you *are* a fit-for-purpose CEO and absolutely the right person to take on the job, you might be screwed. Our world and culture are shifting and evolving dramatically fast. Anyone who thinks they know how to steer a business with complete certainty is full of it, for one, and if you don't take the attitude of being a perpetual learner, the world will pass you by. The only thing you need to continually cultivate throughout your life is curiosity, the belief that there's more for you to learn and plenty of people to teach you, and that you can't be complacent. If you can master those three things, you're in good shape.

In *Mindset,* Carol Dweck tells the story of George Dantzig, who was a maths graduate student at Berkeley in 1939. She writes, 'One day, as usual, he rushed in late to his maths class and quickly copied the two homework problems from the blackboard. When he later went to do them, he found them very difficult, and it took him several days of hard work to crack them open and solve them. They turned out not to be homework problems at all. They were two famous maths problems that had never been solved.'[2] I love this story because it underlines the formative power of a growth mindset. If you assume that every problem is solvable, you're much more likely to figure it out. On the flip side, if you think something is too difficult, and everyone's already tried, and what do you know, you're never going to succeed.

> **New Thought:** Nobody knows what they're doing; your only job is to figure it out, day by day. Do the work, and keep your antennae up and your mind open and curious.

---

### 2. Old Thought: You should naturally be good at things. If it doesn't come easily, it's not for you.

*Knowing what you don't know is more useful than being brilliant.*
– Charlie Munger

I want to double-click on education because it's one of the things I'm asked about a lot. I am not a naturally gifted learner, school was incredibly hard for me and I ended up not finishing. To that point, I'm not 'naturally' good at anything. Not a sausage. This doesn't mean I'm not really good at a lot of things, but you would never take someone like me and pattern-match me against anyone else in the industry and say, 'Ah, there's a winner.'

In the earliest stages of my career, I felt a ton of anxiety about my lack of higher education. It felt like such a void in my life because I left school when I was sixteen and have always felt 'behind' everyone else, and that they learned things I'm also supposed to know. Even though I got a head start in the working world, I felt like everyone who went to university had a head start in life. On some level, I knew this wasn't true, but I still struggled to shake the belief that everything would have been better if I'd been able to stay in school. Though when I reflect on this now, I recognise that following a preordained path – you go to a good university, you get a good job, you retire – can create complacency and passivity. If you assume it will work out because it works out for everyone else, it's less likely that you'll figure it out for yourself.

So, first, yes, get a good education. This is one of my priorities for my kids, and while I have a lot of thoughts about *not* giving my children money, as I don't want to deprive them of the opportunity to figure their lives out themselves, I will *always* pay for their education, including any postgraduate degrees they might want to pursue. While it's not 'formal', I am educating myself all the time. I've put myself through college courses, like Yale University's African American History from Emancipation to 2010. I read compulsively, both newspapers and books. And, if you haven't noticed, I make a lot of phone calls and ask a lot of questions.

Back in the day, when I was trying to figure it out, I got out the Yellow Pages in London and tracked down all the PR agencies. Then, after landing a one-week placement at one of those agencies, I'd take the fashion industry contact bible, *Le Book*, and copy the entire thing. I started calling and writing to people asking if they needed help. It worked – people needed help – and so I did a year unpaid anywhere I could lend a hand. I'd work at various PR companies or designer studios for four days a week, and then I'd spend the weekend working retail to make money to survive.

Often, I'd find myself in a cupboard packing up samples to send out with a twenty-two- or twenty-three-year-old recent university graduate – at first, I felt 'less than' because of my accent and lack of education, but pretty quickly, I realised I should probably get out of my own way on that. We were all equally clueless about life, and none of us had any work skills. In some ways, I knew more than they did, as I had been out for myself for a while. Over time, I came to realise that my lack of education wouldn't be a massive factor in the potential for success – nobody was résumé-checking me for a university degree.

I had worked my way beyond that expectation and was on the same path as these other girls.

Since I wasn't overly formed by a specific university degree in, say, marketing or journalism, I used my internships to help me figure out what I *didn't* want to do. I knew I wanted to be in fashion, that's it. At first I thought I wanted to do PR, then I thought I wanted to be a buyer, then I thought I wanted to be a journalist. Over time I managed to gain a cursory understanding of a lot of different functions while ticking things off my list of career possibilities. I ruled out a lot of jobs via experience. The other upside is that I came to fundamentally understand the business of fashion. I worked every dogsbody job out there.* I really came to know the sausage quite intimately – and how the sausage is made.

Besides getting a taste of every part of the fashion industry, every once in a while, if you were lucky, you'd get a sign of something you were good at. I believe enormously in signs and that the universe is in constant communication with you, if you care to pay attention. At one job, someone complimented me on how enormously organised I am, in another how I could always see around corners and understand the bigger picture and end goals of the clients. I took notice of this and realised I might have a talent to cultivate there – one of my points of genius now is that I can pull many, many strands together at relative warp speed and then sell you on the vision. I see the story, I see the journey, I see how everything is connected, and then I can bring people along on the ride. This is possible only because I have the mentality that keeps me focused on the bigger picture – I'm not sure if I would have focused so intently on developing and maintaining that skill if it hadn't been called out as special early on. In my early days, I used to be in charge of posting health and safety manuals backstage at the shows and making signage – one day, someone

---

* For the non-Londoners, this is code for menial, low-level work.

pointed out that spatially, from a graphic design point of view, I had done a really nice job. My response: 'I don't think you should put up an ugly sign in a really beautiful environment.' And from this, I noticed that I pay more attention to small details than the average person. To this day, I am really, really good at understanding the visual language of an email, store signage or a landing page – I know how to present product really well. I learned I had a knack for negotiation because in the chaos of backstage, I could always bring people together, whether it was the designer's team, the PR team or the production team, and get everyone to cohere and be okay together. This signalled another skill.

When I worked at Quintessentially with a bunch of Eton and Harrow alumni, I really became disabused of the idea that I wasn't smart. I loved a lot of them, but those toffs couldn't organise a piss-up in a brewery. I didn't know until I was an adult with kids of my own who share my diagnosis, but I'm dyslexic. The minute I understood this though, I felt a flood of self-belief that I could figure out how to work with my dyslexia – and that it gives me special powers in the way that my mind is organised. I realised then that I'm not stupid, I just learn differently. I also let go of the belief that everything would have been better if I had been in a fancier school, because it would have still been *me* in the fancier school – and I still wouldn't have understood how I think or learn. I came to understand that the only person who could affect my reality is me, and that I needed to sharpen up and get really good at working with my mind and how it uniquely functions.

One of the superpowers of dyslexia is that I see through problems: I can make everything very uncomplicated and distil it down to its essential nature. I don't get confused or stuck in a bunch of dark side alleys, and it's also why I'm good at identifying all the thoughts that I don't want to entertain.

Every superpower in my life and work is based on my relationship to the world. It has all come from understanding myself through experience. I am incredibly organised, but this goes beyond Excel. It's about seeing the underlying system, what's important and what's extraneous, what's essential and what's a 1 per cent distraction. I care a lot about beauty and small details because aesthetics are critical to customer experience and the success of the product. And I really believe that there are creative solutions to every problem where everyone wins, meaning I'm exceptional at bringing unlikely partners to the table and making people happy. Nobody taught me this, and you won't find it on any school curriculum. It's an attitude. I figured it out by observing myself and the way other people responded to me. I urge you to do the same.

I also urge you to move past the discomfort of asking a million questions. Think about your career as your opportunity to study and learn, with no graduation in sight; because the world is constantly evolving and shifting, your skill set must expand and grow to keep pace. In the time of permanent disruption and change, what works today will not work tomorrow. The people who thrive in this environment are those who live in a growth mindset, continually adapting to the world by paying attention and assuming they know nothing. In my experience, perversely, men are more comfortable in this stance: they don't believe they should have all the answers. As women we need to move past feeling like we are stupid or inadequate for not knowing everything, or that the wrong question will give us away as a fraud.

Again, education is important, but there is no educational degree that will deliver you certain success. I've worked with enough highly pedigreed people that I've learned having all the right degrees from the right schools will not solve your underlying anxiety about not knowing enough. And it shouldn't. What you need to do instead is transform that anxiety into curiosity: ask questions, lean into the valuable white space that's left when you don't rush to fill it because you immediately assume you know best and must have all the answers. What you need to discover is a fundamental faith in your own ability to *figure it out*. Not to have the solutions, but instead to have the mindset required to discover them repeatedly and recurringly. It's important to remember that the solutions will shift and change.

New Thought: **You will bring a particular genius to your career, and it's your job to figure out what this is.**

---

3. Old Thought: **Part of your job is to make other people comfortable.**

*Your energy is your most expensive currency.
And not everyone can afford it.*
– Déjà Rae

This is what I'd like to hear women start to say: Instead of *I can't* _____, I'd like to hear *I won't* _____ . Or even *I don't want to* _____ . Because you know what happens when you tell someone you can't do something? They push. They suggest ways in which you might be able to accommodate their desires by rescheduling your life, or breaking a boundary, or pushing past your own values or limits. I've been trying this for a minute, and when I tell someone I won't come to an event or shift my schedule around, they offer zero retort. It's so final, so assured, so clear. If you don't feel ready for the directness of *I won't*, you can modify the script: *I'm saying no to everything right now,* or *I'm heads-down at the moment. Please ask me again in the new year.*

I understand this might sound stark and maybe even mean in a culture where we are conditioned to be so goddamned nice all the time, but we need to give ourselves and each other a break. While you might *think* it's your job to serve other people's needs and make other people happy at your own expense, it's actually not. Not only that, it's not even your job to ensure that other people are comfortable. I want you to sit with that for a minute because this is big in the psychology of women: so many of us have been convinced by the culture at large and maybe even our parents, teachers or friends that we should sacrifice our preferences, goals and desires to keep other people happy. We steamroll ourselves in the process.

Now, I get that within the function of having a job and being a reliable employee, *you will need to do things that you don't want to do.* This is a reality of working for other people. But there is a line that I want all women to find between work that can sometimes be irritating or an inconvenience – and soul obliteration. When there's choice, make sure you bring yourself into the decision as well: *Do I want to travel and I'm making my kids an excuse for not pursuing more, or do I not? Do I want to take on this additional project, or do I not? Do I want to work on Sunday night, or do I not?*

Saying no for many of us is a new skill, possibly one that's never been exercised before. It's okay to practise in less consequential ways, rather than steeling yourself to defy someone who has more power than you right out of the gate. Practise with your friends – instead of telling lies to get out of Friday night plans, tell them you're trying to be more direct and give them a straight *No, thank you, I don't want to go.* Or *Thanks for the kind offer, I won't be able to make it.* In time, a simple 'no' will become more and more accessible. Don't offer an abundance of excuses; don't justify your 'no'; don't hem and haw; don't apologise. You can be polite and even grateful for the opportunity (you don't want) without selling yourself down the river.

The instinct to dwell on the way other people feel about us is not always a great survival skill – spending a lot of energy trying to make yourself perpetually palatable can really fuck you up. I've heard stories from women who found themselves being convinced to sign additional years-long contracts for jobs they despised. I've heard stories from women who got screwed in their marriages because they were embarrassed to get advice from others. I've heard stories from women who felt like they were being an encumbrance or taking up too much time with questions, so they rushed through the paperwork to please the person offering the pen. And I've heard stories from women who didn't want the person they were negotiating with to think they were mean because they were pushing back. When we don't stay connected to ourselves, we're much more likely to get screwed because *we know*. At some level, you always know. Find that part of you.

Sunita Sah, a physician and professor at Cornell's school of management, explains that insinuation anxiety is that feeling you have when you don't say something for fear of making it clear to the other person that you hold a negative opinion of them. Insinuation anxiety is the reason why we can struggle to speak up about a bad haircut, or send an undercooked meal back, or tell someone we think they might be giving us a raw deal on a car, or a salary, *or* a term sheet. She writes, 'Insinuation anxiety encourages us to act against our values and preferences in order to protect another person's feelings. We do not want to *insinuate* that we think the other person may be biased, corrupt or plain incompetent. So we often comply with a suggestion, keep silent or accept a bad piece of advice, just so that the very person who is hurting us, costing us or putting us at risk can "save face."'[3]

I don't really struggle with insinuation anxiety. I push back, though it's a muscle I had to build. When I'm uncomfortable, confused or I feel like something is off, I *ask* for clarification – and I always ask for time so I can look things over on my own clock (and have my lawyers look, too), without feeling watched for my response. I do this nicely enough – sometimes I even crack a joke or a smile – but I don't rush to please, and this has kept me safe.

I'm somewhat convinced that one of the reasons we hate to say no, or make ourselves say yes to things we want to reject, is that we hate to *hear* 'no' ourselves. I still find it hard to hear *no*, yet I've trained myself to look for the lesson and what the *no* is there to teach me. There's some magical thinking involved where if we say yes to everyone and everything, we'll only get yeses to our requests in response. That, and we sometimes take care of the needs of others, hoping they in turn will then take care of ours (again, magical thinking in action). Hearing *no* can be painful because it suggests that you've over-asked, or been presumptuous, or are pushing too hard – and for many of us, it can be excruciating to hit that type of boundary or wall. This is another reason it would be good for all of us to practise this powerful two-letter word with each other; think of it as exposure therapy.

'No' is not death. A no is not the end of the world. A no doesn't mean that you don't have incredible value, or that people don't want to have dinner with you, or don't want to have you around. A no – particularly in a high-stakes situation like your salary negotiation or when you're doing a deal – can feel scary as fuck, but don't give that word so much power. Ultimately, it's just information, signalling a boundary or line – it doesn't need to shut the conversation or the negotiation down. Use a no to a request for a promotion as an opportunity to ask where you can improve, where you're falling short and what you could do differently. Then drop the defensiveness and listen. Sometimes a no is easy to digest and recover from, but when I hear a no that causes me to stop short, I pause and take a deep breath, and then I ask questions, looking to understand where the other person sits and why. Keep reminding yourself that this is not the end of the world, nor is it the end of your opportunities. As the saying goes, *Rejection is God's protection.* I'm so grateful my first bosses gave me a big, fat, heartless no when I asked them for more money – I'm not sure where I would be today if this hadn't pushed me out the door and onto my own path. There's no version of business and life where you get successive yeses until you die. If you're not hearing no from time to time, you haven't found the edge of what's possible. It's now your job to find that edge and pursue it.

> **New Thought:** Your wants and needs are as important as everyone else's – in fact, for you, when it comes to work, they come first. If you're not hearing 'no', you're not pushing hard enough for those wants and needs.

---

**4. Old Thought:** You should strive for work-life balance.

> *Whenever you see me somewhere succeeding in one area of my life, that almost certainly means I am failing in another area of my life. . . . That is the trade-off. That is the Faustian bargain one makes with the devil that comes with being a powerful working woman who is also a powerful mother.*
> – Shonda Rhimes

In 2025, I went on *The Diary of a CEO* and the host, Steven Bartlett, asked me about interview red flags. I offered that a big one for me is when someone asks me about work-life balance in the organisation. I said, 'Work-life balance is *your* problem. That's yours to figure out.' This line got picked up *everywhere*, and you would have thought I'd cancelled Christmas. Some people were outraged, while others slid into my DMs to thank me, as it's something that they de facto ask in interviews without really thinking about why. I get this: we've been programmed to say it. My issue with the ask in an interview context is that it signals a lack of personal responsibility and autonomy, two qualities I expect from my team.

If you come to work with me, yes, you come in, and yes, you have set hours, but there will always be flexibility within your working life in the same way that you need to be flexible in your home life. Nobody is looking to see who is or is not sitting at their desk – we don't work like that anymore. I don't know if *anyone* works like that. But there is a quid pro quo expectation, if we're being honest, that if you're going to use work hours to do personal things, you're probably using some personal hours to do work things. There's also an understanding that some people are exceptionally efficient and focused and boundaried with their time, and they might get a majority of their work done between the hours of 9:00 a.m. and 5:00 p.m., while some of us are more fluid and unstructured. I don't really care. It's none of my business. My business is that you do your job. And if you have a lot of ambition for yourself, you're probably going to want to do your job and then some.

I know that people prioritise the mythical 'work-life balance', though everyone struggles to define what this means.[4] The lack of definition makes sense, as theoretically this balance is different for everyone, and it brings me back to the idea of trade-offs: you're not going to get everything you want all the time. I can assure you that you won't be running a massive company maintaining a personal policy that you're done working at 6:00 p.m. every night and are unreachable every weekend. Sure, fine, we'd all vote for a perfect, mythical 'work-life balance' in a vacuum. But if you rank work-life balance on a scale against earning substantially more, year-over-year, or getting a really meaningful bonus, people's priorities would change. Those achievements correlate with working really hard. To run an organisation where people get great work-life balance, you need to be profitable. The company needs to be in line with, if not beating, its competition. It's not realistic to imagine that you're going to work at a start-up with the potential for huge upside and be home by 5:00 p.m. every night when there aren't that many people to get the huge amount of work that needs to be done *done*. It *is* realistic to earn a nice salary at a stable business with limited upside and expect to be home at 5:00 p.m. every night. Every job is different, with different trade-offs.

I am in the business of delivering huge upside, and with that comes an expectation that my people are not going to be watching the clock but doing what they need to do to get the job done. This isn't for everyone, but it is the right fit for people who have a similar ambition. When we're talking about a traditional job, I don't think there's an expectation anywhere that you need to work seven days a week. But if you have ambition, if you want to do *the most*, if you want to grow, if you want to be one of the people at the top of the organisation, chances are good that you're going to have to work a little bit more. We shouldn't be angry about that; we should be honest about it! That's the truth. I'm sick of people lying about it. Everyone I know who is extremely successful is a little bit of a workaholic – they work on Saturday or Sunday if necessary. They're looking at emails at night. I do this. I also put my phone down for three hours every evening to have dinner with my kids. I completely check out for a holiday a few times a year. I have many great weekends up in Malibu on the beach where I'm not thinking about work at all. This happens. But I do not lie to myself or other people about shutting work out of my personal life. It's all one thing.

I get that people are tired of hustle culture. People are burnt-out and tired of thinking about being burnt-out. I get it. But figuring out your own limits and your own ambition is a big part of your responsibility to yourself. And my part here is to deliver a level of honesty about what it takes to be really successful. I see it as an obligation not to lie. I refuse to tell people that they can be really successful without giving 150 per cent, without waking up most days and doing some type of work or at least thinking about work. It has not been my experience that people achieve great things doing less. People chafe against this because they don't want to do it. They want all the benefits, but they don't want to do the messy part in the middle of creating success, which requires a lot of monotonous and endlessly grinding work. I cannot stress enough that you will not be able to skip out on this level of consistent intensity and succeed. I get it, it's not for everyone. And if it's not for you, don't do it. That's your choice. *But an extraordinary career is always the result of extraordinary effort.*

It's not the right call for a lot of people. The reality is that most of your colleagues and coworkers don't actually want the tippy-top pinnacle of success. Most people want the security of a well-paying job that allows them to pay their rent or their mortgage. They want to have a nice life, and a nice car, and educate their kids, and go on a couple of holidays. That's what most people want. And should you be able to achieve that without working every night and weekend? Yes, definitely. But if you want an extraordinary life, it will require extraordinary sacrifice.

If you run a modern organisation, chances are nobody in your company will miss a dentist appointment, their turn to be the surprise reader at their kids' school, or a parents' evening. If someone's kid is sick, their kid is sick and will need a parent to be home. Nobody who works for me is waiting to go to the doctor for three months because they can't duck out for a 3:00 p.m. appointment. That's just not how we work anymore. We have a flexible way of working. But do I think that working from home for three days a week is conducive to becoming a leader? No, I don't. First of all, there's an urgency and an immediacy to being together with people that you cannot approximate on Slack. You've got to gather people quickly and do things fast. That is one of the qualities that's made me so successful: we move, we get stuff done. We tolerate mistakes because we optimise for speed. We don't sit and specialise and figure it out three months later. There is an urgency with which we work. There's also proximity, which is key in business, especially in the earliest parts of your career. If you want to sit at the leadership table, remote work isn't going to be in the cards for you – that doesn't mean that you can't anticipate a certain amount of flexibility, but you're not going to run a team effectively from your bedroom. You have to be in the room. You need to be seen. There's a middle ground situation where all employees are able to balance their career aspirations with their home obligations. That was already happening before COVID hit. But I'd be lying if I said that I don't really worry that putting women back at home is not putting women forward.

I actually lose sleep worrying about the impact of remote work on women who want leadership roles. On the one hand, I recognise that it creates slack and relief – chances are, you can swing more pickups or take a break and head down to your kids' preschool to serve snacks. But then you are literally not in the room. Ultimately, I don't think women are served by it because there's a sneaky presumption in our culture that mothers are default caregivers, and that they should be able to do it all – also, that work is kind of a 'bonus job' on top of the primary duties of being a mother. I've heard from very senior leaders at my companies that their husbands argue with them about the necessity of paying for childcare on WFH days, somehow labouring under the belief that being in the house means you can do your job while executing drop-off, pickup and after-school activities. I worry that shit like this is disproportionately going to affect women's ability to step up and become leaders of organisations. There's the belief that if they're working from home, they don't need the help. But they do need the help! Women need all the help they can get!

We've really wrestled with the WFH question at our companies. On any given Friday, the product teams are probably in the office. Otherwise, the office is largely empty. Post-COVID, we've given everyone the liberty of working in the office four days a week, with the expectation that they're putting in a fifth day from home. I have really, really mixed feelings about this. We talk so much about the flexibility of working from home and what Zoom has enabled in business, but we don't talk at all about the rigidity of it, and what it takes from work, and what you miss out on. I can guarantee that if I had been WFH in my twenties, I wouldn't be anywhere close to where I am now. And I don't just mean professionally. I met my husband at work. I made some of my best and strongest relationships at the office, relationships that are the foundation of both who I am and how I find my happiness. The friendships I made early on in my career are some of the most important in my life.

It's so interesting that we have an aversion to the office now, and all want to be as far away from it as possible. I just don't really get it. I'm an in-person person. I want to be with people. I want to collaborate. I love detail and specificity. I want to do things quickly. I mentor a lot of young men and women inside my own businesses. Work culture right now makes this very hard. I can't teach you through a screen – if you're not with me, you won't see how I move or operate. You need proximity to me. You need to understand the flow of what's happening. The way we work now makes me a little sad because I don't think we're having all of those exchanges that are the result of being in a really dynamic environment where you're able to learn from people on the fly. We're simply not together as much as we used to be, and our professional relationships are suffering because of it. Also, it just isn't as much fun: *Drink after work, anyone?* Now I'm really showing my age.

If you work in a business with other people, or you *want* to build a business of scale someday, the idea that you can do it alone is a joke. You are not going to get far unless you surround yourself with people, because nobody is successful working on their own. If you want to lead, or be at a decision-making level at any company, you need to be with your people. I haven't seen it work any other way.

New Thought: **Work-life balance is the wrong focus – alignment to your ultimate ambition is the right one. If you want to go big, what you lose in remote work is profound. The downside is deceleration – a curse for ambition.**

---

5. Old Thought: **You're owed mentorship and opportunity.**

*Nothing will work unless you do.*
– Maya Angelou

While mentoring as many people as possible is now one of my primary intentions in this phase of my life, in my own experience, I didn't have any mentors. I held Oprah in my head as a paragon of what was possible for a woman, and I watched her on TV whenever I could (often when I was bunking off lessons after dropping my younger sisters at school), and I picked up what she was laying down about gratitude, mindfulness, self-actualisation and manifesting your life through action. I wanted to be thoughtful and articulate like Oprah, and I wanted to move like Oprah because I thought she moved so well. She was kind of *it* for me because, as they say, *You can't be what you can't see*. We didn't have podcasts and endless online content when I was coming up, and I'm really someone who learns from watching other people operate. Absent a lot of people to look to in the wider culture, I used what was immediately available. If you're smart, you will make whoever is around you your mentor – both in what you want to adopt and what you don't.

I started my first real salaried job in the fashion industry when I was eighteen, and I just happened to sit directly in front of my boss. All my friends at the office thought this was unfortunate because she could see my screen – while they were online shopping at Net-a-Porter, I was relegated to work, and this was good for me. I listened to every phone conversation she had. When she had a great call, I'd write down what she'd said so I could adopt parts of her pitch. She'd walk out of the room, and I'd pick up the phone to dial for new business, adopting her lines and then making them uniquely my own. She wasn't my mentor, she was my boss (and a bitchy one at that), but I learned a lot from her. I even copied her outfits. She was incredibly formative in my own early success. Look around: there must be people, whether they'd be your first pick for a mentor or not, who can teach you. Emulate what they do. Ask them for feedback on your work and what you could do better. Practice leads to mastery. Everyone starts somewhere, so start by studying the best people in your midst. While we're trained to look at women who are senior to us to teach us things, I've learned just as much from women who are my employees, like Mel Anderson and Lindsey Frawley.

Honestly, anyone who would be a good mentor probably doesn't have time to mentor you. And depending on who you are and your level of exposure to best-in-class businesses and leaders, you're probably not going to be surrounded by the right people anyway. Almost every one of my podcast guests has told me that their mentors all came out of books, and Mark Cuban told me he is currently being mentored by AI: 'If you learn how to prompt it . . . it's like having an entire staff of a thousand business professors.'[5] (He also makes the point that if you're using your job correctly, you're being paid to learn, regardless of where you sit in the company.) So start exactly where you are and figure out whom you have contact with who can teach you things – they don't even need to participate; you can simply study them. They could be colleagues, teachers or even friends. Early on in my career, I'd look for mentorship from my clients, too – if I encountered the CMO or the CEO, I'd ask a question at the end of the meeting. I'd say, 'I have two other questions that have nothing to do with the work we're doing or the brief I'm here to deliver, but I'd love to ask you . . .' Invariably, they'd answer and give me really generous and thoughtful advice. I never wasted the opportunity and I asked good questions. In my experience, people are happy to share their wisdom if they have the time and you ask in a nice way.*

Throughout my life, I've had an insatiable appetite to learn. When you are building something, you don't get to stop growing. You need to stay in learning mode. It helps ensure that you are always asking better questions. You're staying curious. You're refusing to let your ego block your evolution. For me, this boils down to a lot of reading, a lot of self-reflection and a lot of listening. I often have a lot to say, but sometimes I need to stay quiet and observe people operate whom I aspire to be like so I can better understand how they do what they do. Commit fifteen

---

* Too many of us are scared to ask, but the worst thing you'll hear is *no*. Build your durability for hearing no so that it doesn't stop you from asking.

to thirty minutes a day to intentional learning – read a book, listen to a podcast, take a course or watch someone you admire speak. At the end of every day, ask yourself some questions: *What did I learn today? What challenged me? Where are my gaps? What could I do differently or better next time?* These simple prompts keep your brain in learning mode and bring some awareness to how you're operating in a way that's very healthy and hygienic.

Find some teachers in your life – a group of friends, a coworker who is wise and thinks bigger than you do, a more formal mentor if you can find one. But think deeply about where you're spending your time and with whom, as it can really expand or limit your growth. I've been quite systematic throughout my life about shedding people who were not good for me, or who dragged my energy down. You might need to shed people who carry low expectations for you or are narrow-minded. It's just not worth it to stay loyal to people who don't want the very best for you. Throughout it all, stay rooted in your curiosity and remind yourself frequently that you don't know everything – if you can do that, you'll go much further than most people.

One of the most foundational parts of my success has been that I've never felt like anyone automatically owes me anything – I've never had any entitlement about what my career should look like or which opportunities should be rolled out for me. I've forged my own path. I knew it started and ended with me. I meet a lot of people who expect a lot simply because they show up. Maybe they're right to have that level of entitlement, but in my experience, you need to make a career yourself and prove yourself worthy for advancement. It doesn't just happen because you've been there the requisite number of years. It requires an active desire to get better and grow. Nobody can do that for you. You must be devoted to curiosity, learning, flexibility, discipline and hard work if you want to advance.

The three most important words for the advancement of my career were: *I'll do that.* That was me. My whole life, I've had my hand up, offering to do the thing. It didn't matter which workplace I happened to be in; I'd put my hand up. *These boxes need to be packed up and shipped.* 'I'll do that.' *These samples need to be steamed.* 'I'll do that.' *We have a client in town who wants to see the sights.* 'No problem, I'll take them around.' People started to look at me as someone who would always get it done. It's not that I had any particular skill. I simply put myself in the space of giving it a go, every single time. Because I'd never been trained to attack a problem through the lens of a business school, I'd go straight into figure-it-out mode. Nowadays, we call this 'test and learn', but at the time I was just known as a person who would solve the problem by throwing a bunch of things at the wall to see what sticks. I grew a reputation as someone who could make shit happen; from there, my confidence grew that I could, in fact, make shit happen.

If you're hoping to be noticed, if you're hoping to be promoted, the most surefire way to ensure that this happens is to be excellent at what you are doing. I find it really difficult when people come to me and ask me for a promotion, or an expanded job remit, or to do a different function altogether – *I'd really like to do this thing over there; I'd like this bigger opportunity* – when they're not blowing my socks off. I then have to tell them that they're only 70 per cent good at what they're currently doing. On the other hand, I'm always looking at the 120 per cent people in the organisation and thinking about how to grow them. Those people get much wider remits because I trust them to be excellent at whatever it is that they're doing. I don't care so much about whether they have the expertise required, as I'm confident they will figure it out and learn quickly on the job.

I'm much more inclined to hire for attitude over experience. For this reason, I'm very open to moving people around to different functions on the team – and other good leaders share this willingness – because the more the team understands the business as a whole, the better they can function with increasing responsibility and an understanding of the organisation and our goals. If you're an amazing wholesale salesperson who really wants to learn e-commerce and how to buy for DTC channels, I'm going to support that mission. I'm very invested in team members who are interested in the entire business and want to see the structure from outside their current lane or division. I have done sidesteps from one department to another in a few of my jobs, and it has always served me well.

Another essential quality to cultivate is flexibility. This comes back to knowing what you don't know, and acknowledging that the world is changing so quickly, what you know today might not be relevant tomorrow. You've got to *always be learning*, always trying new things, and looking for novel solutions. I hire a lot of people who are in their forties and fifties for senior executive leadership roles, and I'm conscious to rule anyone out who adopts an attitude that's overly fixed, rigid or certain. If you come from a competitor and say, 'The only way to get from here to there is the way I've been doing it for the past twenty years,' we're not going to be the right fit. I want that vast experience to be paired with flexibility, because technology means the customer expectations change all the time.

I'm a generalist who came up in an unexpected way, but most people take a more typical path: they're specialists. If you're working in a function in an organisation, you're a specialist. And some leaders are specialists, too, like Mellody Hobson, who is the co-CEO and president of Ariel Investments. When we spoke on my podcast, she talked about cultivating her expertise in finance – and how she'll never, ever be done becoming an expert. She talked about how when you survey the greats, whether it's Steve Jobs, or Walt Disney, or Warren Buffett, 'they did one thing extremely well and they went deep. An expert is someone who knows more and more about less and less. There's a difference between a general practitioner whom you go to for your routine checkup and brain surgery. I wanted to be the brain surgeon of my field.' Mellody went on to explain that she 'wanted to be known for something that [she does] so well it distinguishes [her].' For her, one of those distinguishing points, in addition to her financial chops, is that she can explain money and financial concepts to anyone, making a complex industry transparent and understandable. And she focuses on this in particular because once you can teach something, you really own it – it forces her own learning and question asking.[6]

If you want to run the place in time, or if you want to start and run your own thing, Mellody agrees with me that you need a level of intensity, a sense of urgency, an indomitable work ethic and a desire to be great. She believes what Jim Collins, author of *Good to Great*, writes: 'Good is the enemy of great.' You can't be a B+ player because then you'll be satisfied with a B+ result. I know I just belaboured this in the section on work-life balance, but you'll probably need to be a little bit of a workaholic if you're going to make your dreams come true. And she feels you need to be incredibly disciplined. This is industry-specific advice – my emails are not like this – but Mellody has someone copyedit every single one of her emails because she feels that an error there could create the idea that she's not fastidious and detail-oriented – and when it comes to people's money, they expect precision and care, not sloppiness. 'A typo could kill an opportunity for us because they will think you're half-assed – as my husband always jokes, "She does not like half-assed – she likes whole-assed."'[7] While spelling isn't important to me, my team knows that I am incredibly disciplined about every aspect of each product. I believe this is a huge part of my success. I sweat every single, solitary detail and rarely use the apparel phrase 'correct and proceed'. Instead, I want to see it, wear it, test it and probably change it again! I will obsess about every part of a store's design, and any copy that touches product, the website, a swing ticket or any part of our business. I don't feel I need to *do* all the work, but I do need to *respond* to the work and give feedback and direction. I out-care everyone else. I pay maniacal attention, so my team does, too. Discipline is contagious in an organisation, and it's contagious in your life. When you take this approach, it will start to positively affect other parts of your life. As the saying goes, *How you do anything is how you do everything.*

Wherever you are in your career, treat every opportunity and experience as leverage – even if you hate it in that moment, skip the sour attitude and think about what it's teaching you, and what you'll eventually be able to bring forward. Early on in my career, I realised that every client who had a show could eventually be useful to me in some way, shape or form. I cultivated all those relationships. Eventually, when I left that company, not only did I have contacts to leverage but I had my reputation, which ended up being even more valuable. I was known as a hard worker, diligent, perfectionistic and someone who would get the deal done. I was also known as having a lot of passion and enthusiasm for the industry and for making the entire experience as joyful and fun as possible. Those contacts became my clients at my agency ITB; those clients then gave me bigger and bigger projects and opportunities once they were certain I would deliver. And eventually, when I needed to do my first raise, I didn't go to a VC or a fund – I went to my clients. I had long working relationships with all of them and a reputation for always delivering on my word. Many of them are still my trusted advisors to this day. So what I'd offer is that rather than getting too fixated on your next step, or where you want to be, think about where you are today and make sure you're as excellent as possible. Start with yourself, and use that as a springboard for your next move.

> New Thought: **You are the creator of your own career, and the responsibility for it is yours, too.**

# 4. Family

*The most important relationship you'll ever have is the relationship you have with yourself.*
– Diane von Furstenberg

Women are overburdened, and arguably none more so than mothers. We all come from a culture in which the needs of women are an afterthought, leading to burnout, resentment and rage. A big part of the reason why this happens is that we leave ourselves out of the equation, expecting and hoping that others will see that nobody is taking care of us and rush to do it – this is a fool's errand. Early on in my life I decided that I wanted to not only understand myself, but I wanted to learn how to love myself and to really value my needs. We all need to fall in love with ourselves before we can properly love anyone else. We all need to love ourselves to feel like we deserve more. To quote Diane von Furstenberg, 'The most important relationship you'll ever have is the relationship you have with yourself.'

The single most important thing I do every day is look after myself. I bet some of you are arguing with me in your head: *But what about your family? What about your four kids? How can you not put them first?* We have a massive cultural blind spot that any woman who doesn't profess to be kid-first exclusively is somehow deviant or defective. We don't fault men for going to the gym, taking time to read the paper without interruption over breakfast, or watching four hours of football with their friends. We expect it. But when a woman starts with herself, we assume she's a selfish bitch who has terrible priorities, and we judge her accordingly. But here's the thing: if I don't take care of myself, who will? And what's more, if I don't resource myself, I'm certainly not resourced to give my energy to anyone else. I know that I get shit done because I value myself – and I value my goals. I don't want either of my daughters to labour under the belief that caring about themselves means they must care about other people less. It's actually bonkers when you put it like that.

Taking care of yourself can mean a million different things, though I'm talking about taking care of myself emotionally and mentally. I'm not talking about splashing hundreds of dollars at a spa or taking myself shopping – we're in a bit of a bind right now as women, where we're equating those types of activities with self-love. It's not exactly what I'm talking about.

I don't always find it easy to love myself, but I begin every morning by talking to myself in the mirror. I remind myself of what I want, I remind myself of my favourite qualities about me, especially when those qualities feel far away, and I remind myself of everything in my life that is working. Usually, I say something like, 'Emma, it's a good day. None of the stuff bothering you matters – it doesn't matter that your hair looks like shit and you don't know what to wear. It doesn't matter that this situation is bumming you out. You are healthy, and today you get to see this person, and that person, and do this, and do that. You have so much choice in your life. Look how far you've come: today, you'll likely be recognised for all you've achieved in some sort of public way, meanwhile it wasn't that long ago when you were begging for money and hoping someone would even listen to your pitch.' It's never, ever a bad idea to remind yourself of everything that's good and going well in your life, and all the opportunities that might unfold.

At a young age, I began to recognise the power I had to predetermine the course of my day – before I even got out of bed. I knew it would be a good day or a bad day – regardless of what might happen – depending on my attitude. I remember Oprah saying something like,

'I thank my heart because it gets up every day, without me thinking about it or telling it to, and pumps blood around my body.' This is so profound. You get up every day, and your lungs are lunging, and your heart is hearting, and aren't we all so fucking lucky?

This is my version of a gratitude practice. If talking to yourself in the mirror feels too corny, you can write it down in your journal, or talk to yourself as you're driving to work, or after you've dropped your kids at school. But I recommend looking yourself in the eye as you do it, ensuring it really lands. The reason I'm so insistent about this – the reason that this is the introduction to a chapter about family – is that if allowed, we will put ourselves off. It's what we've been doing for millennia. And it has to stop. You must begin the practice of loving yourself first, of putting yourself first, before you turn to anything or anyone else. There is plenty to go around. Anyone who has given birth to a second child has worried they won't have enough love to go around, only to find that love seems to exponentially increase. Loving yourself takes nothing, zilch, from the other people in your life. You will find that it means you can love them even more.

### 1. Old Thought: You're responsible for your kids' lives – and it's your job to protect them from the world.

*Don't leave anything for later. . . . Later, people grow up. Later, words go unsaid. Later, you lose interest. Later, opportunities slip away. Later, the day turns into night. Later, you regret not doing something. Later, life goes by. And you had the chance.*
– Toshikazu Kawaguchi

'I think *YOU* should have the piano lessons.' I laugh about this still, but this came from my husband, Jens, and it was directed at me. We have a beautiful piano in our house. Naturally, I had been harbouring fantasies of my kids being virtuosos and all of us huddling around it to sing songs at Christmas like you see in the movies. But I was getting tired of trying to convince all my kids to not only take piano lessons, but *want* to take piano lessons. None of them are musically inclined.

After listening to this hustling from me for many months, Jens finally turned to me and told me that, as this seemed to be my ambition, I should take care of it myself. 'Take piano lessons, Emma. *You* be our pianist.' I laughed, because as much as I love the idea of being a well-rounded savant, I don't yet have the time. It was an excellent reminder though of the way that we can focus so much of our energy on other people – often trying to control them or convince them that we understand their needs much better than they ever will – that we lose sight of ourselves.

That might have been the point that I stopped being ambitious for my children. They have to find that for themselves. This is tough medicine for an ambitious person turned parent. I would love to engineer their childhoods to ensure they hatch well and do important things in the world, but I recognise not only that this is a fallacy, but also that then they'd be living the life I'd choose for them and not their own. Yes, there are a lot of things that I do do – namely, giving them a lot of love and attention; giving them opportunities to try different things and hopefully find activities they're passionate about; enough travel to stoke their curiosity; and a high-quality education that fits their varied learning styles. But beyond setting the table and filling it with nutritious options, I can't do the chewing and swallowing on their behalf. As part of this, I realise I can't make my son's anxiety go away (it's his natural disposition), or solve their learning differences, or make a harsh world less harsh. I can be a soft lap but not a shield. They will need to experience the world and shape their attitudes to it on their own.

We've created a crisis for mothers in defining parenting as something you do *full-time* – or not. I understand that we do this to give parenting equivalency to a career, and we don't want women who don't work outside the home to feel bad about their choices – or lack thereof.* I get that. And still, parenting is not a job. Parenting is way more amorphous and difficult and uncontrolled than that. There's no time clock to stamp, no merit pay rises (or material compensation at all), no annual reviews where someone tells you how you're killing it and where you need to improve. There's *no boss*. It's much, much harder. After all, your child is not a product to be defined, managed and ultimately marketed to the world, as much as our culture tries to convince us that this is our duty, or that certain inputs will result in certain outputs.

When I speak like this in public, when I tell people that I don't get involved with the small details of my kids' lives, that I don't sit on their group chats with their friends (yes, some parents chaperone their kids' chats), that I'm not panicking about scheduling their days perfectly, other women look at me cross-eyed. And some are pissed off or uncomfortable. There is certainly a cultural belief that when it comes to parenting, there's always more that should be done – and always more that *you*, specifically, should do. But I refuse to buy it. I believe this is largely just anxiety that we create and then foist onto each other, creating a type of doom loop where we'll all try to outrun falling short of some sort of cultural ideal. I believe it's largely a function of privilege, too. More resourced families, families that aren't trying to keep their heads above water, are more inclined to think they can control the world – including their children – whereas when you have less cash, just keeping everyone alive can feel like a real accomplishment. Meanwhile, all of us are experiencing the *global privilege* of living in a much safer world than our ancestors – though we have a hard time convincing our

---

* I would never, ever, ever want a woman to feel judged for not having a career. It's none of my business and seriously, no shade or shame. I also understand that parenting and working without support is fucking impossible. I have a partner who is a devoted dad, *and* I have a staff of people who support me at work and help me take care of my four kids and my house. I have a lot of resources. That's the only way any of this works.

fear-driven minds that things are relatively okay and there are no real threats lurking in the bushes outside our homes.

In *Outraged*, professor and psychologist Kurt Gray writes about the idea of 'concept creep' when it comes to harm, and how we're unable to turn off the hypervigilance that's kept us alive for millennia. He points out that when it comes to global natural disasters, for example, more than five hundred thousand people lost their lives in the 1920s, when there were two billion people on the planet. Despite there being nearly eight billion people in the 2010s, we saw a small fraction of that number die from global natural disasters, only about fifty thousand.[1] After living through the Palisades and Eaton fires in Los Angeles in January 2025, it was remarkable that despite stunning damage, only thirty-one people died – the world feels far more murderous than that.

The perception of threat when it comes to parenting is even more prevalent, despite the fact that you don't see many kids' faces on the sides of milk cartons these days. Gray writes, 'Whether you find parenting today to be overly coddling or appropriately protective, the undeniable truth is that our idea of what counts as "harmful" toward kids has expanded. We let our kids do less on their own, and we see more danger in things that used to seem safe. Even though the world is safer, we remain afraid of danger – and perhaps even *more* afraid. Parents during the Industrial Revolution had to worry about their child being dismembered by dangerous machinery while working twelve-hour days in hot, dark factories. Parents today worry about the harm of walking home, or the trauma caused by the cruel comments of other kids. The concept of harm has crept.'[2] I get this wholesale; I believe that most people around me are coddling their children. It's possible that this is easier for me to see because I was decidedly not coddled as a child and certainly found myself in situations that were not safe. Though when I speak to friends who were brought up in entirely different situations, financially and otherwise, it seems like we all experienced a lot more freedom and what you might call, in today's terms, benign neglect. There were no lawn mowers clearing our paths or helicopters observing our every move. And most of us turned out just fine. These days, to be the lone parent who resists over-involvement in parenting makes you an outlier – even though all signs point to the fact that our children aren't doing well, locked inside with their screens. Kids need freedom, they need nature and they need to test their own power and limits in the world. We cannot do that for them. It's easy to be hijacked by fear. It's easy to be hijacked by the anxiety of other parents, or to train your eyes on what they're doing and push to conform your own parenting to their standards. But I'm not sure this does any of us any favours.

I think about Carl Jung's idea that our kids bear the burden of our unlived lives all the time, particularly in the way that so many of us have been convinced to see our kids as containers for us to cultivate our own sense of worth, or fertile ground for us to find our own purpose and then make them live it. I get a lot of dopamine hits from being a mum, and I'm proud of who my kids are growing up to be, but I really work hard to give them a wide berth. I want them to feel like everything they achieve in their lives (or don't) is on them. I want them to take full responsibility *and* full credit. I see my job as providing them with a lot of nutritious fertiliser: good food (though I'm not a nut about this); a willing and nonjudgmental ear; an hour or so every evening of devoted time and attention, including dinner as a family every night when phones and work are put away; access to enriching activities; and unconditional love. When it comes to all things – screen time, TV, junk food – we try to fill their plates with vegetables so there's less room for dessert. But there's still dessert. I ate a lot of shit when I was a kid, and I turned out just fine. It's just not that deep.

When it comes to the hurdles they'll encounter in their lives, those hurdles are their own. There's a reason it's *their* homework and not mine. You will never catch me doing it for them. I'll help out, but I'm not in the lead. As women, we need to have serious conversations with ourselves and each other about the bounds of our responsibility, when we are horribly overreaching, and what we need to concern ourselves with. For what it's worth, I see this at the office all the time – team members will come to me out of concern that another person on the team is working too hard, and I have to ask: *Did they say that to you?* (No.) *Did they ask you to speak to me about it and intervene?* (No.) Stop parenting other adults! The instinct in us to do this is strong. But since we're talking about homework, eyes on your own paper!

Ultimately, this is the question I ask myself constantly: *When it comes to the kids, what is my aim?* I can honestly tell you that my aim is to have happy kids who are kind, curious and engaged. That's pretty much it. I cannot ensure that they're not going to have anxiety. I cannot ensure that they're not going to have learning difficulties. I cannot ensure that they won't suffer bullying. My responsibility is to raise kids who are secure with who they are, who can speak up and advocate for themselves, including when they need help and additional support, and who approach the world with curiosity and an open mind. My responsibility is to raise kids who know they can figure it the fuck out when they encounter all the problems that will invariably arise. It is not my responsibility to snowplough the path or be their constant companion.

The other day at a public speaking event, a woman asked me if I spent my time differently at the weekends and whether I focused all my energy on my kids.

'No, absolutely not,' I responded. 'I'm a max three-hour mum. After a few hours of focused quality time, I'm doing other things. I work out, I read, I do courses on things like Transcendental Meditation. But I don't spend eight straight hours with my kids unless we're on holiday – and I don't think they would want that either!'

Afterwards, my publicist told me that she had groaned at my answer, wanting me to choose something more socially palatable. But I refuse to lie, especially around something that's so crucially important for women. We don't need any more gaslighting. I refuse to set up unrealistic expectations for other mums by lying about my own life. I believe women are in an untenable position because we feel like we can't tell the truth – either about reality or about what we want – and then we try to convince ourselves that we're supposed to feel a different way about parenting, and that we're definitely the only defective mum because we're not excited to get down on our hands and knees to have a doll party on a Saturday afternoon. Some women love that; many women do not. When I asked my publicist if *she* spends eight straight hours with her kids, she acknowledged that no, she does not. I'm very fortunate that I have an engaged co-parent, access to a lot of childcare and household support,* and an ease around screens: I don't give myself a lot of grief for parking my kids in front of a movie or setting up some playdates so I can get some errands done or read a book. I don't think my kids are missing out because I'm not their constant companion. Because guess what? Our kids don't want us to be their primary playmates either. They really don't. They want us to be more like the family cat – available for an occasional snuggle and always there on the periphery but largely giving them space. My kids seem to love 'parallel play', where we read in the same room, or I do work

---

* I have two nannies all the time for our four kids and a team, both at the office and at home. While I've always had childcare, this bigger level of support is relatively new, and I don't take it for granted. It's a huge gift. I'm also honest about it because we don't need to be lying to each other about the help we get. When I turned twenty-nine, I finally felt financially secure enough to splurge on a cleaning service once a week; when we moved to Los Angeles, we had a housekeeper. As my ambition and businesses have scaled, the scaffolding of support I've called in has increased to match the pace. That said, there are plenty of times when I need to use an iPad or TV to babysit my kids. There's no shame in it.

while they play Roblox; they're not looking for me to be their best friend. But I do look for opportunities throughout the year to make really wonderful core memories with them.

Motivational speaker Jesse Itzler speaks very powerfully about time in a way that really connects for me. He points out that if your parents are seventy years old, and you see them once a year, you might tell yourself that you have ten more years with them. But really, you have ten more visits with them total, which is really not so much. You might be better served to be a little more intentional and present with the time you do have left. Itzler takes the concept of time, which seems elastic, endless and infinite, and grounds it down into something that feels a lot more scarce, and therefore more precious. We all saw that now-viral Instagram post that went around reminding parents that if you have a twelve-year-old, you're already 70 per cent through the time you likely have left with them at home. Ideas like this stop me in my tracks.

I use that now to think about the number of Christmases my family has while we're still reliably under one roof, the number of Easter breaks or summer holidays we all get to take together before these weeks become complicated by school trips, sleepaway camps and competing interests, like friends and significant others. It's just not that much time. But rather than letting this spin me out into trying to make every single minute with my kids count, it helps me focus my attention on high-impact, core memory events. I think about all the moments, and the anticipation and lead-up to those moments, too: I want Halloween to be special, I want Christmas to be an *event*, I want to load the calendar with family game nights and theatre trips and other exciting moments that we can really look forward to and then live them hard.

There's a corollary in business, which is doing drop models and limited-edition collaborations that come and go really fast. One of the reasons I love these so much is that they feel like a big event rather than just merchandise that rolls in and sticks around for a long time, making seasons and time indistinguishable. You really get to see where you've come and where you're going when you look at your business in this way. You get to build in anticipation, and you get to build in celebration after and really have a moment where you take stock and say, *We did this thing*. I feel the same way about the big moments with my family. While this seems like a lot of pressure, I actually feel that it's relieved a lot of my anxiety, and conversely, it's taken some of the pressure off every single day needing to feel special and packed out. It has helped me a lot mentally and also given me a lot of incredible moments to remember with my kids.

Every time I get fearful that I'm an inadequate mum, whenever I get swept up in anxiety that I'm not doing enough for them or that I missed an important child-related email, I remind myself of my core aim: healthy, happy, kind kids who are equipped to solve their own problems as they figure out who they are, *not* kids who feel compelled to be who I want them to be. This is weirdly hard, I get it. And there will certainly be times as they get older that I'll want them to choose differently. I'm sure they'll seek therapy when they're older with long lists of my failures, but if I don't give them stuff to work on, am I really doing my job anyway? They'll need some resistance; they need to encounter a not-always-friendly world to work out who they are.

We need to resist the urge to imagine that everyone else's happiness and comfort is our problem – *including* that of our children. It's our job to establish a stable foundation from which they can develop this capacity on their own. I know that when I am happy, peaceful and content, my kids *love it*. This gives them the freedom to focus on themselves without worrying about me. I want to give the children the dignity of their own process, and I believe they will genuinely love me for this as well.

**New Thought:** You're responsible for providing your kids with the nutrients they need to thrive; what they choose to grow in response is the fruit of their own lives.

---

### 2. Old Thought: Don't work with your partner.

*The most important decision you'll make is not where you work, but who you choose to partner with the rest of your life. A spouse who is not only someone you care for and want to have sex with, but is also a good partner, softens the rough edges, and magnifies the shine of life. I have several friends with impressive careers, wonderful friends, and a spouse they love. But they aren't happy, as their spouse isn't their partner. They are out of sync on their goals and approach to life. Misalignment on what's important and a lack of appreciation for the other makes everything . . . harder.*
– Scott Galloway

When people learn that my husband and I are business partners and have been for eighteen years, the response is usually two questions: 'You *work* with your husband? How do you stay married?' They don't understand that we have different, albeit complementary, skill sets in both business and life. If you've been paying attention to this book, you know I would never do business with someone unless we were equal partners. This same mindset holds for our personal relationship: I'd never sign up for a marriage not based on equity.

About two years after the launch of Good American, the opportunity to work with Kim Kardashian on a new venture emerged, and planning for SKIMS started. I think Jens and I were a natural choice to be her partners because I had a long track record with the family after Good American. Given the scale we projected to do out of the gate, Jens took the lead in raising the funds. We needed substantial innovation, we needed a huge amount of inventory, we needed hefty shoot budgets, and we needed a best-in-class team and site experience from day one. Good American was on total fire, we had accelerated to doing $150 million in revenue incredibly fast, and I had learned a lot – but I knew Kim's idea had the potential to be a billion-dollar brand out of the gate. Jens became the CEO, allowing me to do what I do best: I worked on developing the product assortment, with Kim at the helm as creative director, serving up never-before-seen product ideas like the one-legged shapewear we launched with. I'd found my dream role: at SKIMS I oversee design, merchandise, planning and production as the chief product officer. We've built a world-class team of the best talent imaginable in the fashion space, and I'm proud to have been able to have an opportunity to create generational wealth for myself and my family.

We announced the new venture under the name Kimono – a play on Kim's name – which, given the climate at the time around cultural appropriation, was a mistake. People were furious. But we understood the outrage, we apologised for the misstep because we needed to, and we acted decisively to change the name, despite having printed a million units with the Kimono branding. That would be my issue to undo. SKIMS ended up being a far stronger brand name anyway. Aside from that, we were prepared for the company to be huge – though we *still* managed to underestimate demand. We sold out of the collection in ten minutes flat. I honestly thought the Shopify page would implode. I will never forget that day because everything went wrong, and we needed to delay the launch three times, pushing it an hour each time. I sat on the floor of the airport and missed my flight while we worked through site and syncing issues. We couldn't afford to let this many customers down.

This time, though, we had a production calendar set fifty-six weeks in advance and weren't out of stock with nothing to sell for two months. Progress!!!

While I had built ITB as part of the Saturday Group, Jens and I had never worked shoulder to shoulder before SKIMS – but even then, work doesn't subsume our relationship. People assume that we're talking about the business all the time, that SKUs and profit margins are our form of pillow talk, but we speak about the daily grind of work very little outside of office hours – and even then, we manage our own fiefdoms separately, staying in our own lanes. Up until recently, we didn't even have offices on the same floor. We come together for executive team meetings and two weekly ninety-minute one-on-ones. We don't even drive to work together, as we're either rolling calls or dropping different kids at school.

We work hard to stay aligned at the office so no team members ever feel uncomfortable or like they're choosing sides, and he works hard to back me on product, even when the rest of the team is balking at the gambles I want to take. As he says, 'Let Emma be Emma.' After all, my batting average is good: if I think a collaboration is worth the risk, or that I can sell ten thousand of a single SKU, Jens will back me to roll the dice. And for the most part, this has worked out. When it doesn't, we take the hit together. From the first day I met him, long before we were ever romantically involved, Jens has always believed in me, maybe even more than I believed in myself.

Jens is very engaged with our family, and he's there for the needs of our kids. While I don't think he's ever cut any of their fingernails or cleaned their ears (that's my purview), he makes up for it in a bunch of other ways. I haven't booked a holiday in sixteen years, I don't even know where the rubbish goes when it leaves the kitchen bin, and when there's some weird beeping noise coming from somewhere in the house, Jens takes care of it. Among my jobs is to listen for when my kids' toenails get so clawlike they're scraping against the floor. We didn't sit down and commit our duties to paper, but we have distinct roles that we execute without debate. We have such a successful partnership because I don't try to micromanage his stuff, and he doesn't micromanage mine. Ultimately, I knew exactly whom I was marrying: Jens is the most reliable and steadying presence in my life, and he's never boring. And I knew that he wasn't going to dump anything on me or expect me to be his mother.

While my home-life situation is a little unusual, I don't think the qualities of our partnership should be. Because, even if we don't share office space, *we all work with our partners*. Or, if we're going to be in an effective marriage, it's wise to think about it in this way. To that end, talents and competencies should be respected, and duties must be divided. Doing this well requires each partner take on an equal measure of savoury and unsavoury tasks so that the woman isn't left with all the crap while the man takes all the glory. And doing this well also requires understanding the full scope of each person's contributions. As Eve Rodsky outlines in *Fair Play*, making dinner isn't just turning on the stove; cooking also requires planning, shopping, prep and cleaning. While we haven't done her process, we understand this intuitively.

One of the things I love about Jens is that he was able to see me before I could see myself. He is incredibly encouraging at every turn, especially in moments of doubt. Whenever he hears me saying, *God, this feels outside of my comfort zone,* he reminds me of all the things I've done. Jens is a great conceptual cheerleader. I know he has my back, and I have his. And yet, he's not involved in all my stuff. He's invested in my happiness and success by encouraging me to focus on what I want – not by telling me what I *should* want. We both offer each other a lot of autonomy and space. If you really want to go for it in business, that's what you need from your partner: someone who supports your belief in yourself so you can do what you need to do, and someone who is interested and curious about who you are and how you're changing. Jens and I have that in spades. It's fine if you get less than that in your partner, as long as they're not actively working against you, envious or sucking your energy or self-belief.

Jens and I have been together for a long time – and hopefully we'll stay together for a long time to come. But I never, ever take that for granted. Life is weird – shocking really at times – and I don't believe in complacency. Just as I'm always applying myself at work, learning and evolving to stay in touch with our businesses in the present moment,

I work hard at my relationship, too, understanding that what we need from each other today is not the same thing we'll need from each other in the future. Jens and I also have trade-offs: in 2024 to 2025, when I launched my podcast and wrote this book – while continuing to work on SKIMS, Off Season and Good American – Jens took the lead on parenting. How we're going to find a balance between us is something we actively discuss all the time. I also recognise that we're slowly shifting and changing as people, too – I hope we stay connected as we age, but many people don't. This might sound like a wild way to talk about your husband, but I'm more interested in reality than fantasy, and reality would suggest that we all stay awake and alive in our relationships and continue to assess whether they're helping us grow or keeping us stuck.

New Thought: **Your romantic partner is the most important work relationship in your life.**

---

3. Old Thought: **Get your career dialled in before you have kids.**

*Wherever you go, go with all your heart.*
– Confucius

Jodi Kantor looked at me like I was a little crazy. She was moderating a *New York Times* DealBook Summit panel on women and work-life balance, and I was telling her that even though we offer it as part of our packages, I think egg freezing is a bullshit corporate benefit. I explained, 'As women, we have to take partial responsibility for this. I've been one of those women in a leadership position giving women false hope and telling them, "Wait it out, it will be fine." Guess what? It's not fine. Like it really isn't, unless you're one of those people who doesn't *really, really* want to have a baby. But for a lot of women, that isn't the case. They've waited, and they've waited, and they've put their career first. And when they've "chosen" to have a baby, it's no longer their choice. This has been me. My frozen eggs didn't turn into embryos. And my embryos didn't turn into babies. This idea that you can put your life on pause and run at your career and then revisit your life when you're forty-two is bullshit. How many people does this work out for? Almost none.'[3] I refuse to participate in a culture that tells thirty-year-old women to blindly work their arses off for years, and *then* to think about a family when their chances of having a baby are really low – all because, in the USA, there are even fewer benefits for mums and families than in the UK. Understandably, most women feel they need to work and 'get ahead' so they can afford to pay for childcare – and then there's no child to take care of. If we want to give women benefits, we need to give them that: paid family leave, access to subsidised childcare, universal preschool. Not bullshit egg freezing. We've created a suite of benefits as a corporate play that's masked as being really great for us when it's not.

I work with and mentor so many women in my companies who are in their thirties and forties, and there is heartbreak all around me. This heartbreak is compounded by the fact that there's so much shame for women in not being able to have children that it's rarely discussed or shared in a professional forum. Even among my friends, friends whom I know had to do IVF or use surrogacy, lips are firmly sealed while it's happening. It's like we can't speak about IVF until it's all done and hopefully successful. I remember being on a boat with a bunch of friends a few summers ago – each one of those friends had confided in me about a fertility-related issue, and I knew that of the five of us, I was the only one who knew what was going on. It remained unspoken. It felt very sad to me, as I knew we could have a really powerful conversation if people felt they could be more open. This is one of those conversations that we need to blow up in the culture so women don't feel so alone, or so broken.

I've also had my own fertility journey that felt, at times, full of despair – and this was *after* I'd managed to 'naturally' conceive my first two kids. It is devastating to not feel like you have reproductive agency, like you can't control your body. And I mean this in all ways. As a parentified child, I didn't originally know if I'd even want to have kids, as I had spent so much of my childhood looking after my younger sisters, but once Jens and I started, I didn't want to stop. I'm sure many women understand this: once you decide you want a baby, it is entirely consuming. Jens would ask me what I wanted for dinner, and all I could say in response was, 'Another baby.' Except my body wouldn't comply.

After what felt like an endless number of rounds of IVF and three miscarriages at nine weeks, eleven weeks and, devastatingly, sixteen weeks, I felt like I was going to break. I was in the clinic after the third miscarriage, and the woman taking care of me pointed me to a door and told me that it was a match service for surrogacy. While I knew a bunch of people who had used surrogates, I never thought it was for me. In my mind, it was for my gay friends, for those with severe health complications or those who couldn't be bothered to get pregnant. I looked at her like she'd lost her marbles.

'Listen,' she said. 'This is hard on your body and it's not working. You should think about it.'

I went home and I called a friend who had needed the help of a surrogate. She gave me the best advice, reassuring me that her kids are her kids, and she felt and feels the same love for the child who didn't come out of her uterus. I went on to meet a lot of surrogates, but I ended up working with the first woman I met. She carried my twins, the single greatest gift someone has ever given me. It was a profound, incredible experience with an amazing woman who went way beyond our contractual commitment. It was also profound because I'm someone who is used to getting her way by working toward her goals, and I couldn't achieve this without the intervention of a very kind woman.

---

In operating businesses, it's very important to me to encourage the women who work for me to come back into the office after they've had a kid. I know this period of time can feel like emotional quicksand that takes a lot of women out of the game, but if they're ambitious, and they want to actually do the thing, I want them on my team – and if they can't do it at one of my companies, under my watch, I don't know where else they're going to pull it off. Partly, I try to lead by example. I know people are watching me and thinking, 'Okay, if Emma is doing this with four kids, then I can do this, too. If she leaves for an event at her kids' school, then I can leave, too. If she leaves at 5:00 p.m. every day without compromise, then I can, too.' On the flip side, I am incredibly honest about the trade-offs that are required. Recently, a mum on my team came to see me to ask if she could leave every day at 2:00 p.m. She was eating herself up with guilt about not being at home with her baby and convinced that doing this for her kid would be the right thing to do. She was also experiencing a lot of external pressure that she should be at home more.

I had to be candid with her: 'No, you can't do that if you want to stay on track; it's not concurrent with what you want to achieve at work. Let's talk about both sides of this. You want to be home for this tiny baby who is sleeping all the time? You are up in your head. How much of this feels like you think you need to do this because you feel bad, versus what your baby needs from you?' This is the question we need to ask ourselves: is the feeling coming from you that you need to go home to be with your baby, or is it a fear of judgement from the outside? If it's the latter, think again. This is where you have to lean in to start with yourself. You must decide what *you* think and what *you* believe. In working with a lot of mums, and being a mum myself, I know there's no simple compartmentalisation that makes this all go down easier, where nothing gets sacrificed in the process. It is very difficult to go 100 per cent on work ambition and 100 per cent on parenting simultaneously. The math doesn't math. In reality, for work to work for mums, women need to feel like they have agency over their lives at the office and that they're able to make fluid decisions based on all the factors that aren't fully in their control. They need the conditions of the office to not only allow this, but to expect it – and the flexibility and trust from managers to make it work. Honestly, we all need this. If your kid is at home ill, or if you've broken up with your partner, you're not going to be very useful to me or anyone else at the office – it's fine and it happens.

I would much rather that we all operate at a level of honesty where people feel comfortable doing what they need to do, and we all acknowledge that none of us are robots. It drives me crazy when employers approach mums in particular as though they're inclined to take advantage of them if you give them flexibility. There is no woman with kids who takes the piss with flexibility. They don't exist. I have never, ever had an experience with a working mother where she's taken advantage of me and the benefits or the flexibility I've afforded her at work. In fact, the opposite happens: the working mums in my businesses use the flexibility and are without a doubt the most productive and the best at growing teams and results, precisely because they need to be able to make things work for themselves.

I want to caveat that I'm not talking about working dads here because that idea has somehow not punctured the consciousness of America and the UK. Most men do not list 'dad' in their bio, much less think about how to spend their days without sacrificing quality time with their kids. To this end, paternity leave in America is bullshit, too, because *men don't take it.* They feel like they'll be penalised for taking the chance to help their partners out and bond with their babies, and they don't want to take any time off from their careers and eventual ascension. This is a cultural issue, as it's not this way in Scandinavia and other parts of Europe, where you'll see a lot of 'latte papas' taking time away from their careers at the local coffee shop with Bugaboos and babies strapped to their chests. Thasunda Brown Duckett was on a *New York Times* panel with me – she's one of the few Fortune 500 female CEOs – and her husband, a former marine, now looks after the kids. She spoke a lot about what happened in their relationship as he decided to let her career fly, a story that's all too rare in our culture. In Europe, nobody looks at you sideways if you're a man who looks after your family. Theirs is a too-rare example in our culture.

We'll talk about this later in the book, but I also urge my teams to remember that work is *not* your family: we're here to do a job. But there's a balance to this where I see my team members as people and not 'functions'. There is a huge piece of what we get up to at work that has nothing to do with the goals or the strategy of the business. I tell the people who work with me the following: 'Because I care a lot about where the business is going, I need to care a lot about you. If I care about you, I know you'll care about my business. If we both do those things at the same time, we'll be fine.' In my experience, working mums feel like they're making a big sacrifice for their children, and they want to understand what they're getting in return. This is about flexibility and respect, but it's also about offering women a clear path and career progression. They need a bit more than their wage and next job title. Mums need community, a good fucking time and a positive environment that gives us an identity outside of motherhood. And we *all* need a sense of purpose, to be surrounded by people we enjoy, and to have fun.

New Thought: **There's no time like the present to manage both work and life; there is no 'right' time, so don't wait.**

# 5. Building a Brand & Business

*Take a simple idea and take it seriously.*
– Charlie Munger

'Entrepreneur' is a funny word. It's French, and it comes from the idea of 'undertake', you know, to take on an idea. But I love the double meaning of it also being what we call funeral directors. In many ways, building a business is not dissimilar to what happens at the morgue. A lot of things need to die in order to make an entrepreneur's dreams come true – and I also think something needs to die in you for you to feel ready to take on this trip. It's not an easy one, but it might be the most important journey of your life.

I've been entrepreneurial since I was a tween, when I sold 'found' merchandise to anyone who could pay cash on the spot. But I didn't have a word for it other than hustling. I've always been a tirelessly hard worker. This is one of my most consistent qualities, and it can't be overstated: I grind. I've always been able to identify an opportunity and know how to fill it. And I've always liked taking managed risks. (As stated, I don't go backward in lifestyle, so I am not a renegade with money, though as we'll discuss, you need to be willing to gamble a bit to make it in business.)

Compounding is a thesis a lot of business gurus talk about, but if you don't have anything to start with, it can feel like demoralizing advice. How do you parlay a negative bank balance into money, or a lack of experience into exponential success? Don't let thoughts like that deter you though. Start with what you do have – yourself. Begin there. It is *a lot,* I promise, and ultimately, it's what you can control. Realising this is a big part of what has made me successful. I leveraged my grit, tenacity and willingness into a career – and then I leveraged my reputation as a hard worker into my first business. That's all I had, and it was enough – along with a willingness to continually put it on the line and the consistency of a psycho.

As I built ITB Worldwide, I realised I wasn't really taking any risks. I understood my business intuitively and could have kept cranking out deals to enrich celebrities, influencers and brands, but the interest and desire in doing this . . . died. I became an extremely frustrated consultant, enraged that I wasn't materially benefitting from my own ideas, even though this was my fault; I had designed my business to do precisely that. My agency model was built on selling my knack for putting people, ideas and companies together at a fixed rate. There was no model for creating any additional upside for myself – I didn't benefit beyond that single payment, even if the seeds that I planted grew into millions, if not billions, of dollars of revenue. I had done this to myself, and I knew I needed to resolve it myself. From this resentment, my first legitimately entrepreneurial venture was born. In retrospect, it's wild that I thought I could pull something like Good American off – and even wilder that, in fact, I did. For all of you who are thinking, *Yeah, but you had a celebrity cofounder . . .* sure, but we tend to grossly overestimate the impact of celebrity on the creation of enduring brands – in some ways, they are almost at odds with each other. You're taking someone who is timely and of the moment and butting it up against an idea that needs to be larger than any single person's cultural resonance to last. Our world is a graveyard of failed celebrity projects, and very few work long-term. The important thing here is that I had the audacity to think I could start a brand with one of the world's most famous women – and it worked. But before that happened, I had to place the call, take the meeting, make the pitch, create the collection, raise the financing, all without knowing if it would go anywhere after working full days at the office, a job that was already costing me between twelve and fourteen hours a day. That's how much it takes.

I meet a lot of entrepreneurs – people who sit at the head of boardrooms packed with serious investors, and people who are nursing a dream with literal pocket change they've managed to scrimp and save to pay for their first prototype. Regardless of what the cap table might look like – or if there's even a cap table at all – these entrepreneurs all have something essential in common: they have faith in themselves. While every entrepreneurial journey is different, in my experience, great entrepreneurs think in a highly specific way. Most founders I know – including myself – believe in themselves to the point of delusion. Let's get into it now.

### 1. Old Thought: You need to raise a lot of money to start a company.

*The only place where success comes before work is in the dictionary.*
– Vince Lombardi

One of the biggest mechanisms for procrastination in the start-up world of business is the belief that you need to raise a colossal amount of money to get started. Most businesses are not built off an idea and a vast pool of cash though – most are funded with working capital that's fuelling something that's already working. Unless you're a proven builder in a space like AI, which legitimately requires huge amounts of capital to train and develop models, your best bet is to start exactly where you are. And bootstrap as much as possible. There are manifold reasons for doing this, including the creation of a valuation that will drive value for *you* – and the discipline to build a profitable business out of the gate. The days of hunting for profits in five or ten years on businesses that could be run more efficiently are largely behind us, and this is a good thing. You want to build something steady and sustainable from the get-go. Top-line revenue is irrelevant, especially if you're spending more money in marketing and customer acquisition than you're making. (It's true, this used to be how a lot of VC-backed businesses were run – the idea being that the lifetime value [LTV] of the customer would be high enough to eventually put you in the black. It was a kind of insanity, and I'm so grateful that my earliest investors were old-school, and they coached me to chase EBITDA [earnings before interest, taxes, depreciation and amortisation] – and by extension, profitability – out of the gate.)

To build a viable company, you need a spark – you need an idea, ultimately, and from there, you need the belief that you can go out and find what you need to get it done. People struggle with getting started because everybody imagines that in addition to large sums of cash, they need the perfect, dialled-in plan. That's a lot of pressure – and it's fallible, because I can promise you that businesses change *a lot*. In fact, *everything* in your business *should* change except your purpose. A big part of this belief is that many entrepreneurs don't know how to manage what they don't know, so they think they can outsource it by fixating on a model and a business plan – neither of which have been tested by the market itself. They think this is a way to manage risk. But you can't really manage risk when you're starting something – *it is risky* – and so you need to walk into this head-on. Risk is a requirement; playing it safe is the real danger. Risk is the bridge between who you are today and where you're going.

You also need to approach the world with some flexibility, knowing you will get most things wrong. You will fail a lot, though you need to reframe failure as feedback. You are iterating your way to success, and it is painful. This is tough medicine. So many people I meet, specifically a lot of women who understandably feel like they have a lot more to lose, are full of fear – terrified that they don't know what they need to know, scared that they'll fail big and be publicly humiliated for thinking they could have pulled something off. I totally understand this – women are criticised ruthlessly, and it's rational to be freaked – and yet, you can't build shit if you don't start. Just start, even if it's teeny-tiny. Too rarely do people think, *I'm going to start with something small and test it. I'm going to start exactly where I am and learn everything I can by tending to the garden I can reach.* They decide they need to start by buying fifty thousand acres instead. Not only is this an expensive way to learn, but it's also far harder and more pressured than it needs to be.

We live in a culture that glamourises investors and having lots of them. Getting a lot of cash in the bank and a high valuation is held out as a pinnacle of achievement, proof that you have an idea that's valid and worthwhile. Because of these vanity metrics, a lot of people raise money for the wrong reasons: *not* because they need working capital or know exactly how to spend the money to build the business in the right, sustainable way, but because they want cultural proof that they're worthy. The result is usually a disaster. You can't take money for the wrong reasons. As Mark Cuban offered on my podcast: 'Raising money isn't an accomplishment; it's an obligation.'[1]

I meet a lot of entrepreneurs who are confused about the role of the investors. They mistake them as friends and feel betrayed when they are not ride or die, or they see them as irritating pebbles in the bottoms of their shoes. First, your investors are not your friends; they're your business associates who might be kind and pleasant and *friendly* but are ultimately on your cap table to see a return on their investment. And if you fail to deliver on this relationship, things might turn. On the flip side, you can't hate your investors either or hold them in disdain. If you hate your investors, if you're blaming them for pushing you, or for demanding a return on their cash, you raised money for the wrong reasons, or you didn't pay attention to all the warning signs that they weren't the right investors for you. It's rare that investors don't show their true colours before you take their money. Often, entrepreneurs are in such a state of desperation when they're raising capital – they're out of runway, they're worried they'll have to lay people off, they can't keep up with the momentum of demand – that they look the other way. It's a bit like being in love at the beginning of a relationship: you're infatuated, and when the guy across from you lashes out at an unsuspecting waiter, you blame the waiter. But if you chose reality instead, you'd know the waiter is not actually annoying – the guy sitting across from you is just an arsehole and you don't want to face it. Investors are generally plain-speaking, so listen to what they say.

There's an episode of *Sex and the City* where Carrie meets a guy played by Jon Bon Jovi in her therapist's office. She never finds out why he's in therapy, naturally, and they go on to get together. After they have sex for the first time, she lights up a cigarette in bed and asks him why he's seeing their therapist anyway.

He says, 'I'm really fucked up about women. After I sleep with them, I completely lose interest. What about you? What's your problem?'

'I choose the wrong men,' she replies.

It's a common trope in business that many of us take our unconscious relational patterns – being attracted to jerks or cheaters, wanting a parental figure, looking for approval from any external source, wanting to be seen as a serious person – and impose them on our investors. There's a lot of transference that can happen if we're not awake to the stories and thoughts that we're running in our minds. Please, get clear: both about why you need the money and how you intend to spend it and what covert expectations and stories you might be carrying about the people who are giving you a cheque. Be sure you're not also harbouring a (false) belief in yourself that you'll effectively be able to manage or manipulate your investors into something different from what they signed on to do. This is not only a waste of your precious time and energy, it can also be fatal to your dream.

So many founders tell me they took money from investors who told them, quite explicitly, *We don't see you as the long-term CEO.* These founders, whose desperation gave them an inability to hear this as truth, are then shocked and outraged when their investors eventually make moves to replace them with a more seasoned CEO. I guess they thought the investors would change their mind, or that they didn't *really* have the authority or power to do that, or that they'd be dazzled by the founder's leadership prowess once they got further under the hood of the business, but this is one of the most frequent showdowns in companies. And it's unnecessary, as the investor intentions were clearly stated but not heard as the truth. There's a refusal to read the room. You need to see your potential investors as clearly as possible, and take everything they say as a reality, *before* you accept their money. And you also need to decide if you really need the money: *Is it worth it to sign away a certain amount of power, control and future upside? Do you absolutely have to do it? Have you explored other finance opportunities, like bank loans, instead?*

There are other ways to get capital to operate a business, and it kills me that many founders who manufacture products don't know this. I have good friends who found themselves in predatory loan situations because they didn't realise there were other ways to access cash. Though I launched Good American with only $3 million, which wasn't enough to even see us through launch week, I managed to put off raising additional capital for two years, and I did this by working with a bank and a factoring facility to create enough inventory to build our sales. One of the wonderful things about operating a business in America is that there's a business infrastructure there that doesn't exist in the rest of the world. For one, there is a unique financial construct that exists in apparel and other consumer goods in the US called factoring: your factor, for example, will underwrite your order and advance you the cash to make the goods, so long as you have a guaranteed order from a retailer that they know is financially sound.* They take a small interest fee on the loan while giving you the liquidity you need to grow. If you have to use investment funds to create product, you're theoretically spending money that you might not get a return on for months, depending on your production calendar. That's a lot of money running out the door, and it can make it impossible to string a business together for small brands that are running tight.

While it might have been less painful to just go out and get a big cheque for Good American, I knew I could string it along, and I wanted to do this for as long as possible before we took on investment to grow. There were a lot of kinks to work out and a lot of learnings to learn without the added pressure of blowing the roof off the top of the building. Plus, we knew that to expand the brand in the way that would do it justice, we needed retail. Women needed to be able to come in and try on our clothes. And retail requires an intensive amount of cash. Speaking of retail, right when we were about to sign a lease for a shop on Melrose Avenue, Amazon swept in and took our spot – on 10 March 2020. Even though I was pissed off at the time, this saved us from a disastrous retail rollout during COVID that would have killed the brand.

---

Even though I'm now a seasoned entrepreneur, and investors are very eager to give me their cash, it hasn't changed the way I incubate and build brands. Quite frankly, I really only want to do businesses these days that I can fund myself and run with five people in a room (this

---

* I want to stress here that some of my *most important* relationships in business are with my bankers and agents at factoring facilities – I try to see them regularly. This is not the glamourous side of business, but it can be the most consequential. I am hugely indebted to these people for being my partners through thick and thin, and because I've invested in our relationships, they always have my back. They also give me great insight into the entire industry: I know which retailers are in trouble, for example, long before it's public knowledge simply because my factor partner will no longer guarantee those orders.

is the most fun part of any business in my opinion – I *love* the early days). Case in point, for Off Season – which I cofounded with Kristin Juszczyk, an adorable and super-talented woman who is the wife of San Francisco 49ers fullback Kyle Juszczyk – I funded it with a little bit of cash, a team and back-end infrastructure, along with some resources from Fanatics. And we didn't start from zero, either, as Kristin had already tested the market and built an appetite for a brand. Without investing a single dollar, she had a proof concept.

Kristin goes to every one of her husband's American football games and didn't want to wear oversized jerseys or the unfashionable fan apparel – so she began making her own, cutting up old gear and reconstituting it into custom pieces, like patchworked jackets and capri pants. For her inventiveness, she earned a sizable Instagram following – along with requests from the likes of Taylor Swift for her own game-day gear. Eventually, she slid into my DMs, asking me if I'd advise her on building a real business, and I loved her at first meeting. Effectively, we started right where we were – and small, considering the seismic opportunity.

Off Season holds a licence to do gear for all NFL, NBA and WNBA teams. Other founders might have insisted on taking that big of a bite out of the gate, but I refused; I knew we would bankrupt ourselves. We started with five NFL teams – the San Francisco 49ers for Kristin, plus the Buffalo Bills, Detroit Lions, Kansas City Chiefs and Philadelphia Eagles – and built the brand from there. Eventually, we'd do all the teams and all the leagues, but not as our first step.

Ultimately, you have teams who fail to compete and drum up enough fan enthusiasm to create real sales volume, and you're trading on players' names in some cases – each player requires a royalty, in addition to the licensing fee to the team – plus, players often get traded after the merchandise run is complete, making a certain subset of your product immediately null and void. Besides paying double bubble in fees (team and player), it quickly becomes a product assortment nightmare. Not knowing *anything* about sport has been a superpower here, because I can look at the opportunity as a merchant only – with no loyalty to how it's been done – and see, very clearly, why it's been impossible for start-ups to breathe and only monopolies are the result. While I theoretically could have raised enough capital to go big out of the gate, I don't believe it serves any company well to do it that way. I hope Off Season paves the way for other small companies to get involved in sport without risking bankruptcy before they've even begun. We started with five teams, and then we'll do another ten and then another ten, figuring it out as we go.

Ultimately, Off Season is the result of Kristin moving past a dream of a concept by making clothing for herself. In the process, she kicked off a brand, a brand that we are building from there. We didn't need a lot of capital to begin, and we don't want a lot of capital now, because we'd be going too big from the start. What we're doing is a repeatable playbook for the rest of you: start with yourself and start where you are. It's enough, I promise.

New Thought: **You and your sweat equity are all you need. And if you must raise money, take only what you need to get proof of concept. Keep in mind that taking risks is a muscle you will build.**

---

2. Old Thought: **It's always going to get bigger and better.**

*Do not fear failure, but please be terrified of regret.*
– Captain Deshauna Barber

I like to look at houses on sale in Los Angeles, which seems to be everyone's pastime, if I'm honest. A few months ago, Jens took me to see an architectural house owned by one of LA's business titans that needed a lot of restoration.

As we looked it over, Jens turned to me. 'The month before the owner went bankrupt, he was offered $2.1 billion for his company.' This is just one of many cautionary tales that runs in my head. Our world is a graveyard of brands that were the next big thing for a minute before being chucked on the rubbish heap. The only way to create immunity is to prepare for it as an eventuality. And plan. There are so many founders walking around as examples for the rest of us, founders whose egos got in the way of them being truly original with first-class ideas that endured. This type of hubris has become a more common story than the successful exit. There's a saying in business that I live by to ensure I don't also become a cautionary tale: Valuation is vanity. Profit is sanity. And cash is king.

It won't surprise you if you've been paying attention, but one of my principles is to never let boom-and-bust happen to me. I have trained myself to always, always take cash off the table at every opportunity, and I am acutely attuned to the relevancy curves of every company. I'm trained to understand that the first offer is usually your best offer, and fooling yourself into thinking there is always something better down the road is not smart. I'd much rather pull money out over time, stack my cash and invest in other things. I don't need to be rich when I'm seventy; I want to live well now. I know so many people who experienced a crazy valuation and refused to take something off the table and reduce their ownership stake from 25 per cent to 17 per cent – and ultimately ended up with nothing to show for it. I never regret taking money out when the opportunity is there.

A few months ago, I met with the team at Simon Malls. As we were walking around, they pointed out how the shopfronts once dominated by brands we took for granted have been largely replaced by DTC brands in recent years, only for many of those brands to then go bust. Nothing is forever, and all businesses exist in a moment of time – extending that time past a moment takes a lot of intuition and skill. There is a natural turnover in retail every ten years or so if you study it, so thinking you'll be the exception is a dangerous game.

Before I launched Good American, I did my research and sobered myself about the likelihood of success. Remember when there were dozens, if not hundreds, of relevant denim brands? Where's Current/Elliott now? Where's Hudson? Where's Rock & Republic or Earl Jean? When I looked at the landscape, I realised that they all more or less died at the same place – around $150 million in sales. They fell out of style. To me, this reality feels exactly like a street mentality: you're not the hot girl or the cool gang forever. It all ebbs and flows, and it's no different in business. Yet, many people fail to realise this or believe they're immune.

Companies are magical, and you can sometimes get a four-year halo where things go up very quickly – and then they frequently plateau and begin their descent. There are very few companies – Nike, Coca-Cola, Apple – that have managed to maintain relevance and cool factor and outrun this pattern. There are so few, in fact, you can almost count them on one hand. As I tell founders: *What makes you think you're going to be that special?* I also tell young founders that sometimes the first offer *is* the best offer. This is a question worth pondering: *What makes you think it's going to get better than now?* This may sound harsh or negative, but I don't like the relentlessly positive business chatter that gaslights entrepreneurs about reality by convincing them to hold on for their inevitable day in the unicorn sun – too many people lose out on more realistic success. (We'll talk more about the beauty of businesses of every size in the following pages, too. Very few things need to be a billion-pound brand to be exceptional and important!)

Every business exists on a relevancy curve: for most of us, a brand's time will come, it will peak and then it will wane. Don't get confused about this. To survive this eventuality, a brand must evolve and shift with culture without departing from its core values. Madonna is an excellent example of an individual who managed to stay relevant for decades by continuing to reinvent herself. This is a formula – and companies can master it, too. Doing this is difficult though. You need to understand what your cycle is, how to time your business to that cycle – and what your peak might be. And on the flip side, you need to understand the timing of your downturns, which will invariably come. Your goal needs to be to build a sustainable business with operational excellence that can survive a downturn while you're on your way to your peak. Doing this requires speed and agility, but it results in brands that are healthy and durable and have a fighting chance to transition into something with lasting success.

Often to survive a downturn and extend a relevancy curve, everything about your business will need to change except for the principles of the business itself. Take SKIMS as an example. At its launch, we were selling underwear and shapewear. Two years later, we were making SKIMS clothing – out of the gate, nobody would have guessed that people would be falling over themselves to buy a ski puffer and trousers from us, done in collaboration with The North Face. At face value, the product seems entirely different, and yet, at our heart, we are the same: we are a solutions-based clothing business, a business that's focused on solving problems for customers. The solution might be shapewear, it might be a bra, it might be a puffer jacket, it might be a designer collaboration with Swarovski, Dolce & Gabbana or Fendi.

If you are going to extend your relevancy curve, you need to understand how to 'transition on the way up', which is a concept I heard from LVMH CEO Bernard Arnault that I love and swear by. You need to obsess over the specific problems that are yours uniquely to solve. You need to understand what your business stands for and what that allows you to do – and then you need to take that as far as you can as long as it aligns with your core foundational values and principles. You need to do this with extreme focus. Even if you're not solving a problem, but are feeding a need, you still need a principle for existing to use as your base camp. Let's say you're a coffee company and you're not solving a problem but are servicing a need for amazing coffee. And maybe as part of your platform, it is not only excellent coffee, but it's also cheaper because there are fewer middlemen, or it's less water-intensive, or it comes from a special cooperative regenerative farm. If I were running a company that made amazing coffee, I'd think about what else we could do that's less water-intensive, or what else we could grow and pioneer from this regenerative farm, and so on. You want to focus and double down like a maniac on your mission in a way that makes sense for the business.

Keep in mind that once you've captured the attention of a customer and they trust what you say to be true, they will transact with you multiple times. It's your job to work out what that relationship with the customer allows you to do. Companies that endure over time are intrinsically the same as they were when customers first fell in love with them, yet also foundationally different, as they've learned to shift and evolve with the time and the culture. When you look back at their trajectories, there's a natural arc that makes complete sense in hindsight, a story that develops over time.

Another critical component of 'transitioning on the way up' is the understanding that you need to keep moving and changing with the culture. You can't get stuck with whatever is working in the moment because the only thing certain is that it will change. Whatever is working today won't work tomorrow. I can 100 per cent guarantee that the thing that's driving your business in this moment is not the thing that will be driving it in eighteen months. So how are you prepping for the next thing? I am always in preparation mode for downturns while also ready to take advantage of whatever is coming next, because nothing is permanent. Companies that maintain a relevancy curve for a long time – companies that eventually transform into blue-chip entities – really understand this.

**New Thought:** Focus on extending your company's relevancy curve for as long as possible by 'transitioning on the way up', rather than fixating on some massive exit down the line.

---

**3. Old Thought:** You're going to do one big thing in business – if you're lucky.

*When you're through changing, you're through.*
– Bruce Barton

I'm a serial entrepreneur – and I've also invested in legions of other businesses and categories. I am highly diversified. But it took me a minute to get there, as I approached my first business, ITB Worldwide, as though it would be my bread and butter for the rest of my life. It wasn't until I watched Jens and Erik operate for a long time that I realised I needed to expand my aperture and hold not only a bigger vision for my career and future, but a more flexible one, too. So many of us don't know how to let go – or how to hold an achievable intention for what's possible.

One of the first forcing functions for me to think in a grander way about my business was that I really wanted my own money. I knew I needed to create some value for myself and put some money in the bank. I was very comfortable financially – I could fly around the world in the front of the plane – but I still didn't feel entirely safe. And even though we were married, I wasn't going to hang my future on Jens's bank account either (and I still don't). I'd seen Jens and Erik be very successful through acquiring and exiting agencies, so I executed a baby version of what they were up to, recognising that I'd be adding significant value to the core business in the process – and have more assets to potentially build and sell.

Throughout my time building ITB Worldwide, I kept the core competency of the agency at its heart (collaborations and partnerships between creatives, talent and brands) while acquiring many other agencies to extend our capacities and round out our service roster. When enough clients had questions about licensing, I acquired a licensing agency so we could broker those deals as well; when enough clients wanted VIP gifting, I acquired an agency that specialised in exactly that; when a friend came to me with an artist representation business that was powerful and yet needed infrastructure support, I brought them in, too. At the end of the day, I had amassed a group of small agencies and put them under the ITB banner to build a big company that became a smorgasbord of deal-making within the creative and fashion worlds.

At ITB, I always had trouble making cash and balance sheets work. I knew we were making money, but I couldn't work out where the money in the business was. When I started Good American, the first thing I wanted to solve was cash and liquidity. I wanted to be in a business with healthy margins, not needing to string revenue together by chasing invoices and hunting for the next deal. I wasn't a denim head back then. I liked jeans as much as the next person, but I felt I had enough experience with denim clients that I understood the space, and that denim would be the foundation of a sound business – like underwear and bras, jeans are a commodity product and a wardrobe staple. It felt like the right move, as I knew I couldn't run for cash my entire life.

Back at ITB, I also knew I had built myself a bit of a treadmill – a good business that would never achieve scale in a significant way. Everything we did was both high-touch and laborious. I looked around me in London and saw all these pinnacle agencies with founders who were holding on and had to ask: *What are you holding on for?* I knew that I could hold on but might be left holding nothing. I thought, *Get out of it before it gets out of you.* Intuitively, I felt like it was time to capitalise on what I had built.

When I took ITB Worldwide out to sell, there were multiple bidders, and I went through a whole sales process of turning this agency I'd spent a better part of a decade building into something concrete in my pocket. I got a solid return – not *F-you* money, but a nice ROI for my time and energy. I wanted to sell the business because I wanted to put some cash in my pocket. I didn't know if I could build it to be much bigger than it was at the time, and I wondered if its peak had passed. I took the advice I'm offering in the paragraphs above: understand the relevancy curve, transition on the way up, don't stay too long and take money off the table while you still can.

But after the sale – a high point – I experienced one of the worst moments of my life. They didn't want me to stay on to run the company. I was gutted, and if I'm honest, shocked that they thought they could and should operate without me. This was my inner experience, even as I also felt like I was ready to do my next thing. (And I was. I had the idea for Good American spinning cycles in the back of my mind, though I thought I could run both companies in parallel.) Ultimately, the board's decision to not lock me in was the best thing that could have happened to me – it allowed me to move my family to Los Angeles unencumbered, for one, but it still hurt my ego. Letting go of your baby is really hard, which is one of the reasons that founders often stay for way too long.

After the sale of ITB, I kicked off a process that I continue to this day. I took a blank piece of paper and inventoried the experience, asking myself an important question: *What were you trying to do here?* Followed by: *What do you feel called to do next?* I sat and wrote it all down. I wrote that I was going to walk away from a lot, including people I loved and continue to love now – and that I needed to allow myself to mourn. But I also got really clear with myself that it wasn't about just me anymore. The ITB experience was part of my story, and part of what I would go on to do next, but I needed to take everything I had learned there and close the book on that chapter of my life – while pulling the wisdom forward into what I would do next.

I often talk about my life in chapters – it helps to set a temporal framework around experiences and to consider them as complete. I have the consultancy chapters. I have the chapters where I started my first retail businesses, and I have chapters where I was in the second phase of these businesses, figuring out what to do to move them forward. It really offers a good opportunity to reflect on the past and determine how you want to move forward and grow. It preserves the experience while recognising that it's simply one part of a much larger story.

Now, whenever I start a new endeavour, I sit with a blank piece of paper and answer a series of questions: *What was wrong with the last company? What are you optimising for? What are the key takeaways and learnings that you can pull forward? What do you never want to do again? What was magical and special about this company? What parts did we nail? Where did we fail? What is the ultimate ambition, and what does it look like to succeed? When is enough enough?*

I can't stress how important it is to create a vision for what you want to build – this is different from models and business plans; this is the concept of what you're after and what's possible. I make these less about concrete events and more about how I want to *feel*. I meet so many founders who kicked off a company without a real intention for what they wanted it to be and how it would fit in their lives. This is critical, especially in our culture, which pushes the narrative that everything should be as big as possible and that the only worthy glory comes with billion-pound exits or a dazzling IPO. Not everything is supposed to be that – nor is that necessarily the right ride to aspire to.

I often think of my brilliant and talented friend Renata Quaglia, who makes these gorgeous necklaces under the name RENATA.Q. She gives part-time employment to four or five women in New York City who help with the very delicate crochet work, and she sells through Moda Operandi. She's created something beautiful, truly luxurious, uniquely hers, 100 per cent self-funded and owned entirely by her. It offers her a creative outlet and financial freedom. It's the perfect business and the perfect size for her.

Because we're convinced that everything worthwhile must be *huge*, it stops us before we start. This holds in every sphere of our lives. In my conversation with Michelle Obama on my podcast, she said as much about giving back, too. 'Start small,' she offered. 'The power in small change is really real. And sometimes we get ahead of ourselves because we think it has to be big. And look, not all of us will ever have the platform to have a big impact, and that's okay, because big impact is limited. Look, I lived with the president of the United States of America, and there were so many things he couldn't get done because there are limits on that power. . . . Being a good teacher, that's some power. Being a good parent to the children you bring onto this planet, that's some power. Take care of the thing that you have control and power over. And sometimes it's as small as yourself.'[2] Amen, Michelle. This holds with business, too: while you don't want to hobble yourself with a too-small ambition, bootstrapping and building your own sweat equity is one of the best ways to build.

One way to wrap your arms around an intention for your business is to consider the end point before you begin. I know many successful and seasoned builders who back into a goal – they understand the business's ideal (and realistic) trajectory; they know when it would be the right size for a strategic acquisition and exactly what they need to do to get there. This takes some experience, but it's a helpful construct for everyone: rather than trying to be as big as possible, focus on being as big as you need to be to be viable. What can the market tolerate? Are you building something to be acquired, to go public or to throw off cash as a nice, sustainable business? Ultimately, *be intentional*. It doesn't mean you'll always land the plane on that exact runway, but hopefully you'll at least be at the right airport.

And once that particular journey is finished, get ready to dream about the next one. I firmly believe that we all have many chapters and that this type of reframe will give air and space to your life. Nothing is forever. Enjoy the ride while it lasts while recognising it won't be your final one.

New Thought: **Your life contains many chapters – and just as many chances to begin a new adventure.**

---

4. Old Thought: **Passion is the most important ingredient in business success.**

*Inspiration exists, but it has to find you working.*
– Pablo Picasso

There's a saying that nothing is true if it's not a paradox, and that holds here: yes, you probably need to burn hot for your start-up – passion is essential, you'll need that drive to get you through some long and very hard days – but it's not the most important factor. It's certainly not enough. In addition to a great idea, you need endurance, resilience, consistency and focus; you need a willingness to listen and learn; and you need advisors and investors (potentially) who have been there before and can help you find shortcuts so you don't need to reinvent the wheel. And you need to be willing to hustle.

I love doing *Shark Tank* (the US version of *Dragons' Den*), not only because it's fun but also because it's given me the opportunity to meet and invest in some incredible entrepreneurs. The other compelling factor about *Shark Tank* – and why it's a worthwhile watch for anyone in business, or who wants to be in business – is that as investors we understand our lanes. You can admire a business while simultaneously recommending that they need more than their passion and your cash. We all need mentorship; it's one of the most powerful factors to ensure success, and we need mentors who have been where we've been before. If you have investors, ideally they operate like mentors and have experience to lend you. Now, you might not get Mark Cuban as your mentor/investor, but you can still watch him operate in the world and on shows like *Shark Tank* and get some hits of wisdom.

One of the companies I met and invested in through *Shark Tank* is CAKES body, a solution for what its twin founders call NFO: nipple freak-out. It's a washable silicone slice that you can wear in lieu of a bra to cover your nipples and the surrounding area. It's the perfect solution for those moments when a bra doesn't cut it. The CAKES are grippy, not sticky, so they don't move until you peel them off at the end of the day – and while they're thick at the centre, they're paper-thin at the edges, meaning there's no visible line through clothing. When I met them on TV, Taylor Capuano and Casey Capuano Sarai had launched CAKES body because they were both facing being made redundant from their jobs – and decided to take $10,000 in savings and make the leap. The twins not only had an idea, but they had enough experience as customers of other nipple shield brands to realise there was room in the market for them to make a better version. Nobody was taking the need as seriously as they intended to. When they approached the Sharks for investment, they were looking for $300,000 in exchange for 5 per cent of the business. Having spent zero dollars in marketing, they had managed to do $1 million in revenue in their first year, thanks to an excellent product and organic raves on TikTok, and were on track to do $5 million in year two with a 75 per cent product margin. I gave them $300,000 for a 10 per cent stake, which they accepted after Kevin O'Leary called me Grede-y. Sometimes the nickname fits, but I knew that I could take them much further than they'd probably get on their own. It's much better to own a smaller part of something big than 100 per cent of something small.

One of the other reasons I was keen to give Taylor and Casey my money and my time is that they were open-eyed about both the opportunity and, more importantly, where they might struggle – and how I could help. They had clearly studied their competition and were looking for shortcuts to growth, as well as a broader mandate of problems they might be uniquely equipped to solve. They were looking for mentorship on how to build something sustainable and stable. They recognised that while they had tapped into an early groundswell through TikTok – there was clearly a market, a customer need, and they had created a high-quality, high-margin product – they didn't yet have a business. It can be very hard to translate viral moments on a social media platform that you can't manufacture or control into reliable revenue.

In the time since I invested in June 2023, they've grown the business to $150 million with a team of about ten people, mostly by staying focused, adding meaningful products and bringing the right people into their business for the stage of growth they are at. While they know I'm not going to sit and build their financial model (I did connect them with one of my CFOs), they send me results every month and engage with me for advice – they're clear about their needs and actively embrace what I advise them to do, which means that I continue to lean in as well. I can't stress this enough, because I work with a lot of founders, and none of them are as good at getting my attention as Taylor and Casey. It has nothing to do with the size of their respective businesses either; it's because they aren't as prepared and don't use my time effectively. So many founders turn up and say, *What do you think I should do?* My response: *I'm not here to solve this for you.* Or I'll hear, *Just tell me what to do and I'll do it.* My response: *I'm not your mother.* To use your investors and mentors effectively, do the groundwork. Come with options, mapped-out decisions that need to be made, and highly specific questions. Taylor and Casey will come to me and say, 'We could do this or we could do that. What's the best use of capital? We have these two products on our roadmap. Which one do you think is the most commercially viable? We have this deal or we have this deal – these are the factors, which would you take?' They're prepared, they're brilliant and they're going to be so successful. Taylor and Casey can rely on me for guidance on product innovation, building their team and distribution in particular. I encouraged the idea for them to put a nipple on their boob cover, and they've become the de facto brand for any woman who's had a mastectomy. (Meanwhile, the company now gives one dollar from every product sold to women's health initiatives.) They've been smart about playing to the strengths of their investor – be smart, and if you have an investor, do that, too. If you don't have investors, build a team of mentors.

Taylor and Casey didn't really need my $300,000 to build the business; they were making enough to self-fund the growth. But they did need mentorship from someone like me. If you have an investable idea and there are multiple suitors who are interested in working with you, make sure that beyond the cash, they're bringing something to the table operationally that you don't yet have. It's never just about money with investors, as you want to be able to lean on their expertise. Money is easy for a good, investable idea – keep in mind that not all good ideas are investable – so take the experience that you need, which means someone who has proven relationships and experience in businesses in the region or in your part of the market. If you have an amazing opportunity in China, take the investors who know how to operate in China. If you're in the food business, take the investors who know how to roll out food services across the UK. We'll talk about shortcuts soon, but the right investors or mentors can be the greatest shortcut of all.

Ultimately though, you can have passion, connections, the right idea and mentorship and still fail – arguably, one of the most important distinguishing traits of entrepreneurs who pull it off is a willingness to figure it out. And part of that requires a willingness to suffer both rejection and failure. I actually look for rejection now, as it's one of the sharpest stones on which to polish and shape your strategy and refine your approach. You simply need to frame rejection as feedback, not as a loss or as anything personal. I'm particularly hardwired for this because I saw so many women get rejected when I was a kid, and I also came to see that rejection was not final. I don't want to minimise it, as it can feel like death – *but* the more you accept it as an inevitability, the quicker you will recover and move on. At the beginning of this chapter I mentioned that the etymology of entrepreneur is 'undertake', like a funeral home director. There will be times when it will feel like your business is going to kill you. You will have to sacrifice a huge amount of your life in terms of energy and time to make your dream catch flight. And sometimes you will have to raise yourself from the grave and live to fight another day.

We have an impression from social media in particular that the biggest names in our culture were overnight successes. Suddenly, they were helming big businesses or lifestyle empires, empires that came out of nowhere. This is rarely, if ever, the case. Most people toil anonymously for decades before whatever seeds they're sowing bear fruit – they might be new to you, but they're not new to their trade. People imagine that my life magically clicked into place – that I moved to Los Angeles and made it big in an instant. It's a nice story, but it's not the truth. If I haven't made this abundantly clear in the preceding pages, I've been working since I got my first paper round at twelve. You will start with one customer, or one subscriber, or one podcast listener. That might grow to a hundred, or a thousand if you're lucky. From there, growth might come a little faster or it might not. You might need to build your enterprise brick by brick. For a long time, in almost every business or brand, *nothing happens* . . . for an agonizing amount of time. Good American was explosive, but 99.9 per cent of great businesses are about slow, consistent growth.

I want women in particular to know this because we don't talk about it, partly because we don't want to appear too negative or crush anyone's dreams, especially when it already feels so hard for us to make strides in business. But we're not helping each other out when we're not honest about what it takes – and how long it might be before you find any sense of traction. You will have to hustle – and you might still be hustling long after you feel like you've depleted your petrol tank. It's not a glamourous proposition. It's *hard*. I don't want you to have a warped idea about this, so you're ready for the fight. I hear from a lot of female founders who think their passion for the problem they want to solve is enough. Passion is something, but it won't take you that far. You can't manifest your way to a great business. You need to have a business case. You need a customer. And a massive amount of grit.

I was giving advice to a young founder the other day, and a colleague who overheard told me that I'd been too harsh. 'Don't be such a bitch!' As I explained, no, I'm not a bitch – I'm not trying to be purposefully obstructive or negative about something, but I'm also not going to lie and tell an entrepreneur their idea is perfect when it's not, or that their business model will work when it won't. That is not helpful. We all need to be brave enough to cut the crap, specifically when we're trying to help women. We are not served by dishonesty or punches that are held back to preserve our feelings or someone else's comfort. This is not to say that I'm always right or that a founder won't prove me wrong, but if I have an intuition or a piece of wisdom for them, I feel beholden to share it in an unvarnished way. Even if they only take it under advisement but largely stay the course, I'm guessing that it will still help them sharpen their attack in some way. No idea is perfect out of the gate. Every founder must take feedback and iterate. Meanwhile, say the truth, as none of us have any time or money to waste – *particularly* women.

**New Thought:** In addition to passion, the fastest path to business success is still long and steep: you need endurance, a willingness to work, the ability to focus and a desire to listen and learn.

---

### 5. Old Thought: Failure is a signal that you should stop.

*Failure is simply the opportunity to begin again, this time more intelligently.*
– Henry Ford

When I opened an office for ITB Worldwide in Los Angeles in 2013, I failed miserably. This was largely my fault. I really did mess it up. I did every single thing wrong. I was under the spell of being a typical founder where I believed my own bullshit and thought all my ideas were exportable to any place or any culture. Meanwhile, I didn't understand the operating system of Los Angeles at all. I had no respect for the differences in the market or the community. Los Angeles is a community. Everyone went to school together. Everyone likes to use the same lawyers, eat at the same few restaurants and use the same plastic surgeons. It is a highly networked, self-referential place. I didn't understand this at all.

I also didn't understand that Los Angeles doesn't operate with the same moral baseline as where I'd come from. In East London, your word is king. You do what you say you're going to do. You speak with candour, all the time, because to be a liar is to be a fraud. In London proper, this is slightly muted, but people still tell you what they want and are mostly honest. At a new business meeting, you might hear: 'We don't need these services right now, but if and when we do, we will call you.' They might couch rejection in a nicety – there's a good chance you'll never hear from them again – but you don't walk away from a meeting in London thinking something is in the bag if it's not.

In Sweden, you go to a new business meeting, and they'll say, 'There's absolutely nothing we could ever do together.' It's shocking at first, but once you get used to it, you find it refreshing and liberating and absolutely clarifying. (I love being married to a Swede!) Even in New York, where I had a healthy number of clients, I could anticipate our new business pipeline based on who I know and what they told me. But Los Angeles is the world of hopes and dreams, and so much of what's said is *pure fantasy*. I didn't understand this, so when people would say, 'Oh my god, girl, I have so many projects for you, you can't get here fast enough,' I took them at their word. I assumed I could transport my business to Los Angeles because clearly people were eager to do deals with me, and then ... nothing materialised. It's normal for one thing in business to fall through, or maybe two, or even five – but in Los Angeles, *everything* fell through. I couldn't take anyone at face value; people were wholly unreliable. I realised I was in the Wild West and everyone was a cowboy. There were no standard rules of comportment. It was shocking! I literally did not understand how people operated in that way because I'd never experienced it before.

I was so embarrassed. I was completely humiliated. While I could get over the embarrassment and wounds to my ego, I felt tremendous guilt about the people I had recruited to come and work for me and then couldn't keep paying after nine months. I will always struggle with the people part of businesses. It is acutely painful to hit the wall where you must downsize. The only thing that helps is to lean on an enterprise mentality. If I need to let twenty people go, I have to think about the 140 people whose roles I'm saving and whose jobs I'm stabilizing. All of those futures are also in my hands. I'd be lying if I said this gets easier or that it doesn't fill me with anxiety or grief. It never, ever feels good, and it never gets easier.

After ITB Worldwide failed in Los Angeles, I took to the blank page and wrote all day, including the mistakes I'd made – of which there were many. I had underinvested in staff. I had a belief I could be everywhere all at once and it would always work. I failed to appreciate the culture of the place. I brought what I had to sell, not what they wanted to buy. They didn't need celebrity connections: their next-door neighbour was a movie star, and Beyoncé was a mum at their school. I made a list of all the mistakes I would not repeat. Mistakes are expensive and they hurt, and yet they are always the most powerful ways to learn. Through processing everything that had gone wrong, and what had gone right, I found my gratitude for the clarity. In my opinion, the most dangerous time for any business, or any relationship for that matter, is when it hasn't quite failed, but it hasn't quite succeeded yet. That's the danger zone: when it's not terrible, but it ain't fucking great either. In many ways, I'm relieved Los Angeles served me a big lesson – I wouldn't have known how to operate there if it hadn't.

My mistakes with ITB weren't limited to choosing to open in Los Angeles. I made mistakes for years building that agency in whom I hired, how I paid people, how I paid myself, how I entered new territories, how I started new divisions, how I acquired new companies. I was stuck in an employee mentality, for one. I really did almost everything wrong – sometimes catastrophically and sometimes in ways that I could recover. Those ten years felt like a roller coaster, and when it's your first big ride, it can feel like you'll never get over those free falls to the bottom. I learned specific, concrete things, but I learned the big thing, too, the most valuable lesson of all: when you're doing things and making moves, you lose over and over and over again. I realised I couldn't let those failures haunt me, and I determined not to dwell. I always find the lesson and then I move on. Negative energy is wasted energy. I've come to understand that a big part of my success is getting over the hard shit without letting it slow me down.

In our culture, we're living in a moment where we feel like we shouldn't need to experience any pain or rejection, where the world should be friendly and amenable to everything we desire. We are certainly parenting in this way. This is a bit of a crisis, not because I want my kids, or you for that matter, to experience hardship, but because the big downs are necessary for the big highs. With experience and practice at both recovering from the downs and riding the highs, this roller coaster may get a little smoother, but it still exists. Instead of focusing purely on ups, build the muscle of resilience for failure. If there's one thing I want you to take from this book, it's this: use failure as an opportunity to grow and get bigger, better, stronger and smarter.

When we experience pain, rejection and disappointment, we think something is 'wrong', or that something went wrong. I think about it the other way around: it's not like I'm a robot lady who enjoys hardship, but when things are uncomfortable, I know I'm onto something. When I feel fearful, when I'm worried about being rejected, I feel most alive. I really do go out and look for this feeling because it signals to me that there's something big for me there – an opportunity to experience my edge and to expand and grow. You don't get to do this when you're complacent and comfortable and everything is dialled in.

Psychiatrist Phil Stutz describes this as nonlinear growth – and that you don't really feel your 'life force', or that internal capacity to move forward with flow, until you experience some type of psychological death or setback and need to recover. He calls this a 'pruning', like what you would do to a plant to ensure healthier growth in the future – that it feels painful but actually liberates important parts of you to show up to move forward. As he writes in *True and False Magic*, 'The main way you get access to this super potential is in the face of certain disasters, glitches, or failures. It's a bit like being initiated into a greater level of ability. If you can do something that you thought was impossible, that you didn't think you could do, it is much more life-changing than a thousand psychoanalytic sessions. Why? Because it requires some sort of internal revelation or change.'[3] Stutz goes on to explain that potential, for all of us, is out there – it's just not always 'fun' to go find it and realise it. To participate in the great cosmic pattern of growth, we all must learn to 'die' – often through failure and loss.

I feel intuitively that this is so true; I now welcome the hard times. I am terrified if it all feels too easy or too good for too long, I know something will rightsize me again. And that's okay, I welcome it. I'm much more resilient in the face of that type of change. Now that I have so much more experience, I can honestly say that the roller coaster never ends, but the dips don't feel so low, and on the flip side, the highs are not so high. When we got a large valuation for one of our companies, Jens and I were sitting at our dining room table together. We looked at each other and said, *Wow, that's amazing. Should we have a glass of champagne or something?* If you told me that I'd be building brands valued at huge amounts even ten years ago, I'd have done a cartwheel, but now it's just one more turn in the ride. We are never done.

There is little to learn from success, but failing over and over again will teach you everything. Losing makes you think in ways that victories can't. Over time, with a lot of practice, I've managed to not sacrifice my equanimity, to not get rocked by hard things or overblown by great ones. I bring it back to myself and balance my emotions, and get my head on straight, before I take any action. I work hard on my emotional boundaries, to not let bad news take me down into fear or anger or sadness, or send me into fight-or-flight where I'm taking it out on other people. I've worked hard throughout my life to stay with myself, and to be present with my feelings so I don't get drowned out. Finally, as soon as I'm able to properly reflect, I look for the lesson that the failure brings, the opportunity to get stronger, to get steadier and to learn. Sometimes a bit of time needs to pass before you can discern what's there for you to bring forward, but if you look, the wisdom always appears.

**New Thought:** If you're not failing, you haven't found the edge of what's possible. You're not learning and growing or pushing yourself hard enough.

---

### 6. Old Thought: Negative feedback is a negative.

*There is no failure. Only feedback.*
– Robert Allen

When I think about the factors that contributed to my initial failure in Los Angeles, I want to double-click on the lack of honesty I experienced and the way that this is peddled as perfectly normal and acceptable. Nobody told me the truth. Now, first, I take complete responsibility for my own hubris in this situation: I fucked it. But I do want to circle this and underline it, because an unwillingness to say the truth is especially harmful to women. We think we're preserving people's feelings or being 'nice', but in reality, we are screwing each other over. When you tell a woman that her idea is good or valid, or that you'll buy whatever it is she's selling with absolutely no intent to do what you say, you are harming her far more than the disappointment she might feel in the face of a rejecting truth. Even 'I'm not sure I can offer sound advice because I don't think I'm the customer for this product' is better than 'Your business will be huge!' A lack of honesty is harmful to women because we don't have as much access to capital, we aren't given as many chances and we're definitely not allowed to fuck up in any significant way without being held up to the world as an example of a woman who is too big for her boots. We owe each other the truth, and yet, I meet women all the time who have started things – even friends – and I look at the product or I look at the plan and have to ask: *Who told you this was a good idea? Did all those friends who cheered you on to run this down the field tell you they'd buy this makeup, or do events at your experiential space, or wear this shoe?* There is so much dishonesty – again, not because of malevolence, but because we don't want to suffer the discomfort of the truth. We need to do better by each other even when it's awkward. It's too important. (Keep in mind that your friends are welcome to reject your feedback, too, or overrule your advice – this happens all the time – but say what's on your mind. It's way better to be proved wrong than to have held your tongue or told a white lie of support.)

Just the other day, I sat with a friend who pitched me for an investment – and when I told her no and that it was a bad idea, she looked at me like I'd smacked her. She had no tolerance for any negative pushback. She wanted to do a fashion show with a designer whom she felt was a massive, overlooked talent, but what she pitched was nothing more than a spectacle – all fluff, no meat and potatoes. She had no plan or concept for how she would leverage the show into sales for the business afterwards. She was offended by my honesty, but if I had given her a cheque to preserve her comfort (and in some ways, mine) and some BS feedback to go along with it, she would have encountered far more pain after starting something that would never work. And she could have always done it without me, too. In no way should you think of yourself as a gatekeeper to other people's dreams. She could have gone elsewhere for money and assurance that I'm wrong. As a principle, I don't invest in businesses to be nice, I invest in businesses because I believe in them and I believe in the founders. I counselled her to use my resistance to her idea to go back to the drawing board until she'd pushed herself to translate her vision into something viable. I don't know if she'll take my advice, but it is not loving to lie, even if it sometimes feels easier. As Warren Buffett says, 'Feedback is a gift.'

I've seen a lot of successful founders fail publicly the second or third time around, in part because people think they must know something that they don't (i.e., they don't believe in the product, nor would they buy or use it, but this person has figured it out before, so they must know better). And I've also watched founder friends systematically – and probably unconsciously – remove, or lose, all the people from their circle who tell them the truth. These people are often replaced by 'yes' people or sycophants or those who don't feel comfortable pushing back against power. This is a major danger zone, and I'm on high alert for it all the time. Trusting that people are telling me the truth is what keeps me vital and connected to reality. It keeps me sane. When I see people punish truth tellers, I think they've lost their minds. Great entrepreneurs want to win more than they want to be right. You need to have a willingness to be wrong and to be challenged hard. In fact, you should be looking for your blind spots all the time. I keep people in my companies whose primary role is to tell me the unvarnished truth. They are the most valuable to me, precisely because they're the most likely to tell me things I don't want to hear. I would *much rather* hear it from them though than get soundly rejected in the market when it's too late to change the product or the strategy.

Because so many of us feel afraid of conflict, the truth and making other people uncomfortable, we push off conversations that we really need to have. And we hold on to relationships that no longer serve for fear of having the hard conversation and moving forward. I know many fellow people in business who have kept someone on the team out of loyalty, even as they know it no longer serves the business. I don't think this is fair – to anyone. If you are secretly resenting the presence of someone on your team or hoping and willing them to leave on their own because you don't want to hurt their feelings, that isn't kind or good. The respectful thing to do is to have the conversation and endure the conflict, understanding that you'll both be better served by the result. I think this is a specifically female trait, the belief that if someone has done something good for us in the past, we owe them. But you don't owe them a job in perpetuity or endless yeses to their requests. Early on, I decided to be really truthful, even if it's really painful. It's hard, but it has served me well.

Like me, Mellody Hobson functions on honesty and invites criticism into her life. When she was twenty-five years old, Mellody made a commitment to always be intellectually honest with herself, to commit to sticking to reality, explaining that she knew it was 'going to take a lot of work, because we talk ourselves into believing stories and making excuses and having reasons. I wanted to hold myself accountable. Literally no excuses. Either you did or you didn't do something; there is no try. Intellectual honesty forced me to be really clear about when I was not great and also when I was not treating someone well.' As Mellody would hear herself speaking to someone in a way that was not kind, she'd be reproaching herself for the behaviour: *You're being such a jerk. Wow. Be intellectually honest here.* (Mellody also shared that she earned a big lesson from Dick Parsons when they were on the board of Estée Lauder. She asked him for feedback, to give her 'the brutal truth'. He responded, 'I'll be honest, but I don't need to be brutal.'[4] I love this: you don't need to add meanness to honesty.)

I'm also always looking to hear the uncomfortable truth from customers. I never shy away from what they have to say. So many successful businesses have grown by *asking customers what they think*. But if you want to be a nimble, successful operator, you will go out and actively look for those insights and then layer them back into products to fit the stated need. In the early days of Good American, I'd fly all over the US to talk to customers. We'd bring women into the company, ask them questions, hear their feedback on our products, and then take them to the mall to go shopping. We wanted to understand the entire experience from their perspective, and we learned so much. Often, retailers put mirrors *outside* of the dressing rooms because they want customers to engage with the sales team and ideally get upsold on items (or convinced to buy what they're trying on). Our shopper told us how much she *hates* this and sometimes finds it humiliating. We think of the Good American experience as shopping with your best friend, meaning that our sales team will never try to gaslight a customer about a fit – if you don't love how you look in something, we don't want you to buy it. We want you to press on until you find something you feel great wearing and are thrilled to take home. To that end, we fill our dressing rooms with mirrors so customers can see how jeans fit from all angles, and our sales teams are true retailers: they will turn the shop upside down finding the right pieces for someone to try on and never upsell you on a bad fit.

Early on, a customer turned to me in a shop and told me one of the core problems for plus-size women. 'I never spend much money on denim because I get holes in my jeans because my thighs chafe and rub together as I walk – I'd burn right through this fabric. It happens to a lot of plus-size women.' Our jeans aren't cheap and she wouldn't splurge on something that wouldn't last. She offered us a brilliant insight, and in response we realised we not only needed reinforced belt loops, we needed to reinforce the inner thigh panels as well, and develop a test for chafing. As a counter to this in the business world, you'll hear that customers don't actually know what they need or that they have a failure of imagination when it comes to the future, but this is a cop-out – yes, you need to innovate, and yes, you need to hold a vision for how the world is changing and culture is moving, and yes, you need to be able to see around corners to anticipate where we'll be in a trend landscape, but you also need to respect your customers by hearing what they say – *especially* when it's negative.

You cannot become someone who is too fragile to handle dissent or criticism – you have to stay in a position where you're receptive, where you think people's opinions and thoughts are worthy and valid and interesting. I believe I have a leg up on this because I'm not hardwired to take offence. One of my best friends can think about a mean comment for years after, but I am good at letting things go. I don't have the energy to stay attached, for one, because it really is water off a duck's back. And I'm good at taking things at face value, rather than assuming there's a buried meaning or a coded message. This definitely gave me a leg up when we were all dating around in our teens and twenties, as my friends would spend *hours* contemplating what seemed to be quite clear. There was even a book and movie named after this phenomenon: *He's Just Not That Into You*.

When people give it to me straight and frank, I'm grateful. If that's what they think, and I don't think it holds weight, so be it; if that's what they think and it has good information in it for me, I'm happy for the feedback. When I get critiqued, nine times out of ten, it leads to some opening or change in the way that I behave. One of my super-early investors, Duncan Heath, would always give me feedback – and it wasn't always positive. He would tell me about how I had held myself in a meeting, or where I could have exhibited more thoughtfulness. Since I was new to working with celebrities, he told me I'd need to go beyond surface niceties to really engage this type of artist and actually watch their films so I could be thoughtful when I talked to them about their brands. He was always offering me pointers, and instead of getting defensive or scared or thinking that I was 'in trouble' because I wasn't doing it perfectly, I would take a few breaths and think deeply about what he had to say. After all, he was showing me and telling me things about me that I would not have been able to see myself. If criticism seems scary or hard, reframe it to yourself in this way: you can't see what's natural to you; you'll never understand how others experience you unless they tell you. Honest advice in this vein is uniquely helpful. I find it not only tactically valuable, but it will often inform the way I do things going forward. If you can, summon your bravery and seek this type of feedback out.

New Thought: **Seek out people's opinions and thoughts, particularly if you feel scared to hear them – others can see what's otherwise invisible to you.**

---

7. Old Thought: **If you make a good brand and market it well, the rest will take care of itself.**

*We delight in the beauty of the butterfly, but rarely admit the changes it has gone through to achieve that beauty.*
– Maya Angelou

I recently acquired a significant stake in a gorgeous cashmere company called The Elder Statesman, founded by Greg Chait and designed by creative director Bailey Hunter. When we met, Greg had built a brand of exuberantly colourful, highest-quality cashmere knits, but he hadn't – yet – been able to crack the business in a scalable way. Up until this point, it's been a beautiful art project, which has not been enough to make it a brand for more than a small cohort of in-the-know high-fashion shoppers. I believe there's a cool young luxury customer for the colour and vibrancy of The Elder Statesman, and there's a significant place in the market for an alternative to the Loro Pianas and Brunello Cucinellis of the luxury world. All the venerable heritage brands offer a sea of beige sameness. It's exquisite and tasteful, but it's not exciting.

The hardest thing for any brand to achieve is a distinct aesthetic. So many talents fail because they don't have a defined perspective, a space that they own where it's clear what they stand for. You must know what you do and in what aesthetic world you belong, and conversely, what you don't do. Everyone who comes to work at Elder knows that a basic beige cardigan ain't going to cut it – but a beige sweater with an exposed seam, a colourful stitch or a pocket that's been mended, distressed or holey just might belong in the brand.

At Elder, we are working with a group of kids in Haiti. We asked them to draw their dreams. They created an incredible art collection, and we bought the art to fund all of them to go to art school. Now, if we gave that art to another company, they wouldn't know what to do with it, but at Elder, it was perfect – this art turned into the most magical project I've ever seen in my life.

But a beautiful product, a compelling story, a space in the market, a wonderful founder – tenets of a strong and durable brand – are still not enough to build a business that works. And once you have a business that 'works', you still need to figure out how to grow it in a sustainable way. Good American had an explosive start, but I realised very quickly that there were a lot of complexities: all the things I wasn't good at started to go wrong quite quickly, and I often felt like I was in a losing battle. At the end of the day, being creative and a good marketer only gets you so far. Your goods need to be rightly priced, rightly planned and correctly distributed. I had no clue about any of that stuff. I went on a hiring rampage and started pulling people in who were experts in the areas the business needed to thrive, people who had done it before and been successful at competitive companies who could help me do it again.

I have a distinctively good way of beginning things, which involves bringing a unique idea to life, having the ability to get it started, and making a mark launching it – but you don't go straight to the top business-wise until you're ready. A great launch isn't going to cut it. You have to understand all the factors that make a brand a business. I understand what I'm solving for in the beginning, and then I'm never deluded about what we're going to do. Take Off Season, for example: Kristin has a very specific aesthetic – but most people are not interested in wearing a pair of trousers made from football jerseys. It's the essence of who Kristin is – a young American woman from New Jersey who sews things on a machine at home for the games – but we've distilled it into a product assortment that connects to a behaviour that exists for a lot of people. Most ardent fans wear jerseys, which won't keep you warm after September. As I thought about it from a pricing structure, I made a bet that we could move fans who will spend $190 on a jersey that they only get to wear once a week into a winter coat for $400 that can be worn every day – and that we could woo more casual fans into the brand by making something legitimately stylish. I don't know much about sport and I'm still happy to wear one of our puffers.

One of the reasons that I've historically enjoyed partnering with other founders and creatives is that I can triangulate out and take perspective – and put their vision and aesthetic into a commercial context to understand the potential of both the brand and the business. When founders are too close to what they're making, too invested in their own point of view, the result can be coloured by emotion and attachment and be a miss in the market. This can also happen if you don't have enough people on your team who feel emboldened to tell you the truth.

If I'm making a brand for wholesale, I will take it to Nordstrom or Saks and ask their buyers to respond to the product: *Would they carry it? Would they themselves buy it? If so, what would they pay, and what are the closest competitor brands doing?* If you're willing to take real feedback, which means acknowledging that you might be wrong or off, you can learn so much. If you don't have access to department store buyers, you can run tests online, too. There are hundreds of ways to focus group your ideas and products. Don't skip this step, even if you fervently believe in your own taste and instincts. Getting the product fit, distribution and price right – and anchoring into a margin that will allow you to build a sustainable business – is more important than just defining a desirable brand. Product and price come well before marketing, even though many people mistakenly believe that marketing is the big thing instead of just the last thing. (You can't effectively market bad product – it might work once, but customers won't come back, and long-term business viability is built off repeat purchase and brand loyalty.)

For many companies, the majority of their success can be correlated to nailing the relationship between the product and price. It's one of the things that we obsess over – in every part of the business. We recently launched a capri trouser, and I spent an entire flight going back and forth with the merchant. They thought they should be priced at $129, which I thought was too high because you can get a pair of jeans for $129, and in the customer's eye, a capri is closer to a pair of shorts. To price products correctly, you really need to understand how people think about both value and money. Obviously, you need to have a margin target and understand the cost of what you're selling to ensure the product is profitable, but that won't cut it alone. The customer isn't thinking about it in this way. It's important to understand how the customer will feel about parting with their money for the product. What's the price perception of what you're offering? Additionally, people will pay more for a product from a brand they admire, and they'll pay more for a product if it's shown to them in an environment that resonates – there are a lot of levers to pull to get this particular calculus right. One of the things that makes me good at this maths is that my relationship with money is fully intact. I still know the price of everything. Money really matters to almost every single person in the world, and as a merchant, it better matter to me.

I sit with founders all the time who struggle to get their revenue above $500,000. There seem to be natural plateaus in businesses and this is one of them. It's really tough because at that point you often don't have enough operational skill to be able to scale, nor do you have the money in place to test and try new things. In those situations, it doesn't matter how good your idea or product might be – you must be able to find a customer and operate a business. People always want to know how I learned how to operate, and I wish I had a more concise answer for you. It definitely wasn't business school. I chalk it up to trial and error, common sense, stamina, testing ideas compulsively, always assuming I don't know, being willing to ask for advice from everyone and a crazy work ethic. I never expect something to just happen unless I fully lean into it. That has been my formula.

If you've been in business for six years and you can't get above $500,000, something isn't connecting. Limbo land is really tough: it's when businesses are not failing miserably – in fact, they're not a total failure at all – and yet the business isn't tracking or growing in a way that moves it to the next stage. You're never going to get out of this predicament unless you get product, pricing, distribution and marketing working simultaneously in a finessed way. After you've assessed these four things, you need to consistently look for ways to improve. If you're a beauty brand and you're at Sephora, is your product right for their customer? Is it offering something unique? Is it sitting in the right section? Are the product adjacencies right? Is it standing out on the shelf, or do you need to relook at your packaging? Are your customers replenishing the product and buying it again? What do your reviews and social comments say? What feedback are they consistently giving? You need to dissect every detail. And sometimes you need to admit defeat because you might not have a product-market fit, and it's possible that you need to have a come-to-Jesus moment with yourself. You might need to rightsize your ambition and recognise that the potential scale of your business might not be what you thought. It can be helpful to look around and see if anyone else is succeeding where you're failing – in that moment, you might realise that your business proposition is not really a 'thing'. Being in a no-man's-land with your business is really difficult. I never want to suggest to anyone that it's not. It's often the most painful place to be. But the answer is *never* to spend more on marketing, because you're just pouring your resources into a leaky colander and not an intact bowl. Something in the core business isn't working. That must be solved first.

Coming up in the London fashion world, I had a front-row seat to a hundred different beautiful brands who pulled off insane shows and received endless glowing press from *Vogue* and all the other magazines that used to dictate culture. You couldn't buy that kind of media attention at a time when that was all there was. There were no blogs, there was no social media, there was nothing else fighting for consumer attention. The magazines largely dictated what we should want. And even so, I watched so many designers build gorgeous brands – and yet not one of them had a viable business. They were entirely focused on winning the affection of the press, not on solving their wholesale business outside of the one retailer who reliably bought their collections. They weren't obsessing over what customers wanted and what they would pay for.

While many designers might have been the hottest things at London Fashion Week, I don't think any of them were making more than £2 million a year in revenue – not bad, but they all dreamed of becoming the next Yves Saint Laurent. If they tried to launch now – when press is even more diluted and less impactful – they would absolutely fail, even though they make beautiful shows. It is not enough to make beautiful things that won't work in production and get people to write about them. You must focus on the less glamourous thing: product/market fit and distribution. If you don't focus on distribution, you'll never get your pricing right. If one precious store has an exclusive and you only have one retailer, you're not in a competitive landscape. You're not thinking about what it takes to reach various customers. The success of Good American came because we were obsessed with getting to customers who were underserved. There were legions of women who couldn't go to a mall and buy anything of quality in their size. If I could have advised those designers twenty years ago, I would have told them to focus on a hit product that is dependable, durable, reliable and repeatable, and figure out a wider size run and a distribution strategy that would be supported by the press plan. Ignoring all women who are not straight sizes as a business practice is insane. The shoe floor is full, the handbag department is full, the makeup counters are packed because this shopper *can* find her sizes there, while she's out of luck everywhere else in the department store. Catering to this customer would have been a simple growth engine!

---

It's only in recent years that I've become recognisable to some people and a 'face' to anyone. For the first twenty years of my career, nobody knew who I was – I'd only ever spoken to marketing and advertising industry press until Good American blew up. I was reluctant to go in front of the camera. It wasn't in the cards for me; it wasn't anything I had wanted or set out to do. But as I've become more comfortable with it over the years, I recognise that there's a huge upside to being known: strangers come up to talk to me and to tell me that they're inspired by what I've achieved. They tell me their life stories. I get a lot of really nice, positive reinforcement that I enjoy a lot. I would never lie about that. It has really helped people connect with the businesses.

Understandably, we live in a culture that's obsessed with fame and recognition, and so many female founders either have the desire, or more frequently feel the pressure, to be the face of the brand – and as part of that, to build all the marketing around them and their profile, whether it's through showing up on panels or being interviewed by the press, or building a presence on TikTok or Instagram. You really don't see this with men, even when the men are building businesses that are predicated on fashion, grooming or wellness. As a culture, we don't insist that male founders front the product. I know that a lot of female founders feel very stressed by this pressure.

But being the face – unless you're building a business off being an influencer – is ultimately not what makes a business. What makes a business is not the sexy thing we think. If people were as obsessed with pricing and distribution and their customers as they are with press and marketing, we'd see a lot more successful businesses. It's not fun to talk about efficiencies in operations, or recruitment, or to travel to America to take meetings with Walmart, but it sure is effective. I understand why it seems much more fun to put yourself on the top of the pyramid where you can be preoccupied with being a founder and create a brand in your own image. From this vantage point, you think everything needs to come back to you, that if it's not your idea it won't work, that it needs to be an extension of who you are and how you show up in the world and so on. But it's not a durable business if it revolves around you. I do not have this bug at all. I will go out and find experts in every space where I'm trying to create. Not only is this effective, but it keeps me from getting twisted and my ego from getting too overblown.

Even with Good American, Khloé is a partner in the brand, but she *isn't* the brand. We were very careful about this. I had worked with a lot of denim brands and observed the way they moved in the world. G-STAR cultivated a really specific customer, meanwhile Calvin Klein could shapeshift based on who was in the campaign wearing them, whether it was Brooke Shields or Kaia Gerber. When I started Good American, I wanted to make a brand that *anyone* could put on. You could identify with Khloé or you could be a punk girl with a shaved head. Very purposefully, I wanted to create a brand that would be seen as a blank canvas, that wasn't rooted in a single identity or aesthetic. You could put Missy Elliott in it. You could put Madonna in it. We partnered with Cindy Crawford, Queen Latifah and Dolly Parton. It's about individualism. Whoever you are, Good American is a brand that will work for you. In that way, the marketing stays loose and flexible, focused on the needs of our customer while we focus on the product. The marketing shifts and evolves, but the purpose of the business does not.

To that end, marketing is not even the icing on the cake; it's the cherry on the icing. You must focus on making and baking the cake, which is not always the 'fun' part. Many founders don't want to think about the things that actually make a business great. They think, *I have a fabulous idea, and now I'll just market the shit out of it.* But everything in between is what makes a business successful. If you don't have product/market fit, if your pricing is wrong, if your distribution isn't growing, you're never, ever, ever going to make it. You can't effectively market a bad product, nor can you make it work on a product that's incorrectly priced. You will either spend too much acquiring customers if it's priced too cheaply, or you won't find a customer who is willing to pay.

> New Thought: **Be obsessive about product and pricing: if that's not perfect, your brand will never fully take flight. Marketing is the last thing, not *the* thing.**

8. Old Thought: **There are no shortcuts. If building isn't hard, it's not 'real'.**

*If you want something you have never had, you must be willing to do something you have never done.*
– Thomas Jefferson

In the early days of starting Off Season with Kristin, I told her that I was going to see Michael Rubin of Fanatics fame because we needed to bring him into the business. I don't think that's what she envisaged – like many founders, she was labouring under the belief that she needed to lay every single brick of her business herself for it to 'count' – but I told her that we needed to find and take as many shortcuts as possible. You don't get extra credit for making it really hard for yourself or for reinventing the wheel. If you can stand on Michael Rubin's shoulders and use all his experience navigating the system, *then you do it*. Michael spent fifteen years figuring out the complexities of every sports league – international, too – and brokered all the deals with the leagues. In time, he built a giant platform and a customer base. As I told Kristin, if we can email *millions* of customers who are sports enthusiasts on day one, why would we forego that to build it from scratch? It's better to give a piece of the business away for significant, manifold gains than to hold on to the whole thing but end up with a much smaller meal. (Many people end up with 100 per cent of nothing, which is a painful reality in business.)

When I took it to Michael, he was enthusiastic. We negotiated through some other points – we wanted the brand to have its own stand-alone site that fit its aesthetic rather than existing solely on the Fanatics platform, and Michael agreed to both build this site *and* power it with his back-end infrastructure. He got to go on this ride with us – which was a slightly different adventure from his typical sports journey – and we got a massive head start in return. Michael Rubin runs a $30 billion business because he owns fandom, including twenty million email addresses and 220 million customers. This is an acceleration point you cannot buy. This isn't followers on an Instagram account whom you may or may not be able to reach. These are people who have given their credit cards to Fanatics. If you're lucky, it takes *years* to build a business, and if you can find any way to shave some time off, you do it. There's always an easier way, and you should look for that easy way. It doesn't mean you're taking a cop-out. It means you're smart.

Women in sport are having a moment, and because it hasn't been paying attention to the ladies, the sports industrial complex doesn't know how to meet the demand. I could have given ten speeches at the 2025 Super Bowl, which is a little sad because I can barely name the five teams we did Off Season jackets for, let alone all thirty-two. There's so little female energy in the space, and women are screaming to be included at the level we deserve. Female athletes are crushing it – as they have for decades – but the public is starting to pay proper attention thanks to social media. It was much easier to deny the enthusiasm for female athletes before TikTok. We have big ambitions at Off Season, and to that end, I onboarded one of Michael Rubin's key operators – though he was a great sport about my poach. Meanwhile, my president Vicky Picca knows the sports business inside out; she understands all the complexities and is thrilled to be doing something that women are also excited about. As mentioned, I always work to find the right talent. In terms of product, we surrounded Kristin with an experienced design team – she's been sewing on a machine at home, so we needed to scaffold her instincts with a team who knows how to put together a comprehensive product assortment. There is *no reason* she should do it on her own or need to figure out a scaled sports apparel line from soup to nuts, and yet I meet many founders who want to feel like they touched and built every part of the business. While this might have been a possibility when the world moved a little slower, it's not practical in today's ecosystem. Speed is a significant advantage, and you get speed by enlisting people who have played the field before. Charlie Munger is credited as saying many things along these lines: 'You want to be in business with someone who's demonstrated that they've done it successfully and honestly before.' Another relevant gem: 'We're not looking for the smartest guy in the room. We're looking for someone who's already shown he can run the place.'

I will always insist on finding shortcuts everywhere, including the synergy to be had if you resist seeing everyone as direct competition. I meet some founders who not only refuse shortcuts but they also don't even look for them – and I meet many other founders who overlook the one great thing they're good at to chase a much harder dream. For some, if it's not really difficult, it doesn't seem real. I remember meeting a baker on *Side Hustlers,* a Hello Sunshine TV show on Roku that I cohosted with Ashley Graham. This founder fed us this insanely delicious cookie, and then she started talking about her big dream for her business, which was to open a six-thousand-square-foot experiential space where you could go and get your socks blown off through the event programming. Ashley and I looked at each other and were like, *Wait a minute, what is happening here? She doesn't want to build a cookie brand with her obvious talent?*

In this founder's head, it was all one thing: she baked amazing cookies, so it made total sense to her that she'd do an experiential space. For her, there was no leap in logic.

'That's a very different business, one that you know nothing about,' I offered.

She didn't want to hear it and kept insisting that I was wrong and it would be amazing.

'Sure, that might be true, but are you the best person to execute it?' I responded.

She probably thought I was mean and bitchy, but she was making the same error that so many other founders do: before nailing her core business, she was off to the races, adding all sorts of complexities that she was absolutely not capitalised or experienced enough to pull off without a lot of pain – if at all. Meanwhile, she was taking her sizable gift for granted while simultaneously not recognising that an experiential space has little to do with her existing core customer – there is no logic in the world to suggest that someone who stops by for a cookie wants an event experience instead. To her, having an amazing cookie brand was boring or too easy to be worth doing. This is common: to underestimate what we're good at in lieu of going for something that feels 'harder' and therefore more real. Don't abandon your heroes, they will keep you in business. Something doesn't need to be complex to be worthwhile.

Business coaches Gay and Katie Hendricks have a concept called Zone of Genius, which is brilliant, as they clarify where so many people get caught. In their work, they define the Zone of Genius as the thing that comes most naturally to you, but you likely take it for granted or assume it must not be a real gift (rather than seeing that it is in fact your *primary* gift). When you are operating in your Zone of Genius, everything feels easy – so easy in fact that you might not see what you're up to and might need a friend to help you work out what your Zone of Genius is. (As mentioned, my Zone of Genius is finding the right people, seeing and understanding the larger context of any product or business, and putting it all together in a way that lands in the culture.)

In addition to a Zone of Genius, we each have a Zone of Excellence, a Zone of Competence and a Zone of Incompetence. Most of us spend our lives in our Zone of Excellence: we're good here, but it's not the best use of our gifts, though we think it's where we need to be because we can feel the effort required in delivering in this space. The Zone of Competence is exactly what it sounds like: I'm organised and good at making plans, but I decided to outsource a lot of my daily decision-making about small life details because it's not the best use of my time. My Zone of Incompetence would include things like building financial models or working out why a fire alarm is beeping. I'm useless here. Fortunately, I recognise this and let other people take care of my incompetencies rather than beating myself up for not being good at everything. Hint: *None* of us are good at everything. Figure out where you excel and focus on that. Ignore the siren song of the Zone of Excellence or doing it all yourself. Definitely let go of the instinct to try to develop something in your Zone of Incompetence. That is a fool's errand, and you will fail.

I think businesses have their own Zones of Genius in a way, too: these are the products and services that you do exceptionally well. They are your heroes, and they probably drive a huge portion of the revenue. In most healthy businesses, whether you're talking about a family-run bakery, Apple or SKIMS, chances are that 90 per cent of the business is done on 10 per cent of the SKUs. Ask the bakery owner and there's likely one muffin, or one cookie, that pays their rent, even though they might make some stunt-y offerings like a bacon-glazed doughnut. Chances are they sell very few of the limited-edition, buzz-generating baked goods, but those are the items that might bring new customers in through the door. At Apple, the iPhone carries a huge portion of the business. Most brands, including the ones I work on, experience this reality.

Carrying 90 per cent of the business on a handful of SKUs might sound scary, but it's actually a good indicator that something is working – and from that base you can branch out and try a lot of different things. But don't forsake your heroes or take them for granted. I come from a family of professional gamblers, and because of this, I take very calculated risks. It's in my bones to not be tremendously risk-averse, even though I'm also careful to hedge my bets. I've created a system in business in which I know exactly where I can play a little bit and push it without jeopardising revenue or putting too much on the line. For one, I'm laser-focused on building and reinforcing the heroes and pushing the edges from there. I never, ever risk cutting corners on any product, but I do play with scarcity and availability through pulling on the levers of supply and demand. Some things won't be available for more than a day, maybe a week tops – but you will continue to find your favourite T-shirt even if the collaboration product is all gone. This is part of the magic of creating a brand.

There are other practical shortcuts that I encourage all the founders I meet to explore – one is to focus your preliminary wholesale strategy on one 'hero' retailer and perfecting that until you move into more. Through focusing on department stores like Nordstrom, Macy's or Ulta, who have massive distribution footprints, I've been able to take fledgling brands far. Take building a business with multiple small partners: it takes the same amount of manpower to sell to a bunch of small shops as it does to power 167 doors in the United States through Nordstrom. I can get massive scale through one partner, and there are only a handful of people who work on that business internally, which keeps costs low. That's not cheating, that's just smart. It wouldn't be smart to build an entire business around one department store long-term – you want to diversify – but when you're still in a baby business stage, it can be incredibly impactful to double down with a seasoned partner. We often conflate complexity with being a serious business, but resist that siren song – complexity invariably comes as your business grows and you need new space to grow into, but starting out and making it hard at the onset is an unnecessary challenge. Nail the basics, find the shortcuts, find the people who have done the job before, and move forward from there.

> **New Thought: Business is hard, so relentlessly look for opportunities to make the journey as easy as possible for yourself. Embrace simplicity, cherish your heroes and look for shortcuts and acceleration points wherever you can find them.**

---

### 9. Old Thought: Don't get distracted by the competition.

*I look at social media for one reason: so I see what's going on. I follow every one of my competitors. I follow everyone who's interesting. I follow everyone I can learn from. I probably send twenty or thirty posts of different shit to people who I work with.*
– Michael Rubin

We all want to see ourselves as highly original; we all want to believe that we're creating something entirely new. People in business are no exception. And yet, it's very rare, maybe even impossible, to make something that's never existed before. Most businesses are variations on a theme, even those that are referred to as 'disruptors'. There's usually one significant tweak that's distinguishing. For a decade, the very act of DTC was enough to generate a slew of 'disruptive' brands: making mattresses or reading glasses is not new; skipping out on the department store showroom or traditional retail model is. If anything, going 'first' is a terrible business proposition. You don't want to define the market; you want to *capitalise* on the market and learn from everyone else's mistakes in the process. There is glory in trendsetting, but first-mover advantage usually only applies to category-busting businesses. This is exciting, but it happens so seldomly. As one friend quips, 'You don't need to get the first cup of beer – you just need to get to the party before the keg is tapped.'

I am obsessed with studying my competition, though I've come to understand that this isn't a standard approach. I frequently encounter a fear in other founders to even acknowledge the presence of competitors. Sometimes this is naivete. We'll get an idea or a flash of inspiration, and then assume that nobody is solving that particular problem because no company has crossed our transom yet . . . but a quick Google search reveals that there are many players in the space. (This doesn't mean you shouldn't also try to solve the problem – there's plenty to learn from other people's attempts, and even more ways to distinguish yourself in the process. It *does* suggest, though, that maybe you don't know all that much about the space.) Sometimes a refusal to look at competitors is anxiety. Understandably, we're all fearful of being influenced or copycatting someone else's ideas. But if you let this anxiety occupy too much of your headspace, you'll never begin. Get comfortable with the fact that you won't be the first person to do a beauty brand or bakery concept, nor the first person to develop an app for busy mums, and you're not going to get a patent anytime soon for making underwear or jeans. Use the fact that you won't be first to your advantage. There is so much to learn from studying other founders and companies. I urge you to go to school on everyone in your space. As Michael Rubin confessed on my podcast, he spends a significant portion of his days studying other people.[5]

In fact, as an investor, it's a red flag for me when I meet a founder who can't tell me about the competitive landscape they're operating in. They think it's cheating, or a distraction, to look at what other people are doing. But in the process of pitching me, when they tell me everything they're doing better, and all the reasons their idea or product is superior, they can't compare it to anything concrete in the market. You need to be obsessed with whatever you do. When I push them, they say, 'Well, I'm not interested in what those other brands are doing.' My response? 'Big mistake. You need to be *obsessed* with what those other brands are doing. I need to know that not only are you obsessed with your product, but you're obsessed with the context in which it lives.' Early on, Jens gave me great advice here and showed me what this looked like in practice. We spent *way* too much time, for my taste, in department stores looking at brands that Jens felt were his primary competition when he launched Frame. He studied everything, and I learned to do this, too. Whenever I'm starting or investing in a business, I always take aim at a business that feels like competition. I will learn everything about those companies. I probably know as much or more about Levi's than the typical Levi's merchant. I probably know more about the Levi's pricing structure than I do about my own. I know when Levi's is on sale, I know what's happening with the merchandising of their site, I know when they've launched a new product, or fabric, or collaboration. I am obsessed with Levi's.

When you're working on a business, you always need to learn from the best – and even if the idea of a giant in your industry being realistic competition for your teeny-tiny start-up makes you squirm with hubris (as if!), you still set them in your sights and you study them. It's actually hubristic *not* to. It's important to recognise that you have a lot to learn, and that you can go to school on other people's successes – and their mistakes. Levi's, still today, is the absolute pinnacle in the denim space. They are the most successful, best-in-class version of a denim brand. I look to them to learn all the time, *even now*. I don't do this to replicate their business or merch plan – I do this because comparing my companies to other companies helps me define and differentiate what we do. It offers shortcuts because I don't need to replicate mistakes or obvious failures. Because many of my competitors are hundred-year-old, at-scale brands who have achieved mastery and are clearly operating with best business practices, it's safe to assume their choices are predicated on data and deep research of their customers and the space. They are not flying by the seat of their pants.

I consciously choose to overtly own their influence, rather than ducking my head and pretending these companies aren't swimming in the same culture, impacting what we're up to and all retail trends. If anything, being hyperaware of the competition helps me carve a more specific lane, to get sharper and clearer about who we are. (Have you ever heard anyone conflate Good American and Levi's? Nope, they occupy very different spaces in people's minds.) Another important note about studying your competition or worrying about being studied: by the time something we make comes to market, it's old news – we work so far in advance that people can study us all they want and try to knock us off, but we're already on to the next thing. The same is true in reverse: I don't study competition to copy their styles; I study competition to learn from their tactics.

Plus, within a field of competitors, points of distinction are not necessarily going to be huge – we're all making trousers with two legs, in various washes – but they are hugely important. The fabrics at Good American and our waistband and belt loop engineering are singular achievements that set us apart in the hearts and minds of customers. And then there are a million small points of distinction. I really believe in the power of the 1 per cent, as it adds up over time. I pay attention to details and will do things other people won't do. These compounding small decisions are cumulative and accretive. Over time, they have a really big effect. This is hard to teach, as you are either a person who sweats the small stuff or you just can't be bothered. But I will not rest until it's the exact right brush on the trim package of every single rivet that's on the jean. My team thinks I'm nuts – I will go off about a button on a jean if it's a disgusting colour of silver (words I've used before) – but really, really caring about every detail of the product is felt by the customer. And that care is a point of distinction and differentiation in other denim brands they can choose from. To that end, you need to be obsessed not only with your product but also the entire landscape that your business lives in. That 1 per cent really matters.

I've interviewed a lot of CMO candidates, some of the best in the world. I always tell them that I'm essentially a fake merchant, since I didn't come up in the world and learn the business at every level on the way up. But one of them told me something that felt resonant and true: that my knack for merchandising comes from being able to connect all the businesses I'm involved in together – and then connect them to the wider ecosystem of culture. Because I pay so much attention to the 'competition' and because I sit across so many different brands, I can string it all together into a deeper understanding of consumer behaviour. I see a trend happening in one place – baby T-shirts at SKIMS, let's say – and I immediately know that the bottom silhouette is changing. You can't wear a baby tee with a skinny jean. It signals to me that denim will get wider and bigger. I've been able to use those insights to connect the dots. If I'm selling a hundred thousand baby tees a week, women need some good baggy jeans to go with them.

Excellent merchants see everything coming down the pike, and they don't get attached to a specific aesthetic or outcome – they see it as a playing field where they can execute a series of moves without getting fixed on it being a certain way. It's a muscle that you learn to use. It matters what your taste level is and what your personal aesthetic might be, but more importantly, you need to be able to connect trends. This is the difference between someone with amazing taste who can start something and define an aesthetic and someone who can build something. When you are in retail, it's always, always about connected adjacencies. If I know how to create a $20 million product, I know how to create six other pieces that are related to this hero that might be worth $2 million each. If the hero is a specific cut of jeans, I know exactly which tops to make that will sell easily to coordinate with the trend. This is very different from having good taste or a specific aesthetic. I never put myself, or my own preferences, in the middle of any business. It's just not about me. I'm always very clear about that. But it is about a connected landscape of brands – my own as well as my competition.

> **New Thought:** You need to be obsessed with your business and its competitors. You can learn a ton, and they will help you differentiate your offering.

---

### 10. Old Thought: You need to know the right people and get invited to the right events to make it.

> *I love to see a young girl go out and grab the world by the lapels. Life's a bitch. You've got to go out and kick ass.*
> – Maya Angelou

For the past few years, I've been hosting a series of dinners around the world called 'A Seat at the Table'. At the first one, held in the US, I stood up and gave a speech: 'I always wanted to do these dinners because when I was coming up, I was never invited anywhere – I wasn't invited to any dinner, any party, not a sausage.' (Every single American woman came up to me afterwards to ask me what 'not a sausage' means!) But it's true: I wasn't invited anywhere. While I'm a bit of a loner and prefer my own company, I'd be lying if I said I didn't have FOMO. I was convinced that business success was on the other side of the invitation, that if I only knew the right people or was running around with the right group, everything would be easier.

Now that I'm invited to many things, two things are clear: (1) I don't really want to go, as I feel like I don't get enough time with my family or my friends as it is. (2) Nothing much happens at those dinners. They're mostly about ego-gratification – feeling like you've made it and you're important. But going to events like that will have no clear impact on your brand, and showing up to events will not build a business either. Building a business is a very different undertaking from making small talk at the dinner table. And 'networking' is not the same thing as building a network of people who help you get shit done. I fear that when we conflate our social lives with business access, we make business look entirely relational. Not only do you need to have product/market fit, but you need to have the right friends, too. You need to be 'in'. Sometimes this feels to me a bit like a social media sorority – and I really don't want women anywhere to labour under the belief that they need the imprimatur of said sorority to make it in business. (We'll talk more about friendship and business shortly.)

That said, community is important – it's nice to sit with women and commiserate about the highs and lows, particularly if you feel like it's safe to divulge and seek advice and counselling (often we're all putting brave faces on for each other). And it is very true that the right connections can serve as acceleration points – though those acceleration points are typically less glamourous. When I decided to do these dinners, I curated them very carefully, creating a seating plan that felt like a bunch of first dates. One-third of the women I invited had pulled off trailblazing business success or were incredible operators – two-thirds of the women I invited were just like me earlier in their careers, founders who never got invited anywhere. I put a girl with a hot new shoe brand next to Heidi O'Neill, a former president at Nike; Diane von Furstenberg next to a girl with a beautiful line of dresses; Rachel Zoe with a woman building a fashion services brand; Iman next to a young Black founder in the beauty space, and so on. I wanted every young entrepreneur to walk away with concrete takeaways and advice, even if it went no further than the dinner. I also sprinkle in my tactical network, like the people who invested in me when I was tiny and are good for seed rounds, my lawyers who specialise in start-ups, the bankers who manage my money, both personally and professionally, and people like Kelly Granat, who is one of the only women at the helm of an institutional investor. I am very careful about the seating because I want these entrepreneurs to be next to people who can legitimately help them, whether it's with a bridge loan or how to think about their brand during their next steps. What I socialise is the need to help and the ability to ask. I ask that every single woman stand up and speak about a need they have or a problem they need help fixing. I insist that something come of these dinners by the time dessert is served, aside from some tactical advice and solidarity.

I hope these dinners help, I really do, but I want to reassure the rest of you who feel like you're far away from being on a panel or getting invited to a fancy cocktail party with a step-and-repeat. I don't know anyone who successfully networked their way into a business. This is a myth, a myth that's becoming more insistent with social media. Nobody networks their way to success at a dinner. What's more: knowing the right people, or even *being* the right person, will not get you very far. It's not how you build or scale a business. I understand the siren song – I know because I also experienced feeling like I was missing out, or that things would be different or easier if I could only get in the room with women who had more power, or were photographed, or mattered socially. But I can tell you that it doesn't move the needle. And I worry that it's marketed to women as the thing to strive for and that it can easily take us offtrack – we think we need to speak at every conference; we think we need to make the lists of powerful people and get all the press; we think we need to be tagged on Instagram as part of the club. But I promise: we'd be far better off sitting in a conference room exhausting ourselves over the pricing of every SKU in the business and obsessing over the margins. No dinner will give us the kind of unlock that comes from getting the musculature of our businesses right. I'm including myself in this because I have a lot of experience to leverage with each new business venture, and I certainly get a lot of attention and press, but *I still have to build each business*. There is simply no escaping that reality.

The other thing to remember is that by the time you do get invited to those dinners and conferences, there's a perception that you have transactional power because you've probably done the thing. I'm a good example of this: people started inviting me everywhere once I had built and scaled a huge brand. What's not accounted for in that calculus is that the first three years, nobody cared. Businesses require slow growth – three years minimum – but nobody tells that story. We prefer to believe in overnight successes and the idea that businesses are built on hype and press. The reality is far less glamourous: you need to put your head down and do it. You don't need to tell your story before you do it; save it for the after-party. I do a lot of press now, but I didn't do much press in advance of achieving my vision. I didn't have anything of great value yet to share. Now, I really do want to teach and mentor – and I want to reach as many women as possible, not just women who might be seated next to me at an event. We aren't going to get as far as we want to go if we continue to operate under the belief that mentorship must be one-to-one to matter, or that we can't learn from each other unless we're in the same room.

I recently heard another businesswoman on a panel say that she loved conferences because they are so good for networking. I went out on stage after her and reframed the idea: *This is not about networking; it's about building a network. Men use a network like a tool. It's a means to get shit done. This is what we're supposed to be doing. We're supposed to be finding distributors who can ship product from here to there, bankers who can secure the loan, service providers who can unlock growth, etc. We need to be connecting to people who can help us get things done, not post on Instagram. Bringing women together solely so they can feel a sense of community is not helpful in business. That's a social club, not a useful network.* What can I say? I'm here to say the unpopular thing and always the honest thing.

Most of the baller women I know are not rushing around to conferences or posting about their days on Instagram. They're working. Case in point: I've been chasing Diane Hendricks, founder of ABC Supply Co., to do my podcast for almost a year. (Diane, are you listening? Will you please come on *Aspire with Emma Grede*?) Diane, who borrowed $900,000 with her late husband to start her roofing and siding supply company in 1982, is now worth $23 billion, and I'm dying to talk to her about what she's achieved. But as it were, she's not so interested in showing up for panels or doing press or my podcast – it's clear that this type of activity played no role in her massive success. This is way more typical than we realise. There aren't a lot of Diane Hendrickses, but there are a lot of very powerful businesswomen whom you've never heard of. Most of the powerful businesswomen in our midst keep low profiles. Recent years have marked a big shift for me, as my own profile continues to grow. I recognise I'm cultivating a personal brand, but I'm doing this after-the-fact. I've done the deed in business several times now, and in this phase of my career I want to reach as many women as possible – and I need to do that on social media and through podcasts and TV. I believe I've had the type of success that I've had so that I can help other women do the same.

I love women and I love hanging out with women. Most of my favourite colleagues and coworkers are women. I spend as much of my energy as possible helping other founders who are looking for mentorship and want to learn as much from my successes and my mistakes as possible. I want to help women take up so much more space. I get to invest in some of them and work shoulder to shoulder with a few, but most of them I never even meet in person. And that's okay, that's the beauty of our connected world. I want to be clear about where this mentorship happens – and where I meet most of my *own* mentors. It happens through the pages of books like this. It happens through podcasts and long-format interviews. It happens through online classes. It happens in the natural course of your job or building a business with the unlikeliest of people. You can find the mentorship you need without getting on a plane, I promise. Save your time, energy and money for your business. You're not missing out on anything.

> **New Thought: Effective networking isn't a social undertaking. You need to find people who can further your business goals, not burnish your social media profile. You can do this from exactly where you're at.**

---

### 11. Old Thought: Business is about building a community – being transactional is gross.

> *If you're not willing to do more than you're being paid for, you'll never be paid for more than you're doing. Giving is one of the laws of the universe. You've got to willingly give and graciously receive.*
> – Bob Proctor

A young founder who has a beauty brand that's on fire right now sent me an email a few months ago. She said something to the effect of, 'Hey Emma, I have a category-busting idea for a new hair brand. I'd love it if you'd introduce me to X, Y and Z. I think I can build a billion-dollar company.' The subtext: I'm a woman and you're a woman and, therefore, you should help.

I didn't respond immediately. I felt stuck and, if I'm honest, enraged. And then I wrote her back and said, 'J, the reason I wasn't immediate in coming back to you is I was surprised that you asked. If I were in your shoes, I would have structured this enormous request as a transaction. You need to understand why people do things. You need to say, *I'll give you a piece of what I'm building in exchange for making this deal happen.*' After all, what am I? A charity? A favour bank? This is not how people do business, and yet I get asks like this from other women routinely – always under the auspices of #womenhelpingwomen – which makes me think that we're being conditioned to believe that it is. We're scared of being transactional, so we couch our wants under the veil of friendliness or being a kind or good person. We also think that this is how men do business – that they're all friends who help each other out of the goodness of their hearts. This belief and way of doing business is not helping any of us out. If you want something from someone, if you think they can help you drive your business forward in a significant way, you need to make it worth their while.

I give away a couple of percentage points all the time because why should someone go out of their way otherwise? It's not strange, it's how business – which is transactional and not about friendship – works. Effective networking and business relationships are not synonymous with friendship. When I first launched Good American and went out seeking help and advice, I offered a lot of people positions in the company, as well as equity stakes for integrated partnerships. Some people took me up on it, some didn't. But I always, always offered or went into these types of negotiations seeing them as a transaction for legitimate value – not as a relationship where someone should do a favour for me because they're nice or I'm nice, or do something for me because I'm a woman.

I know this is rough. It chafes against all our feelings about how we are supposed to operate, especially in this cultural moment that we find ourselves in – and yet, behaving in this way doesn't get us anywhere except full of resentment. We need to become much more comfortable with overt and clear transactions, not muddling it up as relational favours and friendships, hiding what we want under a hashtag or a cultural expectation that someone is going to be 'nice' to us and give us what we want. I'm personally tired of being worked in this way, too, and I can see it coming miles away: *If I can befriend Emma, maybe she'll do X, Y and Z for me.* I don't even think it's conscious; it's just the way that we're trained. (And I know this because I recognised it in myself in my early days.) I'm not here for that energy though. Nobody wants to feel manipulated – and if we're honest, that is what this is. If you want something from me that has value beyond my free advice, it needs to be a business transaction that makes sense. If it is, I'm all ears and I'm happy to consider it.

We need to make our asks – clearly and directly – with an understanding of reciprocal value generation at the root of the request. I promise this is not weird, it's business. We need to move past the cultural pressure that suggests that you're supposed to go out of your way for other people for free in a business context. I mean, trust me, I get it: I want to be kind, and share the love, and spread the good vibes. It's not for nothing. But I also want women to understand that when we do this, we're sharing ourselves out again and again and getting nothing in return. It is a type of self-betrayal and devaluation. I'm sure many of you want to throw this book across the room, but you know I'm right. We give what we have away – all the knowledge we've built, our reputation and connections – not believing that it has real value. And because we price it at nothing, we set our own value at zero in the process.

There's something about the one-to-one entitlement of 'I'm a woman, therefore if you're a good woman, you'll help me' energy that also drives me nuts. It's all over our culture and something I hear from other female founders as well: they're overwhelmed not only by the demands for time and support but the energy behind it, which suggests that you're 'bad' if you refuse a person's request. Here's the thing: nobody 'owes' anyone anything – unless you're in some type of structured agreement or transaction. I can also offer that I'm interested in helping *all* women, or as many women as possible. I don't want to reserve my largesse or my advice for the people who can get direct access to me. I don't want this idea of networking and favouring to be gated by who gets invited to conferences, dinners and retreats – or who has a reciprocally large Instagram following or network. We do not need to operate businesses in this way. It's also not how businesses grow.

I hate comparing the way that men and women do business, but from what I've observed, men connect in an entirely different way. For one, they are not burdened by a scarcity mindset, so they never see helping someone else as potentially limiting their own options. Jens never thinks that making a connection or getting involved with someone's business success will take anything from him – if anything, it's the contrary – he's always pursuing upside. He has faith that the more he does, the more he's owed, and if they're not going to transact on that in the moment, he'll transact on it later. He is very open and direct about this, which seems to be the norm among men. They're not hoping that if they're friendly and nice, someone will think to do something for them – it's stated outright: I'm happy to help here; you will cut me in, or you will pay me back. Michael Rubin, who is incredibly generous with connections, told me the same: he knows it will come back to him, and he knows he's collecting receipts to cash in when he needs them. Nobody is confused about this. It's all very obvious. Networking for Jens is not about being 'nice' – he's a lovely person, but he would find that to be an absurd concept and motivator – it's a means to an end. He's not going out of his way to do favours in business for free, and nobody expects it or imposes on Jens in this way. I can't speak for all men (or all women for that matter), but my sense is that this is something that happens mostly among us.

There are a lot of women in the world of business whom I love to see and count as friends, but I never conflate the two. I don't get confused. If I'm sitting with someone and pretending to be mates, I promise no business is happening. Meanwhile, nobody is saying the transactional part out loud, but there is an expectation of something in return. We need to say the transactional part out loud. It would be so much healthier for all of us – not only people in the room, but for all the other women who are watching us on Instagram. And when I say that I don't conflate friendship with business, I really, really mean it. Don't confuse the two. You don't need to like someone to do business with them; you don't need to want to have dinner with them or spend a weekend with them either. On the flip side, someone can be your romantic partner, your best friend and the father to your children, and I still think you should keep the business separate.

Some of you who are reading this book, people who work in the service industry or creative sector, for example, probably feel like other people prevail over you in a different way. I hear from creatives all the time, for example, that people ask for advice or insight without offering any compensation in return – and they feel pressure to respond because what is it to them, really? Isn't it just a few minutes of their time? I meet a lot of women in the service industry or at nonprofits who have spent years and a lot of their own money on their education and developing expertise and ultimately wisdom, and yet they have no idea how to monetise or commercialise this skill set. In our culture, there's an insistence that this work should somehow be free. Many of us don't understand how to monetise our value or stop giving away our primary offering for free. This is a transaction, too. If you're not getting anything in return, it's not equitable or fair, and it's certainly not sustainable.

I often think about women who are legends in the world of fashion – women like Isabella Blow and Daphne Guinness and Amanda Harlech and so many others. These women are fairy godmothers, finding and nurturing young talent and then eventually landing them at big houses where they build billion-pound brands. Alexander McQueen was underground, for example, until Isabella

Blow introduced him to Bernard Arnault. And she got nothing for it. Isabella Blow died penniless. Sometimes these women get styling or consultancy jobs at the end of it all, but none of them have been appropriately compensated for matchmaking talent with businesses that turn into global brands. They probably don't know how to ask for what they should receive; they don't know how to put themselves in the centre of these consequential transactions. I believe this is partly because their 'genius' seems easy to them, so they shy away from charging – but it's a crime that they are not compensated for the value they create. It's important here to understand the definition of a favour, and what I'm describing above is not a favour. A favour is something you do when there's a guarantee that you can call something back to you on the same level. I'll do you this favour, and you'll do me a favour in kind. A favour is not a massive, once-in-a-lifetime thing that you'll never be able to replicate and that will never come back to you. That's not a favour; that's a piss-take. There is a really important line here that we all need to understand: the minute that someone will make money off the request, they need to cut you in. It's no longer a friendly favour; it's a business transaction.

New Thought: **Business *is* transactional, no friendship required.**

# 6. Leadership

*It's never too late to become what you might have been.*
- George Eliot

I was finally in my own office, and it was beautiful. I had started ITB in a corner of the Saturday Group office. Once we outgrew that, we occupied part of the parent company's office, Independent Talent, but we had finally outgrown that as well, and I now had my own space on Gresse Street in Fitzrovia. We were in an amazing area, with floor-to-ceiling windows, long desks and campaign photographs on the wall. I had designed the whole thing myself. I had even carefully hand-applied the ITB vinyl to the reception desk. The whole thing was mine, and I was feeling myself – until my first board meeting on the premises. I had dressed up for the occasion and I was sweating profusely. I was *always* sweating profusely before a board meeting. They would twist me into knots. I was a mess before, during and after.

I'll never forget this particular one because it involves probably the most impactful piece of feedback I've ever received. I also remember it because I was furious. While I normally love being married to a Swede, sometimes I wish he could be a *tiny bit* softer and less direct with his feedback – or at least time it better. This moment was no different.

'Why are you so nervous?' Jens was legitimately confused.

I didn't know. While I'm great at chat and an excellent presenter who can sell anything to anyone, when it came time for these meetings, I was full of self-doubt, always on the precipice of falling apart.

'I know why you're suffering, Emma.' He turned to me. 'You have an employee mentality.'

*An employee what???*

I couldn't think about anything else during the meeting, letting the words sink in. Intuitively I knew he was right. After we wrapped up, when I had a chance to regroup and pull myself together, I thought about why. I was twenty-six or twenty-seven years old, and up until that point, I'd only ever been an employee. I hadn't shifted my mindset when I opened my own agency. Instead of being there as the CEO to guide the board to a decision, I was looking for everyone else to tell me what to do. I was seeking their approval rather than coming into the room and stating the direction, convincing everyone to come with me: *This is the direction we're going in, and here's what will be waiting for us when we arrive.* Jens offered me an excellent insight, and with time, I was able to integrate what he said and change the way I came into a board meeting – and how I thought about myself as a leader.

At that point in my career, I felt so fragile in my role, I probably could have only heard that feedback from someone close to me, but I'm offering it to you here because I see it plague so many of us – including women who have been in charge for a long time. These are women who work for themselves as consultants or creatives, as well as women who run their own businesses, both big and small.

For me, it has been a natural urge to look to other people to be my boss. Part of this happens because we feel like we should feel so grateful just to be there. I know that *I* felt that way at those ITB meetings. I had no idea what I was doing and mostly operated on gut instinct – who was I to boss these people around, all of them older and more seasoned than me? I felt totally intimidated. But as I thought about it more, I realised I knew what I was doing. Not only that, I was holding the vision because it was my idea. I just needed Jens to point out something obvious, and yet hard to see: 'You do understand that no one is your boss in that room? You are the boss, and they are waiting for your guidance. They're waiting for you to say, "I see it. Are you in?'" So obvious, and yet so scary and hard.

It takes a lot of effort to rewire yourself out of an employee mentality when it's your turn to lead, but it's essential: you need to trust that you're holding the mission and the vision. I cannot stress this enough. It is your job to hold this vision, reinforce this vision and create the container in which fantastic people do their best work to help you realise this vision. You must manage your team with the ethos of your company at the heart of all your decision-making.

In *Good to Great*, Jim Collins outlines five stages of leaders – Highly Capable Individual, Contributing Team Member, Competent Manager, Effective Leader and Executive – as well as the key traits of a Level 5 Leader. I love the key traits he articulates because they are simple and true: he argues that you need to blend personal humility and professional ambition. What this means functionally is that you want your company to win, and you will set up your organisation to do exactly that. That is your job. Everything you do is not in service to your own ego; it's to serve the larger business as an energetic organism. You must have an enterprise mentality. If something goes sideways, you don't blame yourself; you correct the problem. And if something goes right, you don't assume it was all you.

This sounds simple, but it's not easy. In many ways there's relief in having a boss – it gives you someone to blame if it doesn't work out as planned, and it really is nice to pass all the hard decisions to someone else to make, but I promise, leading doesn't need to be so lonely. In fact, I'm going to offer that building an incredible team is the most important – and joyful – part of creating a successful business. This is one of the things I excel at: attracting world-class talent and highly competent people. But in order to do that, you need to find your footing as a leader first.

People often ask me about my leadership philosophy, and I used to have a reflexive response: *I must have missed that day in business school.* But over the years, I've come to take the question seriously, specifically because I believe the cultures I've helped to build are responsible for the growth and success of the businesses I lead. I recognise that my behaviour determines the behaviour of my teams. I am a model for them, both in how I function and lead at work, but also in what might just be possible for them in their careers as well. Like many of them, I built my life from the bottom up. I've been in the same shoes as everyone on my teams. I've packed up the samples, I've stayed late to prep shoots, I've written the email copy, I've toiled over packaging design. Teams love this, not only because it means that I appreciate their effort and know what it takes, but because I'm a model of possibility. Because we share core experiences, it stands that what I've achieved is within their grasp as well.

At its core, my success in building cultures and leaders revolves around some core tenets that create an environment where I trust my team and they trust me. I've established this trust in part because I tell the truth, and I expect the same in response. There's a popular concept called an exit interview where people who are transitioning out of the company can tell you to go fuck yourself (basically!). I don't do them because they're symptoms of a business culture where people feel like they can't speak up. *You're going to get the opportunity to tell me to go fuck myself at the end? Why didn't you tell me six months ago?* I want people to tell me the truth in the moment, so I bake this into the culture: I give direct feedback and I receive direct feedback. It's an expectation. My teams also trust me because I take responsibility and accountability for when and where I mess up, which means that when mistakes are made, they feel safe to own them, too. I admit when I'm wrong and I apologise, and the standards I hold for the team are the same ones I hold for myself. This means that if I come to someone with a harsh critique, they've probably seen me do it to myself.

I also make people feel seen, heard and represented. It's perhaps not a surprise that this is the strapline of Good American because customers feel this way about the brand. The same is true of the team. Even if inclusivity might not be everyone on the team's passion, specifically, they feel like they are part of a larger mission and that the work means something in the world – and that their part, specifically, is important. I really go out of my way to recognise and acknowledge good work. I often say that culture is who you hire, who you fire and who you promote. I fundamentally believe that not only is this true, but it's the clearest way to express to your team that their dedication will be rewarded. My team also knows that I will always, always back them, and that I never shift to blaming and shaming, only ever accountability and personal responsibility. I start with myself, and I expect them to do the same. Because of this, I will always, always, always go to bat for them if the shit ever hits the fan. I interpret their actions generously and prize effort and speed over perfection.

So, in a nutshell, my leadership philosophy boils down to the following:

- I paint the vision, reinforce the vision and explain to everyone at my companies how we'll achieve the vision. My team can rely on me to uphold the vision and values of the company.
- Per Jim Collins, I practise personal humility and professional ambition. I go like hell to achieve the company's goals and always put long-term success ahead of my ego.
- I prioritise a culture of truth and honest feedback.
- I know what I don't know and surround myself with incredible talent who *do* know what I need to know.
- I find the best people, people who are super-disciplined, self-motivated and can work with autonomy. I let people do their thing and shine.
- I make tough decisions, including letting people go who aren't effective or are dragging the business down.

- I show up consistently. Everyone can anticipate what I'm going to do and what I'm going to say because I'm the same person every single day.

### 1. Old Thought: If you're going to lead, you need to know how to do it all.

*The simple truth is if you play small, you stay small.*
— Anonymous

At the inception of Good American, at my very first investment review where we were planning out the season and taking bets on the product, I failed to do my job. I got lost in an overly complicated Excel spreadsheet that was packed with numbers and acronyms I didn't recognise or understand. I felt embarrassed and humiliated. I felt like I couldn't contribute to the financial conversation and had no place even being there. At the time, I didn't understand that it wasn't my job to do the maths; it was my job to tell the team what the biggest SKU would be and how the product story would link up to connect with what the consumer would want in twelve months' time. When I got over my shame, when I started asking the planners and the merchants in the room to translate the acronyms and paint me a picture in layman's terms, when I stopped being intimidated and waded into the complexity with them, I realised that obsessing about the financial details wasn't actually my job. I needed to know what I needed to know so I could make decisions, but my job was to see the forest for the trees and call the plays. In that moment, I realised I was the only person with the vision to pull the trigger on these big decisions that would determine the trajectory of the company's business along with our product and brand vision.

In short, one of my biggest breakthroughs in business came when I finally admitted that I didn't know everything. The next breakthrough came when I stopped pretending that I did to everyone else.

Like so many other women, I was caught in a perfectionist trap: I felt like I needed to be great at everything and have all the answers. This is a very real fear for all of us, this fear of not being good enough or falling short of expectations. It can be a crippling and overwhelming anxiety. The instinct toward perfectionism makes complete sense, too, as we believe that doing everything perfectly means we get to avoid criticism and rejection. I feel this acutely, I really do. It's never louder in our minds than when we're about to start something new or step out of our comfort zones. But to step out of your comfort zone and start something new, you need to get past it.

I've been the person who sat in meetings and masked what I didn't know. It's excruciating, the hope that someone isn't going to ask you what you think. My reaction to feeling this way initially was to try to counter it, to convince myself that I needed to learn how to do it all before I deserved to start a business, much less lead one. I honestly believed that being in charge meant I needed to have every answer. I micromanaged every decision and every person. I thought if I didn't control every detail, it wouldn't get done right and we'd be exposed as incompetent – what I didn't realise is that this was not a competent way to lead.

I wasn't alone in this leadership style. So many of us believe we're supposed to be able to do everything – we believe if we don't have an innate understanding of every part of every person's job, then we're failing, or we can't mentor or enable that person's work. I felt this way for an awfully long time trying to manage every part of the business. I don't do this anymore. These days, I can't even tell you the ERP* system we run our businesses on, much less how it works, or how to use it – I've never been in it and I don't want to be in it. Trying to understand this would not be a good use of my time.

---

* ERP stands for enterprise resource planning. I even had to look that up. (I HATE acronyms and jargon.)

It took me a long time to get comfortable with this – and I'm still not perfect at it. In fact, it's probably safe to assume that I'm only comfortable forgoing an intimate understanding of the ERP because I've had business success. On one hand, you would be right; on the other, forgoing an intimate understanding of the ERP is precisely what happened to make me successful.

Early on in my career, I micromanaged the shit out of everyone. What this was: my own version of impostor syndrome, which was a desire to control and perfect. What this wasn't: fun for anyone. The moment I stepped back and trusted the people I hired, my business exploded. It completely exploded. I let them manage the business I'd won. I didn't insist on seeing all clients myself. I then translated this into durable leadership success by being honest with myself and crystal clear about what I wasn't good at, and what skills I needed to look for outside myself. I came to understand that I needed to hire to buttress my primary gift, which is about being able to put the whole puzzle together rather than trying *to be* the whole puzzle. It took me a long time to get there, but being willing to hire the best people and get out of their way was a breakthrough for me. It was also part of an epiphany: my gift is not in any one part of the business; it's in finding the best talent and then enabling them to do their best work in *all* parts of the business. I have the vision and consistently bring all departments back to why we do what we do and am able to connect everyone to doing the best work.

I now love nothing more than gathering the best people around me from all over the world. I love working with those people, in part because it means that I get to learn from the best. I am endlessly curious about their talent, especially now that I've let go of the belief that I need to *have* their talent. I never despair that they might be more knowledgeable or have more expertise, or that they might have more experience, or that they might be more articulate or better at something than me – I'm counting on it actually. That's precisely why I've hired them. I've come to understand that surrounding myself with the best people makes me look good, and when I have the best people on my team, I no longer need to go around pretending to be the best person at everything. I can double down on what I do uniquely well. If you are weak at something, find the person who isn't, and then get out of their way and let them do their thing.

Here are some good questions to ask yourself: Do you really know what you don't know? What are things you might be 'good' at but don't enjoy? What are you not great at? What skills do you lack and what are the areas where you need help? Are you being honest with yourself about your weaknesses? We all have them. As mentioned, I'm dyslexic and I find it really, really difficult to read spreadsheets, particularly when they're full of numbers. I need context and I need things translated so that I can make decisions. While I used to beat myself up about this, I now acknowledge that I'm not an expert in finance; I know enough to converse with my CFO, and they know how to create dashboards for me that align with how I understand information.* In that vein, I don't imagine that I need to be a master of logistics and supply chain; I hire extraordinary operators and production experts. When I try to do something I'm not good at, it not only makes me miserable, it works against me. It doesn't make me sharper or better; it blunts my tools.

This doesn't mean that you get to completely bypass your weaknesses and make your job perfectly align with your preferences. You have to learn a baseline understanding of every part of your business. T-shaped leaders are the best leaders. These are leaders with deep

---

* Early on in my career, I did whatever I could to extricate myself from the financial piece, it felt so overwhelming to me. Because I'm so passionate about healing all my money stories, I stopped saying that and took responsibility for my own learning. I hear the same thing from a lot of female founders who are starting out – *I'm really weak at the financial part*. This is fine, and you should find a fantastic CFO/accountant, etc. who can translate the acronyms and information for you and build your Excel models, but I really urge you to build feelings of power around financial fluency.

vertical expertise, but who understand enough about everyone else's vertical to be effective collaborators. You have to be willing to stretch outside your own preferences to work well with others. For example, I have a really short attention span and I hate long meetings, particularly when they're big. I thrive when there are fewer than five of us in a room. I believe the room gets less effective with every person you add. And yet, every single day I'm in a room with forty to fifty people where teams present upcoming collections to me. This is the only way it works. I may not like it, but it's the most efficient path. Because I'm aware of my weaknesses, I've found a way to work in these forums.

I have a lot of respect for experts who spend their lives going deep on a single subject. This is not me, but it brings great value to all businesses. My 'expertise' is in putting it all together. This is true for most great leaders. Yes, you need to innately understand your subject matter, but you also need to understand people – how they work together and how they don't – and how to realise a vision. I sit with powerhouse people who have fifteen years more experience than I do, people who have run much bigger brands and teams. And through hard work, I no longer assume they know more than I do. They have more experience in their specific area of expertise, but how clever am I for putting them all together? If you find yourself micromanaging your finance team or driving your teams crazy, you either don't have the right team or you are not leading effectively.

What inadvertently happens when you're convinced you're the one who can do it all, and that you should do it all, is that all the incredible talent underneath you sees no path for growth – they're frustrated, they feel controlled and micromanaged, they feel untrusted and stunted, and they leave. It is not a good use of talent or the *way* to cultivate good talent. It can create a type of competition within a business, even if that's not the intent – nobody wants to feel like their boss thinks they could do a better job. They want to feel like they have an important and singular role to play in the functioning of the business. Give them that space and that respect. I know it's hard. There's a lot of cultural pressure on us to be perfect, to have all bases covered, to not be an impostor – I promise you it's to our detriment.

Women labour under the belief that if we're going to sit on top of an organisation, we should be the best at everything. Men, on the other hand, like to surround themselves with a team of rivals[*] – they seem to have no issue keeping other men close to them who probably want to take their job. You can see this throughout the corporate world in leadership teams that are largely male: take Disney, for example, where there's incessant infighting because they are all rivals and all ultimately want the top job. Apparently, it works really well for them. They're all specialists, so Bob Iger runs it as a generalist, recognising that he doesn't also need to be the CFO, or the head of parks, or the CMO. You don't need to understand the financials at the level of the CFO; you don't need to be a comparable marketer to your CMO. If that's where you're focusing your energy, you won't have time to hold the vision for the company and lead.

In my humble opinion, a lot of creative founders – yes, particularly women – feel like they're being negligent if they don't take the CEO role. I sometimes hear from them that they feel external pressure or are pressuring themselves to do the 'top job' because giving that mantle to someone else will somehow mean they don't make the biggest decisions. Sometimes I hear that because there aren't that many women up in the ranks, to not hold complete control feels like a disservice to the entire gender. Here's the thing about the CEO role though. It's kind of the pits. It's highly operational, very lonely and not necessarily creative. Even when I hold the CEO title, I always put someone in the number two role as president who is strong and fills in for my blind spots, as being CEO is not where my greatest strengths are.

---

[*] This is the idea that you see everyone as your competition and use their excellence as a challenge to perform your best.

I don't think women with the title always want the top job per se, but they often believe that if you're the person in charge, you need the title. I'm here to tell you, you can still be the person running the company and calling the shots as the owner *and* bring in a skilled CEO to execute. It's worth looking at men for inspiration here because Mark Zuckerberg is a nerdy engineer; he didn't create the culture at Facebook that made them so successful in those early days – he hired Sheryl Sandberg to do that for him. In creative-led companies, you often see the opposite: a lot of underqualified creative directors try to run the business; it's not always the best idea.

We know that we don't get far alone, and yet many of us don't truly believe it, thinking instead that we need to do everything ourselves. Acknowledging limitations is difficult, and yet it's an essential superpower – if we can get over the anxiety of not being in complete control, we will get much further working together. There's a rub that happens where we *want* to give women as many chances as we can, and we really want to see other women succeed, and yet we're not always putting other women in positions of power in our own organisations because it feels too threatening. This is something all female leaders need to be really cognisant of, because it can sneak up on us – we're not conscious of what we're doing. This hiring advice is massive: you must park your ego because you need people who are better than you.

Every time I start something new, I'm honest with myself: *Am I the best person to run this?* For example, with Off Season, I realised I wasn't the best person to run a business that had that level of complexity in a business category that I know very little about: sports. So I hired an exceptional president, Vicky Picca, to contend with the endless licences and the relationships with players, agents and teams that go with it. It took radical honesty to accept this and to not decide that it would be the best use of my time to learn the intricacies of every global sports league. I understand the pull of that type of intellectual curiosity, but I know to restrain myself and find someone who will do it much better because they've done it before.

I always, always want women to have the healthy pride to believe that they can figure something out – that's a huge part of what will make you successful, particularly early in your career. But when you get to a certain level of success, sometimes the 'figuring it out' is figuring out who can unlock that part of the business for you. The business can't afford for you to learn on the job in that way – and you will drive yourself and your team crazy.

Creating leverage is critical for any start-up or business – and leadership is ultimately a leverage game. Everyone wants to feel the synergy of adding their unique part to the whole, to the collective success of the business, so you don't want to deprive them of the opportunity. Nor do you likely have the money or the time to spare by not fully using everyone on your team to your advantage. You hired them and you're paying them – enable them to do their best possible work.

I believe that the red thread throughout my career is that I really understand leverage. After all, I went from working behind the-scenes at fashion shows and seeing a white space for designers who needed partnerships to eventually becoming the queen of collaborations. From there, I expanded the umbrella from designers to include artists and celebrities, tying it all together through my skills as a negotiator. I know how to bring two unlikely partners, people who see the world very differently, together to create something larger than either of them. Next, I made the massive leap of starting my own business by taking the core of what I understood about talent and the ability of talent to accelerate brands and businesses through campaigns. My intrinsic understanding of partnerships was the nugget that built Good American. Then I realised I needed to expand my understanding of partnership and find the best people to execute the vision – and not just any people, but the best people, since that is the synergy that's possible when you put the right factors together in a business. I'd rather have a team of three than a team of thirty if it means I can get the best. These are the people who cannot only teach you everything but also help you realise your vision. Nobody is self-made; nobody does that alone.

**New Thought: Leverage only comes after you recognise your strengths and your limitations and then hire and empower people whose talents surpass your own.**

---

**2. Old Thought: Take advantage of every opportunity that presents itself.**

*You've got to get up every morning with determination if you're going to go to bed with satisfaction.*
– George Lorimer

When you have a start-up, you get the gift of a million problems that invariably come with it. And you're also going to receive not only a lot of competing priorities but a shit-ton of ideas for ways you can play it. It is very, very easy to become distracted by possibility and not wanting to cut off anything that might be the next big thing for your business – and at the same time, if you don't focus, you will run out of time, resources, energy and money. It's one of the big business paradoxes.

Finding this balance is really hard, truly. Saying no is as important, if not more important, than saying yes. Very often, you need to ignore something that's on fire and calling out for your attention to double down on the most important thing, which might not be that thing that's on fire. One of the jobs of an effective leader is to continually retrain people's attention on the most important things – and typically, you can't really have more than three things on that list. (It always makes me laugh when people tell me their ten priorities, as priority literally means THE FIRST THING.) A significant and often overlooked part of focus is developing good daily routines – both for yourself and within the company – because good routines mean more things become automatic processes and you need to make fewer decisions, which frees up space and energy that everyone needs when you're running at full speed. Ultimately, this type of discipline becomes habit, which evolves into culture – this works on both the personal and professional fronts.

As a leader, you need your team to align not only on the three most important things but also on how everyone's work will ladder up to those three things. This is an essential step. It's not enough to proclaim the three things and then leave departments to their own devices. It's human nature, but we often pay lip service to alignment and then continue to prioritise our own preferences. Teams will want to do what they want to do. But when you're in charge, not only do you need to be incredibly disciplined about your priorities, but you must require discipline throughout the organisation if you have any hope of pulling collective focus off. Every time an exciting opportunity pops up that could be a side alley *or* an acceleration point, you need to repeatedly ask the question, *Does this align with one of our three priorities?* I'm going to stress this again and again, because if you can figure out company-wide cohesion and alignment, nothing else matters.

While it's mission critical in start-up land, it's relatively easy to stay in touch across the organisation – probably there aren't that many of you. But what invariably happens in any growing business, particularly if you're moving quickly and team leaders feel a lot of autonomy (a good thing), is that you can get a bunch of fiefdoms. The e-commerce team has its focus, product is doing their own thing over there, while marketing and distribution are tuned in to their own passion projects. In addition to people being pulled toward what they want to do, what they are good at or what they perceive to be the most important, everyone has their own distracting fires to put out as well. You can end up with organisational chaos if you're not extremely disciplined. Good leadership is about constantly galvanising everybody and having clarity of focus in the business and pushing everyone in the direction of your priorities and vision. Compulsively. Repetitively. You want to work out what you can be the best at and double down on that. You want to resist the urge to overcomplicate things. You want to understand the problem you are uniquely solving and what your unique way of solving it is. You want to know what you can be the best at in the world. Then you ask how you can make money doing all of those things.

Sometimes, actually *often*, you won't get to focus on the three things that you think are the most important or the most fun. This is the rub, but it's true. This will be true in your career, in your leadership and in your personal life. But you need to be clear about what you can and cannot do with your precious and scarce time, particularly as it relates to your goals. There are a lot of things I miss doing in the business – I hate having to skip meetings about print and colour, for example, because these meetings are so fun and I'm obsessed with print design. But unfortunately, I don't get to spend my time at that level of the business anymore. We have a great team who are perfectly competent to oversee this function. I've had to let it go. My priorities have needed to shift. I have to give up the things I *want* to do all the time in service to the larger goals we've agreed upon. As much as I want to cheat, I can't. The entire business requires discipline, particularly from its leaders.

Mark Cuban and I had a long conversation about this on my podcast and how successful entrepreneurs must learn to delegate to build efficiency. This is hard for women – speaking for myself, I had to learn how to delegate because I thought micromanaging was synonymous with 'good managing'. But when you hire right, not only is this a disservice to the talent on your team, it creates resentment and makes it a challenge to retain talent. Great people want the wide lane and opportunity to be great, not to be controlled. As Mark explained, 'You have to learn how to trust. Because when you're really, really, really good at something, and it takes more time to convey it to someone and explain what you want, you just want to do it yourself. Let's just get it done, right? We've got other shit to do! . . . But you have to be able to find your mini-mes and trust them so hard.'[1]

At this point in my life, I'm very clear on what I'm good at and where I am most uniquely positioned to make things happen. And I recognise, through my processing of visioning and compulsively writing things down, that focus is a force multiplier. You must be able to drown out the noise around you and double down on the most important things. This is what will propel you forward. When you're someone like me, a complete generalist, it's easy to be in everything. But I can't make a difference in everything. Being able to pull back and hold the bigger picture has given me so many unlocks – unlocks that wouldn't have come if I'd been too deep into the minutiae. For example, back in the early days at Good American, I pulled myself out of the process of sampling all the denim fabrics, as it wasn't a good use of time. When the team felt they'd found the one, someone presented a fabric and said, 'We should call this one hundred per cent stretchability.' In that moment, with my fresh eyes, I could say, 'No, we'll call it Always Fits. It's one-size-fits-all. Instead of creating seventeen sizes, I'm going to create five that fit the full size range, and it's going to be called Always Fits. If you're on your period, or your weight is fluctuating up or down, your jeans don't have to.'\*

That's where I'm at my best: pulling it all together into a cohesive identity – correlating it to what a customer wants and how she feels

---

\* Besides accommodating weight fluctuations (we do US sizes 00–4, 6–12, 14–18 Plus, 20–26 Plus, 28–32 Plus; UK sizes are four numbers higher, so a US 12 is a UK 16), this has been a great initiative for sustainability—we waste a lot less fabric when we're not cutting seventeen discrete sizes.

– and then baton tossing it to an exceptional team to make it happen. I'm excellent at getting things started, and I'm really good at seeing things through the eyes of the customer. If you are in a consumer business, the consumer's experience had better be one of your priorities. I often find that companies get very internal and self-referential and obsessed with themselves, and they lose track of the way customers think. Everything these companies do becomes about their culture and their internal process . . . but your customer needs to be at the centre of all your decision-making.

It is critical for me to stay as objective as possible about what we're doing at the company, which is a practice in and of itself. It is so easy to get sucked into your own self-referential universe where you assume it will make sense to the customer (and matter to her) because it does to you. I avoid this quicksand by getting out of the office. It's one of the best ways for me to create the conditions to be really thoughtful. I take a snapshot of what's happening with my competition. I go on websites, I go in shops, asking the whole time: *What is the customer seeing? What are they experiencing from this brand? What's new and what's happening more broadly?* Then I go back and look as objectively as possible, doing my best not to believe my own bullshit. I've managed to retain this ability throughout the years, and it's a superpower, one that you can also cultivate.

One way to do this is to sit down with your new employees. They will have fresh eyes for the business for the first few weeks, maybe the first few months, at most. At this point, they start telling themselves the same stories that we tell at the company internally. When there are new people in the business, I like to go to them and ask questions: *What are you seeing? Where were you before? How does what you have seen compare to what we have told you about this company? Where is there disconnect?* You can get excellent information about where you're falling short and failing to live up to your own brand and your own priorities, if you're willing to listen to this type of feedback.

**New Thought:** You will struggle to get scale or succeed if you can't limit your focus and align your team on a few shared goals.

---

**3. Old Thought:** If you're a good leader, everyone should like you. You'll never get to the top unless people love you, because nobody likes women who are too overtly ambitious.

*Why any women give a shit what people think is a mystery to me.*
– Alice Walker

'You think you're so nice, you think you're the shit, you think you're so great.' So said a horrible girl I grew up around in Plaistow, who would always talk shit about me and to me.

I remember saying to myself at the time, *I'm not going to be able to get through my whole life listening to this shit,* particularly because I agreed with some of it. I *did* think I was nice and I did think I was great – I didn't have amazing hair, but I did have beautiful skin. (By "nice," she meant "hot," in American parlance.) In that moment, I resolved to get comfortable with other people being made uncomfortable by me. Intuitively, I knew it would be part of my journey. I don't know if it was a thickening of the skin, but it was an awareness that some people weren't going to like me and I couldn't make that my problem. Catering myself to the preferences of an eleven-year-old girl in Plaistow wasn't my goal. In some ways, it was the beginning of having the opposite of impostor syndrome, which is a concept I think about a lot in the ways that it impinges on women. So many of us feel we suffer from impostor syndrome because we're conditioned to be consumed by worrying about what other people are going to think and say about us. We become trained to be so conscious of other people's opinions and feelings that we stop focusing on ourselves. When we're managing the preferences of other people, we're not thinking about how we want to show up. I couldn't change what this girl thought or said about me – not only was it out of my control, but it wasn't relevant. *Who cares?* As a young girl, I realised I wouldn't please everyone, nor did I particularly want to. Likeability could not be my guiding light.

We all need to get comfortable with this reality: if you're going to be a good, effective leader, you will piss people off. In fact, you can't be a people pleaser and a good leader; the two are mutually exclusive. It is not your job to be likeable; it's your job to lead. Respect is more important than popularity. Being authentic, trustworthy and consistent are what teams require from their leaders and what you must be . . . but likeable? Forget that.

While I mostly love building and leading teams, I'd be lying if I said it didn't also come with really difficult components as well. One of the most important skills you'll need to develop, for one, is the ability to say no. I say no all the time, especially if it doesn't align with my goals or the goals of the business. And saying no to people you care about is hard. And secondly, I tell people the truth and I expect their honesty in return. It's that simple. I tell the truth as it pertains to business, which means it's never personal, but people don't always like it, particularly when it threatens their ego or their livelihood. And needing to let someone go threatens both. This part of the business is deeply uncomfortable, but you must build resilience for it because it will happen. I've never heard of a business journey that doesn't have its ups and downs – there will be mis-hires, and there will also be heartbreaking moments when you need to significantly cut back your team. It's really, really hard. I don't want to minimise that. I care deeply about people, and I'm a woman – I struggle with the two sides of the empathy coin, just like almost all the other women I know. Empathy makes us phenomenally good leaders and fantastic at mentoring staff and looking after the needs of the team, but it sure has an underbelly when it comes to downsizing the team or dealing with people's feelings when they're not getting the pay rises they believe they deserve. I've had to build a lot of durability for displeasing people. It's important to know and accept that people will be disgruntled. And people will come for you. I have come to expect this as part of the cost of doing business. You can't let fear of upsetting people hold you hostage and keep you from doing what is best for your company. You have to lead, and many parts of doing this well will make people angry.

I operate under what I call an 'enterprise mentality': to be an effective leader, you need to separate what is good for the business from what is good for individuals. Sometimes what is good for the business is good for individuals, and sometimes it's not. And that is a balance that I try to seek. But everyone who works for me understands that it's not about them, it's about the business. So you have to say no to protect the culture, you have to say no to ideas that don't align with the vision, and you have to say no to protect your people. That's the collective cause we've been brought together to do: business. We don't work for the pleasure of coming to the office every day to hang out (which is, admittedly, often fun); we work for the pleasure of the business. We are there to serve the needs of the customer, meet our mission and create a profit.

I went on the podcast *The Diary of a CEO*, and the host, Steven Bartlett, brought up how many founders tell him they're scared of social media reprisals, particularly if they start to grow their profile. This conversation is one I've had many times, and it's worth sharing it here.

'If you do something wrong, there's a really interesting incentive where the employee can pop back,' he said. 'If you fire me from your company, Emma, and I didn't feel so *good* when I was there, I now have you by the balls a little bit, if you know what I'm saying.'

'Yes, you do,' I replied.

'Because I can post on my TikTok and say, "Emma is not who you think she is." Because you're living under that threat from some kind of activist employee. How do you stop that from changing the way you live with that "enterprise mentality" and do what's right for the business?'

'I don't think you do,' I responded.

"I've had so many founders say this to me in my portfolio: "Oh man, I'm scared of being cancelled."'

'Well, *don't do anything to be cancelled*,' I responded. 'It's a fine line. Look, if you're a leader, you're never going to please everybody, and this is where leadership style and who you are as a person really comes out. I'm somebody who leads with no ambiguity. Nobody is like, "Hmm, I wonder what Emma is thinking." I'm very clear in what I'm thinking. I'm very clear in what the goals are. And the reason we've been able to do what we've been able to do is because of those things. I have a very straightforward management style, and I bring everybody along with me. Now listen, there's always going to be someone, or a fraction of people, who will feel disgruntled. I've gone through various things in different companies where I've had to downsize or let people go, and those things are really unfortunate, and that's just the course of the business. Are you doing those things in a way that's congruent with who you are as a leader? Again, I never have an individualistic idea about that. If I have to look at a company and downsize, I'm not thinking about the fifty people I have to let go. I'm thinking about the four hundred jobs that need to be saved. And sadly, sometimes there is collateral damage. That's part of being in business. I'm certainly not sweating what somebody might do on TikTok, because I know who I am, and I feel good about the decisions that I make because of where they come from. They come from me, they come from my heart, and I know I'm a good person.'[2]

There were a few interesting parts of Steven's question. First, he led by saying, 'If you do something wrong,' and then he brought up fear of being cancelled. Listen, I agree that we've taken the public tribunal and cancelling too far in recent years in some cases, *and* it's not that hard to be a decent person. If you're legitimately worried about being cancelled, there might be legitimate issues with your behaviour. Having an 'enterprise mentality' is not an excuse to be an arsehole. Yes, you might need to be colder than people would like – again, you will displease people – but there's nothing cancellable about doing your job and leading a company with its best fiduciary interests in mind.

You need to have a social contract with your staff: I want you to work really hard; I want you to be disciplined, courageous and consistent; and I'm going to reward you really well.* We're also going to have these moments that are not so easy, and everyone needs to buy into that part as well. I'm going to give this opportunity to you, and you're going to get a level of honesty and openness in return. I believe it's part of my colleagues' jobs to tell their managers the truth – and vice versa – specifically when it pertains to the business. To that end, I try to be as transparent as I can and bring my leadership team along on the journey. I learned this lesson the hard way.

Early on in my career, when I was running ITB and was an unseasoned CEO, the business was in financial straits – rather than letting my direct reports know and sharing accountability with them, I internalised the pressure and then shocked everyone when we suddenly needed to cut fifteen people from our sixty-person team. Not only did I feel like I was going to die of shame – you entice all these people to give up what they have at other companies and join you on a journey, and then you fail them; it's excruciating – but my senior management team didn't think I was a hero for not bringing them in and saving

---

* If you're on a start-up journey and can't reward your team with the top of the percentile in terms of base compensation and bonus, then you need to sell them on a different opportunity. You need to sell them on a ride where they're incentivised by having skin in the game should you all succeed. They really need to believe in what the business will become. 'I can't pay you a million bucks, but if we're successful, the payoff will be worth it.' I have created *a lot* of value for people, and nothing brings me more joy.

them from reality. They felt betrayed. This was a big lesson for me. I hadn't shared how bad things were with them because I thought, *I'm the CEO, that's my problem; they should be able to just come in and out of the office* – but it created a lack of trust for everyone, and they didn't appreciate it. While I don't think you always need to spread anxiety across every level of the business, I believe you owe it to your employees to give them an honest picture of where things are at – partly so they can help you correct the trajectory of the business.

Downsizing ITB felt like the end of the world, but I did create a better company because of it. I created more discipline in the business because it allowed me to see the mistakes I had made – not only in overstaffing, but in running a less-healthy engine at the centre of the business. I didn't have the right people for that phase of the journey. I realised, too, that my primary job at the top of the organisation wasn't to carry all the anxiety and pressure, but to stand on the sidelines and direct the plays with a full view of the field. I'm not great at sport – getting better! – but the team needs to know their roles, the playbook they're following, and the goal. As a leader, you need to bring your team on the journey and get them involved in the problems so they can own the solutions.

When you're working in start-up land, you're going to experience a turnover in staff – in both directions. Turnover is part of any company's growing pains; you won't be able to avoid it. Often the people who can get you to £10 million are not the same ones who will get you to £100 million, and these are not the same people who will get you to £1 billion. The people who operate companies at scale are an entirely different breed (and frequently do not have the temerity or grit for start-up life). It really does come down to personality type as well as skill set. At the beginning, you need people who can plug holes, do whatever it takes, and wear many hats. As the company grows, you typically need functional specialists. I love the early days; it's why I've started so many businesses. While it's benefitted me having an ecosystem of businesses that people can move around in according to their specialty and company-stage preferences and skills, most of us don't have that luxury. You will need to change your team at various points according to the needs of the business. There are some people who can grow with an organisation, but that is very, very rare. This is really difficult, and yet it doesn't need to be a bad thing, particularly if everyone is honest and clear about when they thrive – and when they don't. It is not 'bad', or disloyal, to need different people at different points of the journey. Just be honest about it. The wrong people will never get you to the right place.

There is a lot of power in a business to unleash when you surround yourself with the best people for that phase of the business and then use their expertise to further your goals. A lot of effective leaders change their team every three to five years. Karl Lagerfeld stayed on top for fifty years, but he brought on fresh blood every five. I don't really like this – in fact, I chafe at this level of mercilessness, and I'm very loyal to people, particularly people who are great. But I also understand that Lagerfeld stayed relevant in part because he kept his team moving at the pace of culture. It's safe to assume that when people signed on for that gig, they understood that they'd be participating in a short run – but the experience would be well worth it and lead them to their next job in a few years. I'm guessing he was entirely transparent about it. This, of course, is honest – I don't think he was sugarcoating anything for anyone. We don't do anyone any favours when we avoid hard conversations and pretend reality is something other than what it is. Nobody is getting duped here.

While I mostly let my kids' schools manage the schooling, as that's what I pay them to do, years ago I did have an email back-and-forth with one of them about their discomfort with the truth, which they perceive as being protective of the kids' feelings. I don't like this, as it creates fragile egos. At their school, they don't talk about 'losing', to the extent that one of my kids didn't understand that she'd lost a race.

Their teacher wanted to have a whole conversation with me about it, and I said, 'The problem with not being honest here is how will she know that she's not good? How will she know that she needs to work harder if you don't tell her the truth? I'm not telling her that she did shit (though she kind of did do shit). I don't need to be mean about it, but factually, she lost – and if she wants to get better, she's going to need to train and practise.' We're creating major dissonance when we lie to our kids and teach them that the truth is bad and should be avoided. The truth is the truth, it's neutral, even if it might hurt or be uncomfortable. But I refuse to teach my kids that they can play with reality by telling themselves a story instead. It will not work out for them in the future. I don't want them to be comfortable lying to themselves, or comfortable letting other people lie to them.

I'm straightforward, but I'm not an arsehole. I've employed hundreds and hundreds of people over the years. If you polled them all, certainly some of them would say, *She's an absolute bitch. She's awful.* But I believe that an overwhelming majority of them would say, *Emma is super fair. She's really honest, she's very consistent and she wasn't a bitch. She's hard and hardworking, and honest, and has high expectations for herself, for the company and for the team.* A fair number of them would say, *I got better because of her.* If you are an ambitious person and you come to work for me, you will go places. I'm going to pick you up and take you with me. As you'll notice, I didn't throw 'nice' on that list above, which I know is a quality or identity factor that a lot of us feel pressured to cling to – I don't do that because you cannot control the way other people perceive you. Nice is a feeling; honesty and consistency are hard to argue with because they show up in actions. I could sit here and tell you what a nice, amazing boss I am, but even my best people – the people who have been with me the longest – have said to me, 'There have been times when you were so tough. Remember when you said, "God, what the fuck were you thinking? What are you doing?" That was so mean. You made me feel like shit.' I take responsibility for that. I'm human. I don't ever want to make someone feel like shit, but I'm not going to lie to myself and say it doesn't happen. This is why I don't cling to words like 'nice', as I can't possibly live up to that expectation all the time – nor do I want to, as sometimes the truth ain't 'nice'. I'd much rather be a great leader. For me, this revolves around basic integrity. I'm consistent and predictable, meaning my team can rely on me and my judgement, and I'm consistent with my values and principles, which guide my decision-making and how I show up every day. Focusing on consistency is also essential because as a good entrepreneurial leader, you must show up every day and do the right things, even when you don't feel the motivation to do so. Adhering to these qualities is far more important to me than being liked.

**New Thought: You cannot optimise for likeability or your own popularity. You need to operate under an enterprise mentality: you can care deeply about the welfare of your team, but you have all signed on to serve the good of the business, not individual needs.**

---

### 4. Old Thought: Your colleagues are like your family.

*It takes twenty years to build a reputation and five minutes to ruin it. If you think about that, you'll do things differently.*
– Warren Buffett

After my terrible experience at the fashion production company, I made a promise to myself to be good to everyone who came through my company. Eighty-five per cent of the people who leave my companies will get an email from me. I thank them for their time and service and for doing an amazing job. I will highlight something specific that they did that was really excellent and that I appreciated. And I tell them they can call me if they ever need something. I really mean this. I can tell you hundreds of stories of former employees where I've got them a job or another big opportunity. Seeing my former colleagues be successful makes me feel like a successful leader. I share in their glory. Being good to the people who have worked for me is a big point of pride. This isn't just because I try to be a good person, but it's also good business. You just never know. I had an intern who turned into a fashion director at *Teen Vogue*; another colleague went on to become the CEO of Harvey Nichols. Jamie Girdler, who started with me at ITB before joining Good American as our CMO, is now a best-in-class marketer with his own agency, which is crushing it. There are so many people in my business orbit who have worked for me at some point who have gone on to do incredible things. Why would I ever treat them poorly for leaving me? It's so much better to have emissaries and well-wishers around the globe whom you can continue to do business with. Nothing is more pleasing to me than seeing them do great things. I want people to not only be ambitious for my companies but be ambitious for themselves. Plus, my greatest hope is that employees leave and get great experience and a wider perspective somewhere else and then come back to teach me what they've learned – that has happened quite a few times as well.

In what I've observed in my own experience and among other female founders and even women on my team, it seems like female leaders have a very, very hard time seeing their team members leave and go elsewhere and succeed. There seems to be something in this dynamic that they tend to take very personally. From where I stand, it seems like they believe they created this moment in time and the conditions for the team member who has left to be successful – they take all the credit, and then they can't stand seeing this magic and sparkle go elsewhere. It hits them in a place where they can't be generous about it. Recently, someone on my team was complaining that a woman on her team had left for an opportunity at another company.

'She's going to fucking die there,' she said.

'Why do you think she'll die there?' I had to ask. 'What did you do wrong that she would die there? I don't understand. She should be really set up for success. She was amazing here. Why can't she be amazing there?'

It seemed to me that this woman on my team didn't *want* her to do well – that if she did well elsewhere, it would somehow indict this woman's own leadership skills. When you think about this, it makes no sense, and yet, I also understand. As leaders, many of us take complete over-responsibility, and with this comes a false sense of what's directly under our control. We can feel like we've been left, that something must be wrong with our leadership style if anyone would want to go elsewhere. It's a type of codependency and it seems to strike some of us particularly hard. It's also hard to accept that people are in fact autonomous and self-reliant – it can be a hard pill to take when you think it's all on you. But you are not their parent, you are the facilitator of talent.

A business is not a family and should not operate like a family. We may love each other, but we're not a family. I'm not collecting children; I'm running an organisation. Loyalty has to be to the vision and to the company. We are there because we've gathered together to do something specific in business. You have an at-will relationship: people will go, both at your behest and also at their own. This is the function of a healthy business. Things change, people change, the needs of the business shift and evolve, and it stops being the right fit on both sides. I'm so grateful to people for their time and energy and for coming to work for me every day. I require a lot, but it is always an evenly weighted exchange. If they give me a lot, I will give a lot in return. I will pay the best. I will bonus the best. You're going to have an amazing work experience, and I'm going to invest in your development. I'm going to give you snacks and out-of-control benefits and an amazing office to come to. I'll give you great experience. You can take credit internally and externally, and when you leave, we'll be your best reference. But you are expected to bring it in return. Sometimes that stops being reciprocal and that's okay. We're not married, and these are not my children; we're a team, not a family.

In a nutshell, I think very carefully about how I bring people into my companies and how I take them out. I'm slow to hire and quick to fire, yes, but it's much deeper than that:

- I hire for values and fit and attitude over experience.
- I have high standards and hold people to them. Everyone has to be excellent. If someone isn't, it's not just me who won't tolerate it. Not letting people go who aren't doing a good job is a disservice and injustice to the people who are.
- Be honest *and* kind – there's never a need to be an arsehole. You can always be respectful.
- I expect accountability and high levels of personal responsibility. People can make mistakes; they just need to own them and learn from them.

**New Thought: You need to care deeply about your team, but you cannot tolerate poor performance or misalignment. You need to let people leave with respect and dignity to seek new experiences.**

---

### 5. Old Thought: Everyone is watching you.

*The most courageous act is still to think for yourself. Aloud.*
– Coco Chanel

After I started the 'A Seat at the Table' dinner series, I received an outpouring of messages from women wondering why they had been excluded: *I really need to understand why I wasn't invited.* My response: outrage. What I want to write back: 'Why do you think everything is about you? Do you think I woke up this morning thinking about you, with an intent to exclude you? I had forty spaces at the table. A lot of people are not going to be invited.' (The email I don't mind receiving? 'Hey, next one, I'd love to be in!') If you spend your life assuming you're being intentionally excluded, you're not only wasting your emotional energy but you're somewhat deluded about where you rank in importance in other people's minds. I am legitimately surprised when other people think of me, if only because I know it's natural to mostly think about yourself! I really don't rate what other people think of me, or assume I cross their minds all that much. This is helpful, I promise.

I might be hardwired in a way that's different from other people, specifically in that I'm not hardwired to give a lot of fucks about what other people think. I have so much self-assurance, and so much conviction, that it's not that I don't *care* what other people think, I just don't put a high value on it. I don't believe that people wake up thinking about me, for one, in the way that I wake up thinking about me; I'm thinking about myself far more than anyone else. So as long as I'm good with me, as long as I feel integrity with myself, that's the most important thing. I cannot spend my time monitoring how other people feel about me. Not only is it not that interesting, but I don't think they've thought super deeply about it – because *none of us spend a lot of time thinking deeply about each other.*

But we definitely operate as though we must be top of mind with everyone else. This is a grave misunderstanding. Because we're at the centre of our universe doesn't mean we occupy prime position in everyone else's universe as well. Nobody's watching you. This might sound shocking and bad, but there is *great relief* in this. We need to relax. Go and do your thing, whether you get attention for it or not. And even if you do get attention for it – positive or negative – recognise that it's transitory and nothing to stake your identity on. People move on really quickly.

This can be hard for us, particularly when we've tasted a little bit of success. A friend of mine had a terrible ending at her company – she sold it, but she never really sold it in her heart. And then the transaction went sideways and she got screwed over financially. Because her identity was so wrapped up in the business, because she was so emotionally invested in the company, when it was over, she couldn't let it go and move on – she felt like her identity had been stolen from her and she was obsessed with looking into the past and getting it back. People came to her with incredible offers, but she convinced herself that everyone was watching her in the context of her first company and she couldn't just 'do anything'. This is a woman who is brimming with amazing ideas, but she couldn't act because she was convinced that everyone was watching. Her self-consciousness meant she lost the momentum of all her previous success – if you're not using it, your network and your currency grow weaker as time ticks on. Meanwhile, people *really* stopped caring, if they really even cared that much to begin with. Point being, you cannot operate for an audience or even assume that anyone is watching; chances are they are not.

There's a lot of pressure on women in business, maybe because there are so few of us to stand for that business in public – even to be in its creative and in its marketing. With all of the businesses I'm involved with, my 'identity' has very little to do with how they show up in the world – and even less to do with how they show up in consumers' minds. I'm an operator, not a spokesperson, even if I now do a fair amount of business press. I'm very careful not to get my identity all wrapped up in the business – I don't believe that I am the companies. As it were, the moment you take investment, the moment you start working with other people to realise the goals of the company, it's not even 100 per cent yours – it's a collective concern.

I know, with a fair amount of certainty, that in ten years, I'll be in a mall somewhere and I'll walk past a Good American store and I won't recognise the fixtures or any of the product. I know this for certain. I'll probably get really pissed off that they've got rid of all the digital screens that I fought for in the store, or that the fits have changed or whatever it is, but that's what's going to happen – it will be someone else's product vision. I'm not going to cry about it! I'm a custodian of these brands for a moment, but they are not about me. It won't be a verdict on me that these businesses will change; it's not personal. If you want to build something that's all about you, then you need to make a little, beautiful, 100-per-cent-you thing – I feel this way about my podcast, for now, but if it expands and grows, it will be informed by other people and a moving culture as well.

Listen, I understand why we're so acutely self-conscious. I get why we're self-aware to the point of being self-obsessed. I know about the way you're wired for belonging and primed to fear exclusion – that if we get kicked out of the tribe, we'll die. I know all of this. But I do my best not to let it run my life. After all, the research suggests that if you fixate on yourself in this way – if you're constantly thinking, *I'm a woman, I'm Black, I'm old, I'm too big, My wrinkles are showing* – you'll perform worse in the world. They've studied this over and over again with things like the Stroop Test, where you need to process two conflicting sets of information, e.g., the names of colours that are the wrong colour, like 'orange' written out in blue. When people self-monitor, they do much worse on these types of cognitive tests. Women do best when we focus on what we want to do, not when we're worried about others looking at us while we do what we want to do. It's not a good use of our energy.

Because I'm a Black woman, a lot of people want to talk to me about DEI, but if I'm telling you the truth, I don't know how practically helpful it is to obsess about whether people are appraising you in a prejudiced way from a career point of view. I don't think that monitoring for stereotypes is a productive way to engage in any business conversation. Focus on what you're saying and how you're presenting. Now, before everyone protests, I get it. I don't want to suggest that it's not a significant issue. It is. Big time. But when it comes to work, it's a company's problem and not an individual's problem to solve. Organisations need to be doing their level best to ensure that their hiring practices, and their business culture in general, are on point and not biased. They need to be trying to not only attract but retain diverse talent. This isn't just because it's the socially correct or 'nice' thing to do; it's because you won't have a thriving business in the future if you don't focus on it. Companies need to worry about that – organisations need to patrol their own behaviour and their policies; employees can't be the ones policing encounters and wondering if Joe over in IT is biased. It's not productive for anyone. I don't want any of my employees to obsess over what other people think of them; I want them to do fantastic work, with joy, on behalf of the business. And if you think you can't do that where you're at, leave, and don't waste one bit of energy at a company that doesn't care about its culture.

My sisters think I'm not normal in my ability to not care what other people think. (They particularly hate it when I apply this philosophy to them and post pictures of them that they do not like. For the record, I have stopped this because I really do care what *they* think!) But I refuse to operate with too much self-consciousness, as I know it will stop me before I start. It's a safe bet that every single person on a panel with me is better educated; they're probably more articulate and nuanced in their thinking than I am, too. If I got all up in my head about this, I wouldn't open my mouth, and I know my voice is desperately needed. Back at my first job, when I was the Black girl with the curly hair and the sad lunch, I knew everyone *was* looking at me – I stood out sorely and I was incredibly self-conscious. I'll never forget one of the account directors referring to me as sounding like a 'cockney barrow boy', which they did not intend as a term of endearment. Rather than take huge offence, something inside me said, *It's okay, Emma, you're being noticed. Be happy you're being chosen. You're here to do this work. Let it slide.* This was big for me because at the time I didn't have as much of a handle on my anger.

Once I digested his shitty comment, I realised I had an opportunity to stand out. Rather than letting it make me self-conscious, in that moment, I learned to be unapologetically myself. I've always had differentiating factors – I'm Black, I've always been the young one because I got a head start thanks to no college, and I don't have a posh accent. But I realised all those factors were unique to me, that we all bring something unique to the table. Once I got really good at embracing the idea of who I was, of being myself and understanding myself, it not only became freeing but it was also a type of magic. Because I worked in an all-white office, everyone constantly asked me for my opinion – I took this opportunity to give it to them, whether I knew what I was talking about or not. My difference is my thing. It shows up in the way I act and how I move in the world. I might put an outsize value on my difference, but I see it as a positive. Leaning into being myself – not self-conscious about myself but *being* and *acting* like myself – has got me to where I am today, and it's far less exhausting than the alternative: obsessing over how people perceive me. I choose to be exactly myself every damn day.

Mellody Hobson is one of my business heroes, and accordingly, she was one of the first guests on my podcast. I've known and admired Mellody for a long time, and I relate to her deeply, as she's also the product of a single mum and a lot of scarcity. Today she's the co-CEO of Ariel Investments and oversees about $15 billion for clients – she's also ushered through major transactions, like the sale of DreamWorks, and she's been on many corporate boards. She was telling me the story of going to her first conference immediately after university. As she stood awkwardly at the bar, people began to approach: 'Oh, you're Mellody.' She realised in that moment that she was the *only* woman there. And one of the only Black people.

As she explained to me, she had an epiphany: 'What if I use this in my favour? I'm going to be like Cher or Beyoncé. I'm not even going to have a last name. I'm that Mellody with two Ls – I'm going to use this difference to my advantage. If you can stand out, then have something to say.'[3] In that moment, Mellody determined she'd cultivate the skill to back it up – and be remembered in every room she walks into, in every way.

New Thought: **You are not the centre of anyone else's universe – lose the self-consciousness and get to work in the world.**

---

6. Old Thought: **Business and altruism need to go hand in hand because DEI is a social good.**

*Do what you have to do until you can do what you want to do.*
– Oprah Winfrey

I was in New York, at a dinner that I didn't want to go to, sitting next to a man I'd never met before. As I pulled out my chair, I looked longingly at the other end, where the people I did know were congregated and laughing, including Jens. *Oh well*, I thought. *I'll get through this. Maybe this guy can teach me something interesting.*

I was still at ITB, but I'd been cooking the idea for Good American in the back of my brain for a minute – I knew I wanted to do denim, only because I'd had a lot of experience in the industry working on collaborations for brands, which made me think I knew something. I didn't realise that I knew how to do *denim marketing*, but I had absolutely no idea how to make a denim product. This ended up being a good thing, as I don't think I would have had the temerity to start if I knew what I was in for. Anyway, I got into a chat with the guy next to me who told me that he was an investor in a huge plus-size business in America.

'Emma,' he said, 'this industry is blowing up.' As he told me all about it, I pulled the various e-commerce sites he mentioned up on my phone and then had to swallow my dismay: it all looked awful. There was not a single piece of clothing on Torrid, or Lane Bryant, or NYDJ that I would have been happy to wear.

'Nobody wants to dress in these clothes,' I told him. 'This is such a complete bummer. I don't think I would wear this if my house were on fire.'

'Well,' he offered. 'You're wrong, because these businesses are huge.'

'My guess is that there are no better options.'

Sitting at that dinner, it all came together in my head: *I'm going to create a denim company, and I'm going to make all the sizes, all the time. And I'm going to make everyone look hot.* Ding, ding, ding! I knew I could figure it out. I knew how to book talent and bring them into a brand to create acceleration points, and from a marketing standpoint, I knew what connected with customers – looking at these massive retailers, I knew I could do much better for women than that. That dinner I didn't want to go to ended up being one of the best dinners I've ever had.

From day dot, Good American has been about inclusivity: that's the mission of the brand and its purpose. But it's also the foundation of what I knew would be a very good business. When people talk about DEI as a social good, I like to remind them that usually what's good for customers and serves a real need will actually be a good business. It may not feel that way, but most consumer power is in the hands of people who are not white men. At Good American, we intrinsically understood that a significant subset of customers are left out of the conversation: designers and retailers had determined that if you were north of a size US 12 (UK 16), there'd be nothing cute or actually on trend in the store or on the site for you to wear. People who are straight sizes, meanwhile, get a plethora of options. It was almost like a pact. You'd find petites and plus-size on its own floor in department stores, and the selection looked nothing like the rest of the shop. One of the things that was important to me from the beginning was to create no separation. I didn't decide what a size 16 (UK 20) woman could or could not wear; she decided. When we made a product, whether it was a bodycon dress with a split all the way up the thigh or a teeny fluorescent pink bikini, we would make it in every size – the woman can decide, we don't need to moderate her options or police her taste. We were 100 per cent right with this instinct that larger women wanted these things, too – the reason there was no 'market' for it previously is that this customer had never been given the choice.

One of the most thrilling parts of Good American's early success is that we changed the industry. Not only did Nordstrom take us on, but they took our story and went to every other brand to say, 'You need to go five sizes up and two sizes lower than everything you've ever done and emulate Good American's size and scale. Everyone needs to do this now.' Even some luxury brands eventually expanded their sizing – attributing something like 10 to 15 per cent of their profits from the three new sizes they added, sizes they hadn't done before. Good American had a massive ripple effect on the culture. The point I wanted to make at the beginning of Good American was the opposite of performative marketing: we weren't doing a full range of sizes because we wanted to get snaps for being inclusive – we were doing a full range of sizes because being inclusive is *good business*. Inclusivity is not a reason to buy; nobody is buying for the community. People buy for themselves; they buy because we make their bums look good.

I've never understood why companies position DEI as social

responsibility and not business responsibility. If you are trying to build something successful, and you need to find its audience, doesn't it make sense that the people making the decisions are reflective of the audience you're selling to? This feels so incredibly obvious to me as a basic principle. My job is to make commercially sound decisions all day, and those decisions are based on having a really good grip on what's happening in the world and culture more broadly. To do that effectively, I need a group of different people from different backgrounds with different viewpoints. I would stop myself if I had only white women or Black women in the room. We live in an incredibly diverse culture – smart businesses understand this and play to it.

I remember several years ago when H&M got into a big PR blowup because they put a Black kid in a hoodie that read 'Coolest Monkey in the Jungle' on it. There was a huge outcry, as people thought they were coding racism into their ad campaign. First of all, there is no such thing as a racist company. There are racist cultures and racist practices that can take hold. But in this specific instance, it was operators who had massive blind spots – and we all have them. H&M is a privately owned Swedish company that's mostly run by Swedish people – they all have the same background for the most part. When something like this happens, it's clear to me that they just didn't have anyone in the room who would have flagged that as offensive. Instead, they said, *Look at this cute kid in this cheeky little monkey hoodie.* Now, do I think it would have been helpful if they had some Black people in the room? Yes, I do. If this were at one of my companies, someone would have checked the monitor and said, 'Adorable hoodie, but put it on the white kid.' But do I think one needs to change everything about an organisation because mistakes like that happen? I actually don't. You need to throw your hands up and say, 'Fuck, we made a big mistake. There's a lack of diversity in our organisation, and we need to sort it out.' And then you need to act and put process and policy in place so that it doesn't happen again. Meanwhile, as a culture, we need to forgive and move on. What's happening that's more concerning than mistakes is that people are scared to have conversations because they don't want to say the wrong thing or offend – so important conversations are not happening and people aren't engaging. People are becoming neurotic around each other, and that is not a good thing for any of us. Nobody learns, and you get pushed further into little groups where you feel like you have to whisper to each other.

I promise it's way more fun to build companies with cultures where people can speak honestly and transparently – and ask each other questions. Curiosity is one of the foundational qualities I look for when I hire, as well as temerity. Business requires quick, honest and direct feedback and the freedom to make mistakes – so long as you behave respectfully, learn from your mistakes and recover quickly. Business can also be fun. It has been so fun to build a company that stands for something in the world and to structure it around the customer and the women who make up the team.

As a company, we didn't just stop with size inclusivity. Several years ago, it was important to the team to become B Corp certified because denim is a very pollutive business.* B Corp certification means that you abide by a triple bottom line: a devotion to profits, yes, but also people and the planet – and to achieve this you need to institute and maintain best-in-class environmental and HR practices. It is a very rigourous accreditation to receive and keep. Because our team is made up of mums and we serve a lot of mums, Good American has got behind US nonprofit Baby2Baby in a significant way (I'm also on the board). There are a lot of young people at the company, and it's important to them to work at a place that cares about the world they live in – they want us to be sure that we acknowledge that we could always do better, and so we always try to do better. I love building

---

* Tip: become B Corp certified from the jump, as it's very time-consuming and expensive to retrofit your supply chain – their bar is very high!

businesses that chime with my own values, too. If you can take a problem that you really want to solve for the world and put it in the centre of your business, that is a magical formula – and far more effective than trying to sanitise your company's image by giving some money away. It's also worth noting that when your team loves what you stand for in the world, it's much easier to attract and retain incredible talent. It feels good to align your career with your beliefs.

I speak to a lot of founders who, before they're even profitable, have figured out a mechanism to give back and donate a certain amount of proceeds. I always tell them that doing something like this is for really successful businesses – it's the preserve of the few and *not* a given. What is helping you grow and move your business forward, versus what is performative marketing? What are you doing as a mea culpa – one hand that feels dirty washing the other – and what are you doing because it's legitimately formative to your brand? If you want to launch a B Corp and fundamentally run the business differently, that's a beautiful thing, but you better have a very high-margin product, because being a B Corp costs money – you can't do it for marketing, you have to do it because it's foundational to your company's mission and values. We want to believe that consumers are checking the B Corp site to work out where they're going to spend their dollars, but very, very, very few people use things like this as a filter for their purchasing behaviour. We like companies to do the right thing, it's true, but not because they're manipulating us to think they're good actors – we want them to do the right thing because they have integrity and a moral compass. We like brands that build problem-solving into the baseline of the business, to know that whatever they're doing is creating a better product or solution for consumers and the world. But inserting sustainability or not-for-profit elements into your business because you expect customers to gravitate to you because of it will be a costly mistake.

Another misstep I see a lot of founders take is to assume that people shop their values – they make the presumption that because they've got a good story, or their product is better for the environment, that consumers will get in line to support them. This isn't how consumers think. They might buy something once, to be supportive, but they are generally not looking up the backstory of the founders of the company when they're in the grocery aisle or at Sephora. They're just not. If people simply wanted to do good for the sake of doing good, wouldn't our world be a better place? People aren't bad, not at all, you just can't guilt them or shame them into purchasing your product as an acquisition strategy. It won't work. Instead, make a superior product. Solve a real customer problem. And do it in a way that's better for the world or a specific customer. That's a winning strategy.

I meet a lot of Black founders who pitch me on why their haircare product will be different for textured hair. I always push them to go in a different direction, to expand beyond this idea of textured hair as the only viable avenue for a Black founder. Create a brand and sell to *everyone*. 'Everyone' as a quantity is much bigger than an identity group. I've said it five hundred times already, but it bears repeating: Black-owned brands aren't just for Black people, so we need Black founders to create more businesses with a wide customer base in mind. Products that Black people use don't just come from the Black community, *and* you can create a business that is for everyone. I understand the compulsion to do something for your community, and yes, historically the Black community has been underserved, but there's no good reason why you can't make a lotion for anyone who suffers from dry skin. You have a much higher chance of building a successful brand if it's not gated at its start.

Plus, I hate to say it, but a compelling founder is not enough of a reason for someone to buy something or change their purchasing behaviour, particularly on commodity products – particularly if those products are priced at a premium. This goes back again to the obsession people have for being the face of their business – whether it's an external or internally applied pressure to be the spokesperson and representative of the company – it's a new thing, and we need to question whether it's a good one. Ten years ago, we didn't know or care who made our toothpaste or our face mask. They were just brands, being distributed and marketed to us through retail channels. I don't think we need to cement ourselves into the centre of brands and create them literally in our image for them to be worthwhile ventures.

So many female entrepreneurs have a real sense of purpose and a broader vision for doing good and having a positive impact on the world – it's really stunning to behold. And many of us can struggle to put a price on it. But as I try to remind founders, *Wasn't the reason you set out to do this to change the world? If that's the case and if you're going to continue to do it, you have to figure out how to charge for it.*

I started getting heavily involved in nonprofit work when I was at ITB, first at Women for Women International, where I sat on the board for seven years. And it's interesting, because I didn't think of it as penance for creating too much for myself; I thought of it as penance for creating too much money for influencers and celebrities and brands. I wanted to share some of my experience and expertise with charities, as they're always trying to get a paltry share at the end of a celebrity collaboration. I wanted to get brands to actually work with a nonprofit. And this guides my nonprofit work today, whether it's for the Fifteen Per cent Pledge, Baby2Baby or the Obama Foundation. While we try to do a lot of good things at the companies I build, and they all have very robust corporate social responsibility (CSR) strategies, which I think of as table stakes and an essential social tax, I think of my own nonprofit work as an entirely different sphere – one I treat separately. I like to think of them as a different form of business, businesses that might benefit from my acumen for marketing, connecting with both donors and end consumers, and selling a vision for good.

**New Thought:** Create a business that solves problems and is good for the world. Now *that's* a powerful CSR strategy.

---

### 7. Old Thought: If you're too successful, people will want to destroy you.

*In the name of elitism, we do a crabs-in-a-barrel number and pull down any of our number who get public attention or a small success. As long as we're into piranha-ism and horizontal hostility, honey, we ain't going to get nowhere.*
– Florynce Kennedy

When Veronica Garza and her family, the owners of Siete Foods, a tortilla and crisp company based in Austin, Texas, sold the brand to PepsiCo for $1.2 billion dollars, people went nuts, accusing the Garzas of selling out. Something similar happened to my friend Monique Rodriguez when she sold her brand, Mielle Organics, to P&G. The response was outrage: *How dare you? They're going to change the ingredients. You stood for Black women and now you sold us the fuck out!*

Whoa. Whoa, whoa, whoa. My friend Aurora James, the designer of Brother Vellies who started the Fifteen Per cent Pledge in 2020, which asks retailers to sign an agreement to give at least 15 per cent of their annual buys to Black and Brown founders (I'm the chair of its board), jumped into the comments to not only defend Rodriguez but set the record straight. 'This is what we want. She sold her company for a billion dollars. That is precisely the point. You build a great company, and you get to sell it. The best way to infiltrate massive organisations and foment change is from the inside out. Now she's there. Now she's going to teach them how to care about Black hair care and how to look after this customer. She's going to teach them about the culture. She'll probably be on the board one day. *This is a good thing.*' It *is* a good thing. For one, people stop being marginalised when they move into the centre of culture, especially a corporate culture like PepsiCo or P&G, which are two of the biggest global consumer conglomerates. And two, the purpose of business is to build a company, generate a profit and get a fantastic result for you and your team. When you do this, you create wealth for a lot of people – and when you inject wealth into communities, it has a knock-on effect. Everyone who touches a successful business – employees, vendors, customers, retailers – is improved by it. I want a world populated with wealthy women. It's so interesting though because when these female founders do the thing and get a fantastic exit, they get *nailed*. I can't think of a time when this has happened to a man for the same reasons.

Some of this is 'horizontal hostility', a term coined by civil rights attorney Florynce Kennedy in the seventies to describe the way that groups of people who have less political power – women, people of colour, the LGBTQIA+ community and so on – punch across and down because they can't send their rage to the people on top of the hierarchy (white men). Well, power and money are tightly connected, and because of this, building a successful business can transform many lives and shift power structures. As someone who grew up in poverty and around a lot of lack, I can attest to this reality. I have a lot of power. I don't take it lightly. Insisting that we all stay small is not a way to ensure that people who weren't born at the top of the heap can get there too.

Business can do a lot of things – and because of our debased politics and the loss of faith in our institutions, consumers are looking to businesses to solve social issues and both represent and stand up for their values in this world. This is a beautiful thing, but ultimately, a business is for . . . business. Hopefully, you get to look after a bunch of employees and make a great place for them to work with excellent pay and benefits, and maybe you get acquired by a larger conglomerate where you can make even bigger change. But a hair-care brand isn't going to transform the Black community unless it's pushing more money and power into the Black community – and that won't happen if we insist that Black-owned businesses stay solely in Black communities. There is great, essential stuff that can be done on a larger stage. If you're making products outside the system because those products don't exist in the system, then your goal is to ensure that the problem you're trying to solve is no longer a niche concern. When it becomes big, I promise that's good for everyone. More investment follows, more optionality and more opportunity – for everyone. When we look at these founders, they're still doing something that's better than the way that it was – are we really going to hang them out to dry for making some money off it? Do you know how hard it is to build and scale a $1.2 billion food brand? Hats off. Where does the American dream stop? Where do you say, *Okay, my idea of pursuing this dream has a cap on it somehow because I can't upset my community – if I'm too successful, I'm going to get torn down.*

And these are the women who actually make it. Have you seen what we collectively do to the women who fail, in a big and obvious way? We hold these women up as cautionary tales for why you shouldn't have a dream for yourself, why you should keep yourself small and why you shouldn't even attempt to do something big. Meanwhile, 98 per cent of venture money goes to men (yep, not a typo). Seventy-five per cent of venture-backed companies fail to return any money to their investors.[4] You do the maths. That's a lot of men eating shit. And yet, that's not the prevailing narrative.*

---

* To that end, on *The Diary of a CEO,* Steven spoke admiringly of Adam Neumann, who blew it with WeWork (and *still* managed to raise another huge round of capital). For Steven, Adam represents someone who didn't undersell himself. Fair, but as I said to him, 'Steven, you know what happened at the end of that story?' His response:

There's a fair amount of risk that comes to any woman who is visible. You don't need me to tell you that. We see takedowns every day; some seem to be based on sound reasoning (Elizabeth Holmes comes to mind), others much less so. I get asked about this a lot, in part because there's an expectation that I must be holding my breath, waiting for the guillotine to come for my head. I'm not. Not because I don't think it won't happen, but because if it does, so be it. I don't really care. As we've established, I not only have thick skin, I have a preternatural ability to turn down the volume on what other people think of me. I wish I could transpose that on all of you. But I *do* know that the more of us who endure takedowns without being dissuaded from moving forward, the more models there are for the women rising up in ranks behind us, the less dangerous it becomes to be celebrated and seen. I believe that's how we move and shift the culture, I really do.

Meanwhile, we can make it a little easier for ourselves and for each other if we watch the way we're policing other women.

New Thought: **People may want to destroy you, but you can't let that stop you. If more and more of us push through it without being deterred, the culture will change.**

---

'Yeah, but listen, the guy still walked away with a billion dollars.' I cannot imagine anyone ever admiring a woman who blew it in that way. I can't even imagine a woman *being* in a position to blow it in that way.

PART FOUR
# ACTION!

*Risk is a requirement. Playing it safe is the real danger.*
– Anonymous

It was a dark day. I'd told my board at ITB that I was cooking a little business, but when Good American launched, some were pissed off. I may have underplayed it a little bit, but I did the whole thing by the book, crossing my T's and dotting my I's. They still felt (erroneously) that I should have given them a piece of the business. They felt like I had fucked them. I countered that not only had I not fucked them, I'd delivered an incredible return on their original investment in me: I'd started the agency earning a £45,000 salary with some equity and delivered a hundred times back to them.

I'd always assumed after I sold ITB that I'd be asked to stay on to run the thing – I'd built it, so how could it possibly function without me at the helm? I hadn't thought through the logistics – and assumed I'd just fly back and forth between Los Angeles and London with my two- and three-year-olds in tow (nuts!) – but they made the decision for me. They did not give me a lock-in and cut me loose. Jens told me it was the best thing that had ever happened to me, but in that moment, it really didn't feel that way. Some of it was personal. I felt like I was abandoning my entire team by moving to Los Angeles. I had pulled a lot of people and agencies into ITB, and I felt I owed it to them to stay until the bitter end. It pained me massively to leave them. And some of that pain could be attributed to the fact that my ego couldn't handle being dismissed. I felt like I was the company. I wouldn't have known what to call it then, but I had founder's syndrome.

Founder's syndrome 'is the difficulty faced by organisations, and in particular young companies such as start-ups, where one or more founders maintain disproportionate power and influence following the effective initial establishment of the organisation, leading to a wide range of problems.'[1]* Ultimately, ITB carried on without me, in many iterations, and I carried on as well, learning to become less emotionally attached to my businesses. I also came to understand that they are not the vehicles for my identity either. My identity stays with me. Ultimately, you are failing in business if you are not constantly training your team to replace you. If that's not your goal, if your business relies on you for its success, then you aren't building a durable company. You should be able to look through the ranks of your company and see a multitude of stars and stars-in-the-making – people you help thrive and grow. And, if you have a functional business legacy, you should also be able to see many stars from your company now doing their thing in the wider world. If you're building a business that can't exist in your absence, you're building a vanity project. That's fine, but it's a different kind of thing.

It's interesting, but in this next phase of my life, I'm more inclined to building one of those. Rather than building companies with partners and the prospect of exponential commercial growth, I'm interested in creating a small container that can house my curiosity. As I mentioned, I talk about my life in chapters, and I think a lot about how you end one chapter and begin another. I believe I'm done – for the minute – building new brands. I've done it a lot. I'm thinking more about what it looks like to reach people's minds and to teach what I've learned. And I'm also looking to create

---

\* If you fear you have 'founderitis' and want to read a brutal Wikipedia entry, the one on 'founder's syndrome' is for you.

something with more meaning for myself, where I can continue to learn alongside you.

For most of my career, I've been focused on growth and making things as big as possible; now, I want to do things that are small, yet maybe even more impactful. I want to build something that can be done in a single room with five people – yet reach millions. I want to understand what it would feel like to live with a little bit more space in my life, where each day isn't compressed with meetings and I have a bit more time to think, or even have a coffee after school drop-off – can you imagine that this has happened to me just once?! I'm curious to see what might happen in the absence of so much pressure, or how I might act with even more room to breathe. As always, I'm interested in action.

If you've been tracking the structure of this book, you'll know that we started with VISION before MANAGING OUR EMOTIONS and then addressing OLD THOUGHTS. It's my belief that if you can get a handle on how you feel about the world around you and clear your mind of limiting stories, then you're in the best possible position to take the correct ACTION! While I can't prescribe the specific actions that you should take in your life or in your business, I can show you how I set myself up to take the right ones – or at least actions that are most aligned with where I want to go in my life (back to VISION). I act all the time. It's how I learn, it's how I get my energy, it's how I understand the world.

I learned about action growing up in East London, where everyone is always on the go, hustling. Anyone reading this from my old neighbourhood will recognise these principles as our basic operating manual, and they continue to guide how I show up in the world today. None of them will surprise you; they're woven into this book, and they're dead simple:

1. Do what you say you're going to do, show up.
(Decide what you're going to do with a clear heart and mind.)

2. Your word is king, always tell the truth.
(It doesn't have to be the 'brutal truth', the truth is good enough.)

3. Stay in motion.
(You always have to be learning to be in contact with the world.)

That's it. These are the basic principles that guide the actions I take in my life.

I want to reiterate another point I've made throughout this book: you can't build anything of value by yourself. Everything you do will be better by bringing other people into it, to teach you what you don't know, to add strength where you might be weak, to give you leverage on your time and energy, and to give you an honest reflection of how you're showing up in the world. I always hear from people, *Emma, you do so much*. I really don't. When it comes down to it, I make decisions and I make decisions quickly, and those are often the right decisions because I have a lot of practice and I pay a lot of attention to the world. You can learn to do this, too.

But never underestimate the impact or importance of a team. There is an army that helps me, both at home and at work, and I never want to lie about that to other women, because it keeps the whole story going that we should do it all with grace and a full face of glam. I don't do it all. Not even remotely. I don't cook (though I love to), I don't clean, I don't mow the lawn or water my plants; I have two nannies at all times for my four kids, I have a personal trainer who comes to my house, and the budget for self-care. I largely get to do what I want because I've created a lot of optionality in my life through stacked success and an excellent team. You can do this, too. Don't laugh, you can. It might take a minute, but it is absolutely possible to build a supported life where you get to dream big and deliver against the vision you have for the world. I'm proof positive that this is a potentiality. I'm incredibly privileged now, but at one point, in the not very distant past, I was a young Black girl with absolute shit for prospects. I knew I had enough, though, because I had myself. You, too, can start there.

## MY BASIC RULES FOR SUCCESS

1. I shifted my mindset from blaming the circumstances of my life to taking complete responsibility for myself.
2. I worked really hard in my twenties, which is a defining decade for everyone.
3. I included details in my plans for my future: how, when, where and what, though I mostly focused on what I wanted it to feel like.
4. I found a really supportive partner.
5. I established myself in my career before I had babies.
6. I made selfish professional decisions, like leaving opportunities when the time was right for me – it's okay to be most loyal to yourself.
7. I leveraged every job, position or contact to help me do the next thing.
8. I moved far away from people who didn't serve me.
9. I learned to call BS, including on myself.
10. I failed up. I stepped into jobs that were bigger than the reality of my experience.
11. I got up after I failed and continued to get up, learning each time.
12. I embraced crisis and used my own suffering as an opportunity for transformation.
13. I worked on things I care deeply about, like women's rights and economic justice, putting them at the centre of my businesses without making them about marketing.
14. I refused to be afraid of anyone.

And to this day, I always start with myself.

# Acknowledgements

There are so many people I want to thank, but in the spirit of Snoop Dogg, I need to Start with Myself. No seriously! I'm so proud of myself for doing this.

What I *also* know is true is that it took a hell of a lot of people to get me to the point where you can hold this actual book in your hands. First, I would like to thank my wonderful husband, Jens, for encouraging me and supporting me every single step of the way. I'm so grateful to have a partner in business *and* life who understands the meaning of true partnership and how to take the lead with our family to give me the freedom to pursue yet another project. Jens, your love, patience and kindness know no bounds.

To my beautiful children, Grey, Lola, Lake and Raffi: I hope one day you read this book and take a sense of pride in what I do and understand why it is so very important to me. To my entire extended family, for always looking out for me, for your never-ending love and for giving me a sense of security that has set me up for life. To my mum, Jenny-Lee: thank you for raising a girl who truly believes anything is possible – so long as you're willing to work hard for it. I have my mindset because of you. To my sisters, Charlotte, Rachelle and Katie-Beth, who know every part of me: I love you all dearly.

To my incredible team: first, my right hand Derrick Brown (my numero uno) and my agent, Caroline Simionescu-Marin: I literally would never have written this book without you both. I'm grateful every day for the endless work, friendship, encouragement, patience and belief that comes from the two of you, and I'm so happy you have each other to commiserate with! I love you both. To Jill Smoller: thank you for being a no-BS agent and never lying to me. To Alyssa Reuben: I appreciate your unwavering support, for really pushing me to do this book and for answering all my basic-bitch questions along the way. To my wider WME team: I'm grateful to know you all and have you on my side making everything I do make sense and make money! Thank you to Amanda Silverman and my team at Lede PR. Thank you to Jazmin Zamora for having my back. Last, but not least on the team front, thank you, Brittany Smith, my incredible EA, who keeps me on track, helps me organise my work and thoughts, and keeps everything else together: I'm grateful beyond measure.

I write in this book – and speak all the time – about finding the right people to work with to bring every project to life, and this book is no exception. I am beyond fortunate to have found Elise Loehnen, who worked side by side with me to help write this book and guide this project. Elise was the perfect choice and a serendipitous match given her work around the cultural conditioning of women, herself a *New York Times* bestselling author of *On Our Best Behavior: The Price Women Pay to Be Good*. Elise understood exactly what I was trying to do in these pages and brought a depth of knowledge and experience, serving as a critical thought partner for me throughout the process. I'm forever grateful to Elise and her brilliant, brilliant mind.

My immense gratitude goes to Shannon Welch at Avid Reader Press: Shannon, thank you for believing in this project from the very beginning and for editing and publishing my book. It was my dream to have someone so supportive, someone who would not change what I wanted to do – you lived up to all my ideals. Thank you to the entire Avid Reader Press team for your careful attention and stewardship of this project: Meredith Vilarello, Ilana Gold, Jofie Ferrari-Adler, Ben Loehnen, Alison Forner, Clay Smith, Alicia Brancato, Megan Noes, Annalea Manalili, Jessica Chin, Kayla Dee, Chelsey Drysdale, Elisa

Rivlin and Katya Wiegmann. Thank you to Erik Torstensson for putting his magic touch on the cover design.

An immense and heartfelt thank-you to my teams at Good American, SKIMS, Safely, *Aspire* and Off Season. I'm endlessly inspired by the talented women and men who make these incredible companies work. A special mention and immeasurable thanks must go to Melissa Anderson and Lindsey Frawley, who have both given so much to me personally and professionally. I have learned so much from both of you since moving to LA and would never have experienced as much success as I have without the knowledge and expertise you have shared with me.

To my business partners and investors Andrew Rosen, Josh Kushner, John Howard and Nick Brown: thank you for your ongoing guidance and support. Thank you to Kim Kardashian, Kris Jenner and Khloé Kardashian for the years of partnership.

Thank you to every guest I've had the opportunity to learn from on my podcast, *Aspire with Emma Grede*, especially Mellody Hobson, Michelle Obama, Mark Cuban and Michael Rubin.

There are so many people in East London who helped me grow myself up. There is no place like it, and so I have to thank the whole of East London for making me who I am. I want to give a specific shout-out to Perry, for being so good to me when I had nothing to offer in return.

Thank you to my best friends Chenelle Hall, Melissa Wolford, Holly Scott Lidgett, Etty Bellhouse and Poppy Bartlett: you are my greatest cheerleaders while also being honest to a fault – this keeps my feet on the ground. You are the best friends a girl could ask for.

Last but by no means least, I am so thankful to the community of followers and listeners who have joined me on this journey. As I explain in the book, I don't think I've been so successful simply so I can make a lot of money or just live out my dreams. I think I've been successful so I can help other people do the same. Nothing makes me happier than passing on what I've learned to all of you. I hope you find yourself Starting with Yourself, too.

# Notes

### PART ONE: VISION
1. I go through this process in depth in a birthday-timed podcast of *Aspire with Emma Grede* called 'Plan Your Life Like a Business'. This episode also includes many tips and tricks for planning and habit stacking.

### PART TWO: MANAGING EMOTIONS
1. James J. Gross et al., 'Gender Differences in Emotion Regulation: An fMRI Study of Cognitive Reappraisal', *Group Processes & Intergroup Relations* 11, no. 2 (April 2008): 143–62, https://pubmed.ncbi.nlm.nih.gov/29743808.

## 1: ANGER
1. Prentis Hemphill, *What It Takes to Heal: How Transforming Ourselves Can Change the World* (Random House, 2024), 81.

## 2: FEAR
1. Gay Hendricks, *The Big Leap: Conquer Your Hidden Fear and Take Life to the Next Level* (HarperOne, 2010), 17–18.
2. Kelly McGonigal's *The Upside of Stress: Why Stress Is Good for You, and How to Get Good at It* (Avery, 2015) is a great read on this topic.
3. Barry Michels and Phil Stutz's tool 'Reversal of Desire', which you can read about in *The Tools*, is an excellent tool for moving through fear and pain.

## 3: GUILT
1. Elise Loehnen's chapter on 'Sloth' in *On Our Best Behavior: The Price Women Pay to Be Good* (Dial Press, 2023) covers a lot of this ground if you want to understand where some of these stories about women and work come from.
2. C. G. Jung, 'The Collected Works of C. G. Jung, Volume 15: Spirit, Man, Art, and Literature' (Bollingen Series: 2023), para. 4, https://jungiancenter.org/wp-content/uploads/2023/09/vol-15-the-spirit-in-man-art-and-literature.pdf.
3. Michelle Obama, 'Aspire with Michelle Obama and Craig Robinson: The Power of Knowing Your "Why"', *Aspire with Emma Grede*, 24 June 2025, Audacy, 1:17:33, https://podcasts.apple.com/us/podcast/aspire-with-michelle-obama-and-craig-robinson/id1811878340?i=1000714315259.

## 5: JOY

1. Mark Cuban, 'The Aspire Playbook: Mark Cuban's Day-1 Blueprint for Startup Success and How AI Is Changing Entrepreneurship Forever', *Aspire with Emma Grede*, 15 July 2025, Audacy, 29:29, https://podcasts.apple.com/us/podcast/the-aspire-playbook-mark-cubans-day-1-blueprint-for/id1811878340?i=1000717298123.

## PART THREE: OLD THOUGHTS

1. Summer Allen, PhD, 'The Science of Gratitude', Greater Good Science Center, UC Berkeley, May 2018, https://ggsc.berkeley.edu/images/uploads/GGSC-JTF_White_Paper-Gratitude-FINAL.pdf.
2. Snoop Dogg, 'Watch: Snoop Dogg Thanks Himself After Receiving Hollywood Star', 23 November 2018, Euronews, YouTube, 0:31, https://www.youtube.com/watch?v=NfF3bThOW0Q.

## 1: TRADE-OFFS

1. Obama, 'Aspire with Michelle Obama and Craig Robinson', at 1:13:51.
2. Ellen J. Langer, *The Mindful Body: Thinking Our Way to Chronic Health* (Ballantine Books, 2023), 75.
3. Langer, *The Mindful Body*, 72.
4. Langer, *The Mindful Body*, 73.
5. Elise Loehnen and Phil Stutz, *True and False Magic: A Tools Workbook* (Random House Trade Paperbacks, 2025), 98.
6. Dr Sunita Sah, *Defy: The Power of No in a World That Demands Yes* (One World, 2025), 24.
7. Per one meta analysis, 'attractiveness increased one's chance of getting a job' (Jonny Mattson and I. M. Jawahar, 'Sexism and Beautyism Effects in Selection as a Function of Self-Monitoring Level of Decision Maker', *Journal of Applied Psychology* 90, no. 3 (May 2005): https://pubmed.ncbi.nlm.nih.gov/15910150/), the assessment of employee's potential (Madeline E. Heilman and Melanie H. Stopeck, 'Being Attractive, Advantage or Disadvantage? Performance-Based Evaluations and Recommended Personnel Actions as a Function of Appearance, Sex, and Job Type', *Organizational Behavior and Human Decision Processes* 35, no. 2 (April 1985): https://www.sciencedirect.com/science/article/abs/pii/0749597885900354; C. M. Marlowe, C. E. Nelson and S. L. Schneider, 'Gender and Attractiveness Biases in Hiring Decisions: Are More Experienced Managers Less Biased?', *Journal of Applied Psychology* 81, no. 1 (1996): https://psycnet.apa.org/doiLanding?doi=10.1037%2F0021-9010.81.1.11) and the likelihood to obtain recommendations for salary raises and promotions (Heilman and Stopeck, 'Being Attractive, Advantage or Disadvantage?'). However, beauty can be 'beastly' for female candidates. Attractive women were considered less qualified, were less likely to be recommended and were perceived as deserving lower salaries when being evaluated for male-typed jobs (e.g., D. S. Burns, T. F. Cash and B. Gillen, 'Sexism and Beautyism in Personnel Consultant Decision Making', *Journal of Applied Psychology* 62, no. 3 (1977):

https://psycnet.apa.org/doiLanding?doi=10.1037%2F0021-9010.62.3.301; Madeline E. Heilman and Lois R. Saruwatari, 'When Beauty Is Beastly: The Effects of Appearance and Sex on Evaluations of Job Applicants for Managerial and Nonmanagerial Jobs', *Organizational Behavior and Human Performance* 23, no. 3 (June 1979): https://www.sciencedirect.com/science/article/abs/pii/0030507379900035); Elisabetta Crocetti et al., 'The "Ginevra de' Benci Effect": Competence, Morality, and Attractiveness Inferred from Faces Predict Hiring Decisions for Women', *Frontiers in Psychology* 12 (May 2021): https://doi.org/10.3389/fpsyg.2021.658424.
8. There's a great discussion of this in Renee Engeln, PhD's *Beauty Sick: How the Cultural Obsession with Appearance Hurts Girls and Women* (Harper Paperbacks, 2018).

## 2: MONEY

1. Mellody Hobson, 'Aspire with Mellody Hobson: What I Learned from My Business Hero', *Aspire with Emma Grede,* 6 May 2025, Audacy, 43:28, https://podcasts.apple.com/us/podcast/aspire-with-mellody-hobson-what-i-learned-from-my/id1811878340?i=1000706489071.
2. Lynne Twist, *The Soul of Money: Transforming Your Relationship with Money and Life* (W. W. Norton & Co., 2017), 65.
3. *Chris Rock: Kill the Messenger,* written by Chris Rock, directed by Marty Callner, aired 27 September 2008, on HBO, https://www.hbomax.com/movies/chris-rock-kill-the-messenger/ef53f4c5-8a37-45f1-9f2f-bd635f320c9f.
4. Obama, 'Aspire with Michelle Obama and Craig Robinson', at 1:29:35.
5. Hobson, 'Aspire with Mellody Hobson', at 41:30.
6. Mori Taheripour, *Bring Yourself: How to Harness the Power of Connection to Negotiate Fearlessly* (Avery, 2020), 9.
7. Hobson, 'Aspire with Mellody Hobson', at 44:43.
8. Taheripour, *Bring Yourself,* 50.
9. Taheripour, *Bring Yourself,* 14.

## 3: CAREER

1. Michelle Obama, 'Michelle Obama: "I Still Have Imposter Syndrome"', *BBC,* 4 December 2018, https://www.bbc.com/news/uk-46434147.
2. Carol S. Dweck, PhD, *Mindset: The New Psychology of Success* (Ballantine Books, 2006), 58.
3. Sah, *Defy,* 54.
4. M. Isabel Sánchez-Hernández et al., 'Work-Life Balance in Great Companies and Pending Issues for Engaging New Generations at Work', *International Journal of Environmental Research and Public Health* 16, no. 24 (December 2019): 5122, https://doi.org/10.3390/ijerph16245122.
5. Cuban, 'The Aspire Playbook', at 41:26.
6. Hobson, 'Aspire with Mellody Hobson', at 10:44.
7. Hobson, 'Aspire with Mellody Hobson', at 35:59.

## 4: FAMILY

1. Kurt Gray, *Outraged: Why We Fight About Morality and Politics and How to Find Common Ground* (Pantheon, 2025), 89.
2. Gray, *Outraged*, 92.
3. 'Women, Power, and Money in 2024 and Beyond', DealBook Summit 2024, 11 December 2024, *New York Times Events*, YouTube, https://www.youtube.com/watch?v=5gxCXYJAgwA.

## 5: BUILDING A BRAND & BUSINESS

1. Cuban, 'The Aspire Playbook', at 1:23:44.
2. Obama, 'Aspire with Michelle Obama and Craig Robinson', at 54:29.
3. Stutz, *True and False Magic*, 51–52.
4. Hobson, 'Aspire with Mellody Hobson', at 54:21.
5. Michael Rubin, 'The Founder Playbook: How Michael Rubin Built Fanatics by Betting on Obsession', *Aspire with Emma Grede*, 13 May 2025, Audacy, 29:30, https://podcasts.apple.com/us/podcast/the-founder-playbook-how-michael-rubin-built-fanatics/id1811878340?i=1000708288260.

## 6: LEADERSHIP

1. Cuban, 'The Aspire Playbook', at 1:20:45.
2. Emma Grede, 'The Woman That Makes Millionaires: They're Lying About Work-Life Balance! I Built SKIMS Without Fashion Knowledge!', *The Diary of a CEO* with Steven Bartlett, 4 May 2025, Flight Studio, 41:09, https://podcasts.apple.com/ca/podcast/the-woman-that-makes-millionaires-theyre-lying-about/id1291423644?i=1000706316314.
3. Hobson, 'Aspire with Mellody Hobson', at 31:39.
4. Faisal Hoque, 'Why Most Venture-Backed Companies Fail', *Fast Company*, 10 December 2012, https://www.fastcompany.com/3003827/why-most-venture-backed-companies-fail.

## PART FOUR: ACTION!

1. 'Founder's syndrome', Wikipedia, Wikimedia Foundation, last modified 16 September 2025, https://en.wikipedia.org/wiki/Founder%27s_syndrome.

# My Favourite Books About Business & Life

*Mindset: The New Psychology of Success,* by Carol S. Dweck, PhD
*Principles: Life and Work*, by Ray Dalio
*What I Know for Sure,* by Oprah Winfrey
*What They Don't Teach You at Harvard Business School: Notes from a Street-Smart Executive,* by Mark McCormack
*Trillion Dollar Coach: The Leadership Playbook of Silicon Valley's Bill Campbell,* by Eric Schmidt, Marcus Rosenberg and Alan Eagle
*BE 2.0 (Beyond Entrepreneurship 2.0): Turning Your Business into an Enduring Great Company,* by Jim Collins and Bill Lazier
*Daring Greatly: How the Courage to Be Vulnerable Transforms the Way We Live, Love, Parent, and Lead,* by Brené Brown
*The Five Dysfunctions of a Team: A Leadership Fable,* by Patrick Lencioni
*Good to Great: Why Some Companies Make the Leap . . . and Others Don't,* by Jim Collins
*Management in Ten Words: Practical Advice from the Man Who Created One of the World's Largest Retailers,* by Terry Leahy
*Lean In: Women, Work, and the Will to Lead,* by Sheryl Sandberg
*The Moment of Lift: How Empowering Women Changes the World,* by Melinda French Gates
*The Power of Habit: Why We Do What We Do in Life and Business,* by Charles Duhigg

*The Tools: Transform Your Problems into Courage, Confidence, and Creativity,* by Barry Michels and Phil Stutz

*Tools of Titans: The Tactics, Routines, and Habits of Billionaires, Icons, and World-Class Performers,* by Tim Ferriss

*The Untethered Soul: The Journey Beyond Yourself,* by Michael A. Singer

*What Happened to You? Conversations on Trauma, Resilience, and Healing,* by Bruce D. Perry, MD, PhD, and Oprah Winfrey

# Thoughts

## THOUGHTS

# THOUGHTS

# THOUGHTS

# Index

ABC Supply Co., 214
abundance, 98, 99
action, 269–75
   guiding principles for, 273–74
adjacencies, 209–10
aesthetic, 191–93, 209, 210
affiliative care, 32
agency, 48
alignment, 235
Allen, Robert, 185
alloparenting, 32
Amazon, 162
ambition, 60, 62, 63, 70, 120, 121, 124, 172, 195, 223, 225, 248
   for children, 136
   motherhood and, 151
   too-small, 173
   in women, 239–47
Anderson, Melissa, 105, 125
Angelou, Maya, 124, 191, 210
anger, xiii, 17, 19–23, 42, 184
Anthony, Carmelo, 77
Apple, 166, 203
   iPhone, 105, 204
Ariel Investments, 83, 129, 255–56
Arnault, Bernard, 167, 219
*Aspire with Emma Grede* podcast, 33–34, 75, 91, 93, 148, 173, 206, 214, 236
attractiveness, 71–73
Aurelia PR, 8

Baby2Baby, 260, 263
banks, 161, 162n
Barber, Deshauna, 164
Bartlett, Steven, 119, 241–43, 266n
Barton, Bruce, 169
B Corp certification, 260, 261
beauty, 71–73
Bel Air, 37, 43
Black-owned businesses, 262, 264–66

blame, 21–22, 49
blind spots, 187
Bloomingdale's, 107n
Blow, Isabella, 219–20
body dysmorphia, 72–73
*Book, Le,* 111
boom-and-bust, 164–65
bosses, 28, 29, 118, 222–23
boundaries, 23, 115
brands, 263
   Black-owned, 262, 264–66
   celebrities and, 156–57
   disruptive, 205–6
   DTC (direct-to-consumer), 165, 205–6
   founders as face of, 197–98, 262–63
   heritage, 191
   loyalty to, 193
   personal brand and, 70
   *see also* building a brand and business
*Bring Yourself* (Taheripour), 96, 98, 99
British National Party (BNP), 26
Brother Vellies, 264
Brown, Rita Mae, 51n
Brunello Cucinelli, 191
Buffalo Bills, 163
Buffett, Warren, 54, 129, 186, 247
building a brand and business, 155–220
   and adding complexities to core business, 202
   business plans in, 158, 172
   competition and, 205–10
   and doing one big thing, 169–74
   failure and, 180–84
   and getting bigger and better, 164–68
   and good brand and marketing as all you need, 191–99
   and knowing the right people, 210–15
   negative feedback and, 185–90
   passion and, 174–80
   and raising capital, 157–64

building a brand and business (*cont.*)
  shortcuts in, 199–205, 208
  transactional relationships in, 215–20

cab drivers, 39
CAKES body, 175–77
Calvin Klein, 198
cancellation, 241–43
Capuano, Taylor, 175–77
career, 101–31
  ambition and, 60, 62, 63, 70, 124
  and asking questions, 114, 126
  and being naturally good at things, 110–15
  and being qualified for the role you want, 102–10
  child-raising and, 54–59, 63, 148–53
  effort in, 121–22
  genius and, 115
  and making other people comfortable, 115–19
  mentorship and, 124–31
  opportunities in, 61, 67, 68, 124–31
  and putting yourself first, 61–62
  responsibility for, 131
  self-care and, 59–60, 62
  wants and needs and, 119
  work-life balance and, 119–24, 130
celebrities, 156–57, 190, 233, 263
CEOs, 231–32
  replacement of, 161
CFOs, 229, 231
Chait, Greg, 191
challenge stress, 27–28
Chanel, Coco, 250
change, 158, 169, 183, 191, 249
  small, 173
children
  honesty and, 245–46
  *see also* motherhood and children; parenting
Christmas, 142
choices, 53
  *see also* trade-offs
CMOs, 231
Coca-Cola, 166
Coelho, Paulo, 45
Cole, Pinky, 78
Collins, Jim, 130, 223, 225
comfort zone, 227
community, 211, 213–14
  Los Angeles as, 180
  transactional relationships and, 215–20
comparison, 69, 89

competition, 196, 201, 205–10, 238
  investors and, 206–7
  shortcuts and, 208
  social media and, 205
  within businesses, 230
complacency, 183
compounding, 155–56
compromise, 62
concept creep, 138
conferences, 213, 218
conflict, 187
Confucius, 148
connected adjacencies, 209–10
control, 51
cool factor, 166
COVID pandemic, 162
Crawford, Cindy, 198
creativity, 192
criticism, 159, 188, 190, 227
  *see also* feedback
CSR (corporate social responsibility), 263–64
Cuban, Mark, 41, 43, 126, 159, 175, 236–37
culture, 168, 172, 182, 197, 208, 209, 216–17
  leadership and, 224, 225, 235, 238, 241, 245, 254, 259–60, 267
curiosity, 109, 110, 114, 126–28, 136, 140, 260, 272
Current/Elliott, 166
customers
  feedback from, 188, 189
  pricing and, 199
  underserved, 196–97, 257–58, 262
  values and, 261–62
  viewpoint of, 238

daily routines, 235
danger, 138
Dantzig, George, 109–10
DealBook Summit, 148
death, psychological, 183–84
decisions, 28–29, 231, 235, 247, 274
  customer and, 238
  intuition and, 66
  rightness of, 63–68
  vibe and, 66–67
*Defy* (Sah), 66
DEI, 254, 256–64
delegation, 64–65, 236
denim, 166, 170, 198, 209
  chafing and, 189
  Frame, 102, 207

Good American, 37, 102–9, 144–45, 148, 156, 161, 162, 166, 170, 171, 178, 188–89, 192, 196–98, 207–9, 216, 225, 226, 233–34, 237–38, 248, 253, 256–58, 260, 271
   Levi's, 207–8
depression, 36, 65
details, 130–31, 208–9, 227
Detroit Lions, 163
*Diary of a CEO, The,* 119, 241–43, 266n
differentiation, 209, 210
discipline, 130, 235
Disney (company), 231
Disney, Walt, 129
disruptors, 205–6
distribution, 196, 199
diversity, 254, 259
downsizing, 181
downturns, 167, 168
Doyle, Glennon, 25
*Dragons' Den,* xii
*Dreams from My Father* (Obama), 91
DreamWorks, 255
dressing rooms, 188–89
DTC (direct-to-consumer) brands, 165, 205–6
Duckett, Thasunda Brown, 152
Dweck, Carol, 109

Earl Jean, 166
EBITDA, 158
Edelman, Marian Wright, 1
education, 110–13, 136, 219
ego, 223, 225, 232, 245
Einstein, Albert, 51
Elder Statesman, The, 191–92
Eliot, George, 221
Elliott, Missy, 198
Emmons, Robert, 47
emotions, xiii, 15–18, 29, 37, 44, 184, 273
   anger, xiii, 17, 19–23, 42, 184
   as body-based, 18
   equanimity and, 184
   fear, xiii, 17–18, 25–30, 42, 57, 102, 158–59, 183, 184
   guilt, xiii, 18, 31–34, 49, 55, 57–59
   journalling and, 37–38
   joy, 41–44, 54
   sadness, xiii, 35–40, 184
empathy, 240–41
employee mentality, 28, 92–93, 221–23
employees
   employer partnership with, 101–2
   exit interviews and, 224
   hiring of, 228–29, 233, 240, 250, 254, 260
   letting go of, 225, 240–44, 249–50
   new, feedback from, 238
   promotions and pay rises for, 128, 225, 241
   social contract with, 243
   teams, 223–25, 228–31, 235, 236, 240, 244–45, 248, 272, 274
   turnover of, 244–45
empowerment, 49–50
end point, 173
energy, 41, 59, 72, 115, 127, 134, 253
   focusing on other people, 136
   negative, 182
enterprise mentality, 223, 241, 243, 247
entitlement, 127
entrepreneurs, 155–57
   etymology of word, 155, 178
   founder's syndrome and, 272
   and selling company, 264–65
   serial, 169
   women, 231–33, 248–49, 252, 263–67
   *see also* building a brand and business; leaders, leadership
equanimity, 184
ERP (enterprise resource planning), 227–28
Estée Lauder Companies, 101, 188
eustress, 27–28
event invitations, 210–15
excitement, 27
excuses, 188
exit interviews, 224
expectations, 34, 60, 127, 227
experts, 129–30, 230

Facebook, 232
factoring, 161–62
failure, 70, 158–59, 164, 177–78, 180–85
   leadership and, 266
   learning from, 184–85
   as opportunity, 183
   resilience for, 183, 184
   as signal to stop, 180–84
   women and, 266
fairness, 22–23, 88–89
*Fair Play* (Rodsky), 147
fame, 197
family, 133–53
   career and, 55–59, 63
   colleagues as, 247–50

family (*cont.*)
  time spent with, 142
  and working with your romantic partner, 144–48
  work-life balance and, 119–24
  *see also* motherhood and children
Fanatics, 75, 163, 199–200
fashion designers, 9–10
fathers, 152–53
favours, 220
fear, xiii, 17–18, 25–30, 42, 57, 102, 158–59, 183, 184
feedback, 158, 179, 185, 190, 193, 195, 224, 225, 260
  from customers, 188, 189
  as gift, 186
  negative, 185–90
  from new employees, 238
  rejection as, 178
fiefdoms, 235
Fifteen Per cent Pledge, 263, 264
finances, *see* money
fires, 138
first, being, 206
first offer as best offer, 165, 166
flexibility, 129, 158
focus, 236, 239
focus groups, 193
FOMO (fear of missing out), 210, 212
*Forbes,* xi, 107
Ford, Henry, 180
forgiveness, 23, 41
Fortune 500 companies, 152
founder's syndrome, 272
Frame, 102, 207
Frawley, Lindsey, 125
friends, 35–37, 39, 211
  business and, 219, 220
  investors as, 159
  networking and, 216
Furstenberg, Diane von, 133, 211

Galloway, Scott, 144
Garza, Veronica, 264
genius, 115, 220
  zone of, 202–3
Gerber, Kaia, 198
Gharani Strok, 8–9
Girdler, Jamie, 248
giving and receiving, 215
goals, 70, 173, 225, 236, 239, 240
Good American, 37, 102–9, 144–45, 148, 156, 161, 162, 166, 170, 171, 178, 188–89, 192, 196–98, 207–9, 216, 225, 226, 233–34, 237–38, 248, 253, 256–58, 260, 271
*Good to Great* (Collins), 130, 223
Graham, Ashley, 201–2
Granat, Kelly, 212
gratitude, 47–48, 50, 135
Gray, Kurt, 138
Grede, Emma
  childhood of, x–xi, 3–7, 18, 20, 26, 31–32, 37, 41–44, 68–69, 90, 91, 138, 150, 178, 239, 240, 265, 273, 275
  dyslexia of, xi, 7, 113, 229
  education of, xi, 110–13, 125
  fashion school attended by, x, xi, 7–8, 22, 32
  father of, x, 43
  fertility issues of, 149–50
  gratitude practice of, 47, 135
  house of, 3
  internships of, 9, 94, 112
  jobs of, 6–11, 37, 39, 60n, 67–68, 76, 86–87, 94–95, 112–13, 118, 125, 178, 254–55
  journal kept by, 37–38
  meditation practice of, 38–39, 140
  mental illness in family of, 36
  mother of, x–xi, 6n, 7, 20, 31–32, 41–43, 55–56, 64, 68–69, 79–80, 90
  motherhood and children of, xi, 3, 31–34, 35, 38, 41, 42, 44, 47, 54–59, 63, 64, 80, 102, 111, 121, 133, 134, 136, 137, 139–43, 149–51, 183, 245–46, 271, 274
  nannies of, 141n, 274
  nonprofit work of, 263
  piano lessons and, 135–36
  podcast of, 33–34, 75, 91, 93, 148, 173, 206, 214, 236
  recognisability of, 197, 214
  'Seat at the Table' dinner series of, 210–12, 251
  sisters of, 31–32, 39, 68–69, 125, 150, 254
  yearly plan of, 11–13, 58–59
Grede, Emma, businesses of, xi, xii, 36, 37, 42, 43, 60, 67, 169, 233, 272
  collaborations in, 193, 233, 263
  Emma's identity and, 252–53, 272
  employee departures from, 247–48
  equity deals and, 103
  Good American, 37, 102–9, 144–45, 148, 156, 161, 162, 166, 170, 171, 178, 188–89, 192, 196–98, 207–9, 216, 225, 226, 233–34, 237–38, 248, 253, 256–58, 260, 271

ITB, 60, 92–93, 102, 103, 106, 131, 145, 156, 169–72, 180–82, 221–22, 243–44, 248, 256, 263, 271–72
  Jens and, 144–48
  leverage and, 233
  Off Season, 148, 163–64, 192–93, 199–201, 232
  Saturday Group and, 67, 94–96, 102, 145, 221
  SKIMS, 144–45, 148, 167, 203, 209
Grede, Jens (husband), xi, 3, 28, 33, 42, 44, 47, 56, 71, 72, 80, 96, 123, 135, 146, 147, 150, 164, 169, 184, 207, 218, 271
  as Emma's business partner, 144–48
  on employee mentality, 92–93, 221–22
  Frame business of, 102, 207
  Good American and, 103, 106
  marriage proposal of, 25–26
  money and, 79, 83–84, 90, 169
  networking and, 218
  Saturday Group business of, 67, 94–96, 102, 145, 221
  SKIMS and, 144–45
grief, 37
growth, 178, 184, 213
  mindset, 110, 114
  nonlinear, 183
G-STAR, 198
guilt, xiii, 18, 31–34, 49, 55, 57–59
Guinness, Daphne, 219

Haiti, 192
H&M, 259
happiness, 42, 44, 65, 123
  of others, 143
Harlech, Amanda, 219
harm, concept of, 138
Harvey Nichols, 248
having it all, 53–54, 63
Heath, Duncan, 190
Hemphill, Prentis, 23
Hendricks, Diane, 214
Hendricks, Gay and Katie, 202–3
Hobson, Mellody, 83, 93, 97, 129–30, 188, 255–56
Hoffman Process, 41
Holmes, Elizabeth, 267
honesty, 179, 187, 188, 190, 193, 201, 274
  brutal, 188, 274
  children and, 245–46
  from customers, 188, 189
  leadership and, 224, 225, 232, 240, 243–47, 250, 260

  Los Angeles culture and, 180–82
  women and, 185–86
horizontal hostility, 265
Hrdy, Sarah Blaffer, 32
hubris, 165, 185, 207
Hudson, 166
humility, 223, 225
Hunter, Bailey, 191
hustling, 121, 155, 179
hype, 213
hypervigilance, 138

'I can't' versus 'I won't', 115
identity, 252–53, 272
Iger, Bob, 231
Iman, 211
imposter syndrome, 109, 228, 239
Independent Talent, 221
individualism, 198, 242
Industrial Revolution, 138
insinuation anxiety, 117
inspiration, 174
Instagram, 56, 57, 104, 142, 163, 197, 200, 212–14, 218, 219
instincts, 30, 66
integrity, 34, 247, 251, 261
intention, 172, 173
internships, 9, 94, 112
intuition, 66
investors, 159–60, 174, 177, 186
  CEO replacement and, 161
  competitive landscape and, 206–7
  as friends, 159
  as mentors, 175–77
  relational patterns and, 160
  seeing clearly, 160–61
  *Shark Tank,* xii, 174, 175
  VC funding, 82–83, 131, 158, 266
iPhone, 105, 204
IPOs, 172
ITB Worldwide, 60, 92–93, 102, 103, 106, 131, 145, 156, 169–72, 180–82, 221–22, 243–44, 248, 256, 263, 271–72
Itzler, Jesse, 142
IVF, 149, 150

James, Aurora, 264
James, William, 15
Jefferson, Thomas, 199
Jenner, Kris, 103
Jobs, Steve, 129
Jordan, Michael, 102
journalling, 37–38
joy, 41–44, 54

Jung, Carl, 33, 139
Juszczyk, Kristin, 163, 164, 192–93, 199–201
Juszczyk, Kyle, 163

Kansas City Chiefs, 163
Kantor, Jodi, 148
Kardashian, Khloé, 103, 104, 198
Kardashian, Kim, 144–45
Kardashian family, 106
Kawaguchi, Toshikazu, 134
Kennedy, Florynce, 264, 265
Kimono, 145

Lagerfeld, Karl, 245
Lamott, Anne, 88
Lane Bryant, 257
Langer, Ellen, 65
Latifah, Queen, 198
Lauder, Estée, 101
launch, 192
leaders, leadership, 32–33, 102, 221–67
  Black, 262, 264–66
  CEO role and, 231–32
  and colleagues as family, 247–50
  of creative-led companies, 231, 232
  culture and, 224, 225, 235, 238, 241, 245, 254, 259–60, 267
  daily routines and, 235
  decision-making and, 231
  DEI and, 254, 256–64
  and doing it all yourself, 226–34, 237
  empathy and, 240–41
  employee mentality in, 28, 92–93, 221–23
  employee turnover and, 244–45
  enterprise mentality in, 223, 241, 243, 247
  expertise and, 230
  failure and, 266
  and feedback from new employees, 238
  female, 231–33, 248–49, 252, 263–67
  five stages of, 223
  hiring and, 228–29, 233, 240, 250, 254, 260
  honesty and, 224, 225, 232, 240, 243–47, 250, 260
  identity and, 252–53, 272
  legacy of, 272
  and letting people go, 225, 240–44, 249–50
  leverage and, 233, 234
  likeability and, 239–47
  limitations and, 232–34
  micromanagement and, 227–28, 230, 236–37
  opportunities and, 234–38
  philosophy for, 224–26
  priorities and, 234–36
  remote work and, 122–24
  self-consciousness and, 250–56
  and social contract with staff, 243
  social good and, 256–64
  successful, backlash against, 264–67
  and success of former employees, 248–49
  team of rivals and, 231
  teams and, 223–25, 228–31, 235, 236, 240, 244–45, 248, 272, 274
  T-shaped, 229–30
  vision and, 223, 225, 226, 228, 233–34, 236, 237, 241, 249, 253
  weaknesses and, 229–30
learning, 6, 109, 113, 114, 124, 126–29, 136, 174, 180
  from failure, 184–85
  from the best, 207, 228
leverage, 233, 234
Levi's, 207–8
licensing, 163, 170, 232
life chapters, 172, 174, 272
life force, 183
lifetime value (LTV), 158
likeability, 239–47
limbo land, 195
limitations, 232–34
Lincoln, Abraham, 92
loans, 161–62
London, ix, xiii, 4–6, 9, 19, 25–26, 35–37, 39, 57, 60, 69, 86, 90, 103, 111, 170, 195, 271, 273
  candour in, 180
  Fashion Week in, 9, 196
  Plaistow, 3, 5, 7, 26, 43–44, 239
London College of Fashion, x, xi, 7–8, 22, 32
loneliness, 35, 39
Lorimer, George, 234
Loro Piana, 191
Los Angeles, CA, 4, 39, 41, 60, 102, 103, 171, 271
  Bel Air, 37, 43
  as community, 180
  fires in, 138
  lack of honesty in, 180–82
  property in, 164
love, 39, 133, 135, 136
loving yourself, 134, 135

loyalty, 187, 245, 249
LVMH, 167

Macy's, 204
Madonna, 166–67, 198
Malls, Simon, 165
Marcus, ix–x, 7, 32
marketing, 191–99
　around founder, 197
　performative, 261
marriage
　working with your spouse, 144–48, 219
　*see also* family
matchmaking, 219–20
Maze, the, 22–23
McCullough, Michael, 47
McQueen, Alexander, 9, 219–20
media
　press, 196–98, 213
　*see also* social media
meditation, 38–39, 140
mentors, 124–31, 149, 174–75, 177, 213–15, 241
　investors as, 175–77
micromanagement, 227–28, 230, 236–37
Mielle Organics, 264
Milk Studios, 104
*Mindful Body, The* (Langer), 65
mindfulness, 65
mindset, xiii, 18, 29, 48–49, 65, 115
　both/and, 63, 76–77
　challenge stress and, 28
　either/or, 54–63, 76
　growth, 110, 114
　scarcity, 85–92, 98, 218
*Mindset* (Dweck), 109
mirrors and dressing rooms, 188–89
mistakes, 182, 224, 260
Moda Operandi, 173
money, 28, 42–43, 60–62, 75–99, 155, 169, 229n
　abundance mindset and, 98, 99
　distorted relationship with, 77
　facing and thinking about, 85
　healing relationship with, 78–79
　as foundational, 76
　investing, 81–82
　loans, 161–62
　men's ease in talking about, 83–84
　negotiating and, 92–99, 118
　as neutral, 84–85
　pay parity and, 88–89
　prices, 80, 194
　and putting yourself first, 92, 99

　raising capital, 157–64
　and reliance on boyfriend or husband, 79, 81
　reluctance to talk or think about, 75–85, 101
　and satisfaction with what you have, 92–99
　scarcity mindset and, 85–92, 98
　value and, 194, 219
motherhood and children, 31–34, 54–59, 63, 133, 135, 173, 183
　ambition and, 151
　and being kid-first, 133–34
　career and, 54–59, 63, 148–53
　childcare and, 141, 149
　egg freezing and, 148–49
　fertility issues and, 149–50
　and judgement for not having a career, 136–37
　parallel play and, 141–42
　and parenting as full-time, 136
　parents' unlived lives and, 139
　and responsibility for children's lives and safety, 135–44
　returning to the office after having a child, 150–51
　work flexibility and, 152, 153
　and working from home, 123
　*see also* family
Munger, Charlie, 110, 155, 201

natural disasters, 138
NBA, 163
negotiating, 92–99, 118
negative energy, 182
negative feedback, 185–90
Net-a-Porter, 108, 125
networking, 211, 212, 218
　effective, 215
　friendship and, 216
　versus building a network, 211, 213–14
Neumann, Adam, 266n
*New York Times,* 148, 152
NFL, 163
nice, being, 115–17, 185, 216–18, 246–47
Nike, 166, 211
no:
　hearing, 117–19, 126n
　saying, 115–18, 240, 241
no-man's-land, 195
Nordstrom, 107–9, 193, 204, 258
North Face, The, 167
NYDJ, 257

Obama, Barack, 91–92, 173
Obama, Michelle, 33–34, 53–54, 91–92, 109, 173
Obama Foundation, 25, 263
Off Season, 148, 163–64, 192–93, 199–201, 232
O'Leary, Kevin, 175
O'Neill, Heidi, 211
opinions, seeking out, 191
opportunities, 61, 67, 68, 89, 118, 124–31, 135, 155, 183
  children and, 136
  failures as, 183
  leadership and, 234–38
optimism, 43, 65
originality, 205
*Outraged* (Gray), 138
ownership stake, 165

P&G, 264–65
paradoxes, 174
parenting, 173, 183
  by fathers, 152–53
  of other adults, 140
  *see also* motherhood and children
Parsons, Dick, 188
Parton, Dolly, 35, 198
passion, 174–80
paternity leave, 152
P. Diddy White Party, 9n
PepsiCo, 264–65
perfection, 30, 54, 65, 68–73
  beauty and, 71–73
  effortless, 70
  perfection bias, 71
  perfectionism, 227, 228
  social media and, 69–70
Perls, Fritz, 27
personal brand, 70
perspective, 191, 193
Philadelphia Eagles, 163
Picasso, Pablo, 174
Picca, Vicky, 201, 232
Plaistow, 3, 5, 7, 26, 43–44, 239
plateaus, 194
play, 41–42
point of view, 193
power, 50, 265
pricing, 80, 194, 199
  distribution and, 196
priorities, 234–36
problem-solving, 27, 39, 109–10, 113, 114, 128, 167–68, 206, 236, 244, 261, 262, 264

procrastination, 157
Proctor, Bob, 215
product/market fit, 199
profitability, 158
promotions and pay rises, 128, 225, 241
proof of concept, 164
proximity, 122–24
pruning, 183
purpose, 158, 198

Quaglia, Renata, 172–73
qualifications, 102–10
Queen Latifah, 198
questions, asking, 114, 126
Quintessentially, 9, 113

racism, 259
recognition, 197
Rae, Déjà, 115
regret, 65, 67, 135, 164
rejection, 118, 178, 180, 182, 183, 227
  as feedback, 178
relationships, 23, 37, 39, 123, 131, 133, 187
  friendships, 35–37, 39
  investors and, 160
  and working with your romantic partner, 144–48, 219
  *see also* family; friends
relevancy curves, 165–69, 171
remote work, 122–24
RENATA.Q, 172–73
repeating patterns, 67–68
reputation, 247
requests, 215–17
resentment, 216, 236
resilience, 183, 184, 240
respect, 240
responsibility, 21–22, 41, 49, 61, 131
Rhimes, Shonda, 119
risks, 155, 156, 158, 164, 204, 269
Robinson, Craig, 33
Rock, Chris, 90
Rock & Republic, 166
Rodriguez, Monique, 264
Rodsky, Eve, 147
Rogers, Will, 31
Rosen, Andrew, 105
routines, daily, 235
royalties, 163
Rubin, Michael, 75, 199–201, 205, 206, 218
Rule of Thirds, 36, 42
ruminating, 65
Russell, Bertrand, 19

sacrifice, 62, 85
sadness, xiii, 35–40, 184
safety, 138, 269
Sah, Sunita, 66, 117
Saint Laurent, Yves, 196
Saks Fifth Avenue, 193
Sandberg, Sheryl, 232
San Francisco 49ers, 163
Sarai, Casey Capuano, 175–77
Sassoon, Vidal, 157
satisficing, 65
Saturday Group, 67, 94–96, 102, 145, 221
scale, 194, 195, 204, 239, 244
Scandinavia, 152
　Sweden, 181, 259
scarcity, 85–92, 98, 218
Schwartz, Barry, 65
'Seat at the Table' dinner series, 210–12, 251
self-care, 59–60, 62, 133–35
self-consciousness, 250–56
self-monitoring, 253
selling out, 264–65
Sephora, 195, 262
*Sex and the City*, 72, 101, 160
Shakur, Tupac, 37
*Shark Tank*, xii, 174, 175
Shields, Brooke, 198
Shopify, 104, 145
shortcuts, 199–205, 208
*Side Hustlers*, 201–2
Siete Foods, 264
SKIMS, 144–45, 148, 167, 203, 209
skinheads, 26
Slutty Vegan, 78
Snoop Dogg, 49
social good, 256–64
social life, 211
social media, 40, 42, 69–70, 176, 178, 196, 200, 211, 212, 214, 215
　competition and, 205
　Facebook, 232
　Instagram, 56, 57, 104, 142, 163, 197, 200, 212–14, 218, 219
　reprisals on, 241–43
　TikTok, 175, 176, 197, 201, 242
*Soul of Money, The* (Twist), 87
South Africa, 25, 26
Sowell, Thomas, 53
specialists, 129–30, 231
sport, 163–64, 192–93, 199–200, 232
　women in, 200–201
spouse, working with, 144–48, 219

stress, 28, 47
　challenge, 27–28
Stroop Test, 253
Stutz, Phil, 22–23, 65–66, 183–84
success, 39–40, 48, 51, 60, 90–91, 101, 122, 156, 157, 172, 182, 201, 239
　backlash against, 264–67
　family and, 55–59, 63
　models of, 89
　overnight, 178, 213
　passion and, 174–80
　personal brand and, 70
　rules for, 275
Super Bowl, 200
supply and demand, 204
sweat equity, 164, 173
Sweden, 181, 259
Swift, Taylor, 163
synergy, 233–34

Taheripour, Mori, 96, 98, 99
taste level, 209–10
team of rivals, 231
teams, 223–25, 228–31, 235, 236, 240, 244–45, 248, 272, 274
*Teen Vogue*, 248
thoughts, 44, 50, 51, 273
TikTok, 175, 176, 197, 201, 242
time spent with family, 142
Torrid, 257
Torstensson, Erik, 67, 94–95, 103, 169
Toshiba, 10
trade-offs, 53–73, 76
　both/and mindset and, 63, 76–77
　child-raising and career, 55–59, 63, 151
　either/or mindset and, 54–63, 76
　opportunities and, 61, 67, 68
　perfection and, 68–73
　planning and, 58–59
　and rightness of decisions, 63–68
　self-care and career, 59–60, 62
　work-life balance and, 119–24, 130
transactional relationships, 215–20
Transcendental Meditation, 38–39, 140
transitioning on the way up, 167–69, 171
trendsetting, 206
*True and False Magic* (Stutz), 22–23, 66, 183–84
trust, 237, 244
truth, *see* honesty
turnover, retail, 165
Twist, Lynne, 87

Ulta, 204
upselling, 188

valuation, 165, 184
value, and money, 194, 219
values, 34, 72, 167, 225, 247, 250, 260–61, 265
    consumers and, 261–62
    insinuation anxiety and, 117
VC funding, 82–83, 131, 158, 266
vibe, 66–67
vision, 1–13, 62, 172, 193, 273, 274
    leadership and, 223, 225, 226, 228, 233–34, 236, 237, 241, 249, 253
    yearly process in, 11–13, 58–59
*Vogue*, 5, 196
von Furstenberg, Diane, 133, 211

Walker, Alice, 239
Walmart, 198
weaknesses, 229–30
wealth generation, 265
weekends, 38
Westwood, Vivienne, 9
WeWork, 266n
wholesale strategy, 204
Wilde, Oscar, 68
Will.i.am, 103
Williams, Pharrell, 103
Williamson, Matthew, 9
Winfrey, Oprah, 22, 31, 75, 125, 134–35, 256
WNBA, 163
women, 214
    ambition in, 239–47
    attractiveness and, 71–73
    and being nice, 84, 115–17
    criticism of, 159
    empowerment and, 49–50
    entrepreneurs and leaders, 231–33, 248–49, 252, 263–67
    failure and, 266
    fear and, 158–59
    and feeling inadequate, 114
    helping other women, 215–18
    honesty and, 185–86
    money conversations and, 75–85
    motherhood and, *see* motherhood and children
    personal brand and, 70
    and putting others first, 61–62
    in sport, 200–201
    success models and, 89
    work benefits for, 148–49, 152
    and working from home, 123
Women for Women International, 263
Wooden, John, 63
work ethic, 60, 102, 121, 128, 130, 155, 156, 157, 174, 180
working from home, 122–24
working with your romantic partner, 144–48, 219
work-life balance, 119–24, 130
wrong, willingness to be, 187

Yale University, 111

Zoe, Rachel, 211
Zone of Genius, 202–3
Zones of Excellence, Competence and Incompetence, 203
Zuckerberg, Mark, 232

# About the Author

**EMMA GREDE** is the ultimate modern mogul, turning big ideas into some of today's most influential consumer brands. She's the co-founder and CEO of Good American, the founding partner of SKIMS, the co-founder of Safely and Off Season and now the voice behind the *Aspire with Emma Grede* podcast.

A leader with purpose, Grede also lends her time and expertise to global impact organisations, serving on the board of directors for the Obama Foundation and Baby2Baby, and has recently become a King's Trust Ambassador. Her journey proves that success and substance go hand in hand.

Grede lives in Los Angeles with her husband, Jens and their four children.